Bonanza Books • New York

THE
CUSTOMS AND LEGENDS
OF THE
THLINGET INDIANS
OF
ALASKA

by

O. M. Salisbury

Copyright © MCMLXII by Superior Publishing Company
Library of Congress Catalog Card Number: 62-14494
All rights reserved.
This edition is published by Bonanza Books
a division of Crown Publishers, Inc.
by arrangement with Superior Publishing Co.
a b c d e f g h
Manufactured in the United States of America

Dedicated To

ALMA

TABLE OF CONTENTS

TABLE OF CONTENTS—Continued

LIST OF ILLUSTRATIONS

LIST OF ILLUSTRATIONS—Continued

FOREWORD

Anthropologists, or students of mankind, have long deplored the "Missing Link" that prevents them from tracing man from earliest dawn on down through the ages. However, the record, though not nearly complete, is reasonably adequate on the North American Indians from prehistoric times through the first decade of the present century. With the sociological branch of anthropology in its ascendency, much is being written about them as they are now, but there is an ever widening gap that bids fair to become a new missing link, the transitional period between the aboriginal and the present civilization, the years between 1910 and 1940.

The halfway mark in the transition period between the primitive and the modern has long since passed, unrecorded and unnoted. Among the Thlingets of Southeastern Alaska, the oldsters who could look back and tell of potlatch and Shaman, council house and Raven Clan, have gone to join the great "Ke-an-Kow." Their only records were word of mouth and for the most part passed with them.

Now fourth and fifth generation Americans, the descendants of these oldsters, dance the "Twist" instead of the ceremonial, read True Romances, instead of listening to the legends, and in the manner of youth everywhere care little about the thoughts and dreams of their ancestors. Neither did the early white historians do much in this respect, for theirs was the monumental problem of recording the physical things. Though some must have cared, none had the time to explore the minds of the people with whom they were working.

My father, Oliver Maxson Salisbury, was a man uniquely qualified to pursue the study of mankind. First as the son of a man who headed a post-Civil War Negro school in Atlanta, Georgia, next as a trained teacher, then as an officer in command of colored troops during World War I and later as a captain in the American Red Cross, working with the war torn people of France, Albania, Czecho Slovakia and Ruthenia.

Though never an orthodox church member, his deep religious feeling gave him an insight into the lives, even the minds, of the people with whom he worked that was keenly analytical, yet kind and warmly human.

Father and his wife Alma, my mother, were government advisor and bookkeeper to the store, principal of the school, teacher and father and mother in general to the community in the ancient Thlinget Indian village of Klawock on Prince of Wales Island, at a time when the influence of the oldsters still showed its mark on the culture of the tribe. Some sons and daughters of the oldsters were at the crossroads, leaning toward the new, yet falling back on the old, going to a Christian church yet practicing witchcraft, being vaccinated for smallpox but consulting the shaman in order to play safe.

Here we have an important work written in the mid 1920's that gives insight into the thoughts, the dreams, the joys and the sorrows of both oldsters and moderns of these simple people, bridging the gulf between the old and the new. Written with kindliness of heart, it neither deplores, criticizes nor praises the changes, but examines them with curiosity and wonderment as they occur.

It is, in fact, a little journey into the primitive.

THE
CUSTOMS AND LEGENDS
OF THE
THLINGET INDIANS
OF
ALASKA

Chapter I

OUR SITUATION

We are in Southeastern Alaska, which is a perfectly definite section of that great country, and comprises what is known as the Panhandle; and we are on what is known as the "West Coast" of Prince of Wales Island, over next to the Pacific and therefore off the beaten trail between the States and the North Country which follows up the Inland Passage in the shelter of the myriad islands which fringe the coast of the mainland for a thousand miles north of Seattle.

Our latitude is about a thousand miles north of New York City. As of this writing, October, everything is as green as in summertime, except that part of the leaves have fallen from the deciduous brush, although the buds are so swollen and green they look as though they might burst forth almost any day.

Of course it rains more or less of the time. It does that way in Southeastern Alaska; but there are scattering days, even an occasional week, when the mellow amber light of our low sun illumes the verdure with entrancing beauty.

Mountainous islands of assorted sizes, and varying expanses of salt water meet the eye on every side.

The islands are rocky tips of sunken mountains, so their beaches are of broken rock rather than sand, and the only soil is the water-logged, partially decayed vegetation which is rarely over a few feet deep and is so spongy and loose that if one steps off a windfall onto what looks like mossy ground, he is liable to sink up to his armpits before he hits bottom.

Klawock is located on a long narrow inlet that merges with the waters of a tidal bay into which Klawock Creek empties; and three or four miles up stream is Klawock Lake—the spawning ground of countless salmon.

We reached the village at the close of the spawning season and the beaches at low tide were covered with the carcases of thousands of dead salmon which had fulfilled their mission in life and passed on, leaving ripe and luscious food for the myriads of gulls, ravens and crows which fill the air with their clamor.

We have been told that later the herring will crowd into the inlet in a great flood, and along with the herring will come king salmon, sea lions, hair seals and other denizens of the deep with a hunger for fish, while whales cruise around in Big Harbor outside.

This is strictly an Indian village, there being no whites here except the Government personnel of a nurse and four teachers; and several "Squaw men"—whites who have married Indian women—and we like it better on that account. A mixed population is responsible for many complications and rivalries.

Like all Alaskan fishing villages, it lies along the rocky shore with the water for the front dooryard, in which the fisherman's automobile, a gas boat, either floats at anchor at high tide, or rests in a sort of cradle which keeps it upright when the tide is out. The backyard rises into the wilderness jungle of the mountainside.

The one street is of plank construction on piles, under which the water flows at high tide. On both sides of this plank street are the houses. Some are on the rocky hillside and others on spindling legs, overhanging the water, and while there are a number of fairly modern looking cottages, the older buildings are either large community houses of sawed, but unpainted lumber, or the smaller, older "smoke houses" of earlier days. The latter have no chimneys —simply a sort of roofed hole or ventilator, through which the smoke escaped from the fires burning on a bed of earth on the floor, or from a decrepit excuse for a stove.

This is still a Government Reservation so there is no private ownership of land, and while the owners can sell their houses, that is all to which they have title. Because of this lack of ownership of land, the buildings have been located without any relation to anything else other than the inclination or whim of the builder. Here a building has been torn down leaving only the floor stretched on piles over the water, and there a building, because it hasn't been torn down, is falling down on its own responsibility.

There are three docks at which ocean going boats can tie up, with salmon canneries on two of them which are owned and operated by natives. The third, owned by the native cooperative store, is in the nature of a public dock and connects with the main street at a point which many years ago was the burning ground for the dead, for until the white man introduced his ideas of the disposal of the dead, the Indians cremated those who departed hence.

This ground was held in sacred and superstitious awe and remained many years as a gap between the two sections of the town; but in time some one willing to brave the spirits of the dead and the disapprobation of the living, ventured to make use of the desirable location and built upon the spot. It was a good while, however, before others ventured to intrude in the locality. Now the native store stands on piles across the plank street and the sentiment connected with the spot seems to be a thing of the past.

The Government schoolhouse stands higher up on the hillside in a commanding position, while the so-called *teacherage,* huddles under its wing and corners on the old burning ground. This building, an unattractive two-story shell of a structure, originally stood in another part of the village near the old mission school, and was slid down the hillside several years ago, loaded on a raft, floated around at high tide and dragged up to its present location by a winch, and one of the natives has told me that he and one other did the dragging. It would appear to be quite an undertaking for men trained in such work, but the native skill of the Indians seems to make nothing impossible to them.

Chapter II

THE THLINGETS AND THEIR VILLAGE

The natives among whom we are working are the Thlinget Indians, who, with the Eskimos of the Arctic regions, constitute the main native population of Alaska. The Hyda Indians have a different language and are considered a different race of Indians, but their number is not large. In different portions of Southeastern Alaska the Indians go by different names, such as the Chilkats, Sitkans, Stikeens, but they are considered to be Thlingets with such variations in language and customs as would be natural with groups isolated from one another; and they get their names from the locality in which they are found.

It seems to me a misnomer to call these people Indians, but they have to be called something. We have very definite ideas about the North American Indians as a race—their appearance and traits, but these ideas do not fit the natives of Alaska at all. We expected, when we came up here to find the copper-skinned, taciturn Indian of tradition. The Thlinget however, cannot be called copper-skinned. They are dusky—not black; there is more of the tawny cast of the oriental to their duskiness, than the red hue, and many of them have a slant to their eyes which is very Asiatic. In almost every other respect also, except in the primitiveness of their lives, they failed to fit in with our preconceived notions.

In build, there is more of a tendency to a short stockiness, than to the tall litheness of the traditional "Redskin."

Among the tribal customs and individual traits there are many points of resemblance to the Japanese; however, there has been a mixing of blood ever since the first Russians found their way to this side of the Pacific, and today there are probably few Alaskan Indians with unmixed Indian blood. The influx to Alaska during the summer months for fishing, mining, etc. of the mixed population of whites, orientals, Kanakas, and others of ship and cannery crews has further corrupted the native population.

They are far from being phlegmatic like the Indian we have known, but among themselves are just as sociable as their white brothers; they have a keen sense of humor and are not a bit averse to showing their appreciation of fun. They are fine and appreciative and courteous. As we walk along the plank street we meet men who can scarcely express an English greeting, who nevertheless, lift their hats with a courtesy of spirit which is never outdone by our own people anywhere.

One of the squaw men, a big Swede who has lived a good part of his life among them, has told me that to one who knows the savage state of the natives thirty years ago, the progress they have made in the direction of civilization is almost impossible to believe.

In their native state they lived the life of primitive people. Their homes were of the simplest—not the skin tepee of the Indians further south, for they hadn't the vast herds of buffalo that ranged the plains, to furnish the hides, nor swarming elk, deer and moose to draw upon—but before the advent of the white man they had lived in crude shelters made of logs and bark.

With the coming of the white man with tools such as the saw and axe, they took on some of the white man's ways and built houses, though very different from the white man's. And because it was their practice to live together in family groups, presided over by the chieftan of the clan, they built communal houses—one house for all. In the building of these houses, all members of the clan participated and were generously paid for all that they did in skins or blankets or other articles of barter, although they later became tenants of the houses themselves.

The houses were all of one pattern, though varying in size, which was regulated by tribal custom in accordance with the prominence of the chief of that particular clan in comparison with other clans of the community. They were square or rectangular in shape, one-storied, and were first made of logs thirty to sixty feet long and often of large diameter, which were held together at the corners by withes or thongs of rawhides, or both. Later the cedar logs were split and were rough-hewn into great planks several inches thick which were set on end against a frame of big hewn logs supported on corner posts. The roof of heavy planks swung across big log timbers, was almost flat and was further covered with bark.

The earlier houses were windowless and were entered through an opening high up on the side which took the place of a door and was reached by crude steps. The hole was covered with a curtain of matting woven from bark fibers or the fine roots of the spruce. From the platform at the opening which served as a door, two or three steps led down to another platform several feet wide which ran entirely around the inside of the building. This shelf, or platform, three or four feet above the floor, was apportioned off into sleeping space for the various families occupying the house, and into other spaces used for storage. Sometimes rude curtains of skins or mats were hung up and furnished a measure of privacy, but more often there was nothing of the kind and everything that transpired was in the presence of all. Privacy wasn't a thing they craved and naked children tumbled around their more or less blanketed elders indiscriminately.

Below the sleeping platform and on the ground, was another of hewn planks, which might be considered the "sitting room," while the central space was bare ground where the fire was built under the smoke hole. There all the cooking and household functions were carried on.

The only furniture were chests adroitly fashioned without nails, which were used to hold cherished belongings; piles of blankets and the skins of animals; and weaving frames.

Cooking utensils, articles used as dishes made of wood, wooden and horn spoons, and clothing, lay in heaps on the floor, though each family had its own heap, and each had its own corner of the fire.

From the walls and roof timbers hung drying fish and game, skins of animals, fresh meat, bladders of fish and seal oil, and old dirty clothing—all reeking with grease and highly odoriferous; and as refuse and offal were often thrown in a corner or cast to one side and forgotten, and many lungs were breathing the same air and bodies tainting it, the condition of the atmosphere was such as only an Alaska native could survive; while the dingy, smoked and sooted walls were barely illumined by the flickering fire.

The building of such a house was a great undertaking. As there was no means of transporting the logs they had to be cut along the wooded shores of the islands, dragged into the water and towed by the Indians in canoes to the place where they were to be used; and of course building sites had to be close to high tide line.

With so much labor involved, all of it having to be paid for in some manner, the construction was often much prolonged, but the final completion of the structure was always followed by a great feast or potlatch, in which all who had taken part in the work joined, and at which there was great giving of gifts by the chief of the clan and often a slaughter of slaves—sometimes as many as 200 being killed if the clan were a large one and the builder of the house a "Big Man."

There was often extensive carving of crude totemic figures on the corner posts, and in the course of time totem poles would be erected in front, which would record family history and tradition.

The builder's resources frequently became exhausted before the plans were all carried out, in which case the house was occupied "as was" and the payment of obligations would be long delayed, but never forgotten, either by the debtors or the debtees.

Besides the big community houses in the winter village, each group would have its seasonal camp at its fishing or hunting grounds—generally rude structures of poles, fir and spruce boughs and bark—where they dwelt during the season of special activity; for they lived on wild game, berries, and things from the sea—the "manna" furnished her children by Nature. Each clan had its own hunting, fishing and trapping grounds, its bird-egg-island, its herring spawning ground, and its salmon stream, and those claims were held inviolate or war followed.

It was in this way that the village of Klawock was established by the Henya group of the Thlinget Indians, whose winter village had been at Tuxikan, in a sheltered spot tempered by a warm sea current which swept near the north end of Prince of Wales Island. I have been told that Tuxikan was a much better place to live in during the winter than this, but it was eventually abandoned.

Klawock Creek is a "fish creek" which has a six-mile-long lake for its headwaters. It empties into a tidal bay where the fresh water of the stream meets and mingles with the salt water of the sea which comes in at high tide through narrow channels and makes an island of the wooded point on which the Indians used to camp. The tidal bay in turn empties into a long, narrow, deep inlet which also, in turn, connects with the larger channel outside.

Under these varying marine conditions the natives caught their salmon, and trout which were such an important feature of their diet. Here they caught that native tidbit, the crab, and in special localities found another delectable morsel, the abalone. Herring crowded the inlet and channel in the late winter months and their spawning ground was not far distant.

In all the country about deer were plentiful on the many islands, and bear came to rake the salmon out on the banks of the stream with their huge, but deft paws. Waterfowl flew up the water courses or floated in sheltered spots along the shores; the island jungles abounded in berries of many kinds in varying seasons, while wild celery grew everywhere in great profusion. Nature's larder was well supplied so it was natural that, with Tuxikan for their winter home, this fish-creek region should become their summer camp, and here the greater part of the summer would be spent.

Such were the conditions of the pre-missionary days. The new village was a departure from the old. I have not learned how it came by its name, but the squawking ravens sound the word "kla wock" perfectly at times and may be responsible for it.

The natives spent so much time here that the Presbyterian missionaries undertook to start a school and mission among them in the 80's and because the school was here, many of the people stayed throughout the year and eventually the entire population made Klawock their permanent home. Tuxikan was abandoned completely; their totem poles and old communal houses were left behind, and to some extent, their ancient practices.

It was a new life they entered upon in Klawock with the coming of the missionaries; but while they abandoned their totem poles, which were in a way a symbol of their old life, they cherished their memory, and the mayor has told me he has been advocating that they transplant their poles to Klawock.

Today the situation is very different from the primitive conditions of the old days, although the lapse of time has not been great. The people are very receptive and have gone a long way under the tutelage of the missionaries.

They no longer wear blankets and deerskin moccasins. They are suitably dressed in most cases in modern attire—girls and women trimly bobbed—men well barbered—yet they are not the same as ourselves. There are differences besides that of color. One sees it in the depths of the dark eyes—feels it in a thousand ways—the mind tingles with the mystery sensed. Is it a psychic influence one feels? Does a challenge come forth from the black eyes of these dusky people to meet the white man's vaunted superiority? This is only the beginning of my wondering.

Of course when it comes to accepting the white man's ways and ideas concerning many things, they suit themselves. Their villages have always been small, so they have not the problems to meet that arise from the massing of large numbers in small spaces. Sewerage means nothing to them. They are not informed on germs and infection, therefore do not take them into account. If we could show them germs as big as the ravens and gulls that scavenge the beach, they would think they were a good thing, but when they are told that little things no one can see, are responsible for sickness and death, they know better. Everyone knows that it is evil spirits that make the trouble, and witches, which in the language of the Bible, are those "possessed of the devil." A devil to them, is an evil spirit in the wrong place.

With the grandeur of nature surrounding them, they give no thought to landscape gardening. Why shouldn't they throw their tin cans and other refuse out the front door if they wish? Anyone so fussy as to take offense at that can look somewhere else. With so much room to circulate in, no one can say such things are in the way; as for dead dogs on the beach, if their ancestors didn't mind the carcasses of slaves, why should they bother about dead dogs? Besides, if the tide wants to bring them in and leave them stranded, whose business is it to remove them? What is a little smell among friends? So each tends to his own affairs and lets his neighbors do likewise—merely an application of *laissez faire*.

Aside from their clanal obligations, no such things as public spirit has existed in the past. There was no occasion for it. There was no village government—the chiefs were such only in their own clans. There were no city offices to be filled, therefore there were no politicians to curry favor with the public. The present village government is merely a cloak that the paternal United States has encouraged the natives to wear. They don't need it, but if it makes the "Big Man" at Washington feel any better, it's all right with them.

Numerous traits and practices of the Thlingets are supposed to be due to oriental influence, as the sequestering of young girls at the approach of womanhood, and the taboo placed on pregnant women; but those same customs are to be found among the red men of the States, who confine their unmarried girls in teepees at certain periods, and consider the mothers of new born babes to be unclean.

The practice of marrying young girls to old men, and boys to old women; of a brother taking a brother's widow to wed; early marriage; the late weaning of babies; the father's having no relationship to the children; the subservience of the husband to the wife's family; the property of the dead reverting to the opposite clan; and many others, may exist, as claimed, among the Japanese, but they do not prove anything concerning the Thlingets. Squatting on the haunches may be an oriental practice, but I have seen the Albanians also squatting, as naturally and as much at ease, as the frog; but I fail to see any significance in it. They had nothing else but their haunches to sit on and that is a condition found with all uncivilized races. As for tatooing, they are a maritime people and tatooing is a practice of sailors the world over. Possibly the sailors contracted the practice from the savages in remote places—also, the savages may have caught the habit from the sailors.

There are certain traits among them however, which may be more significant such as their exceptional skill with their hands in basket weaving and carving, their aptness at imitation and adaptability to progress, which separates them widely from the red men; their lack of inventiveness; their talkativeness, sociability and fondness for amusement of all kinds; which show a marked resemblance, it is claimed, to the Japanese; but probably in no respect is the resemblance more striking than their lack of definite religious beliefs.

Human nature is human nature the world over, so it is a foregone conclusion that there will be great similarity between the simple practices of simple people, wherever found, therefore it seems far-fetched to attempt to relate the Thlingets to the Lost Tribes of Israel, as has been done, because of certain similar customs; or to connect them with the Aztecs for similar reasons, as some would do. Differences are often more significant than resemblances, and the variations of the Thlingets from the North American Indians are so radical as to clearly show a different origin, which of course prompts the natural question, "If not North American Indians, then what?"

It is easier to ask questions than to answer them, but if one studies a map of the Pacific and its northern environs, considers ocean currents and winds, a possible answer promptly suggests itself. Add in the physical resemblances, traits of character and similar practices, and one gets at least an interesting possibility to consider. Against the great distances that separated early habitable Asia from early uninhabited North America, the turbulance of the sea, and the crude water craft of the ancient Asiatics, there stands the great Japanese current with its sweep to the eastern shores, and the lure of the fish and the seals of the northern waters, as an incentive to take chances.

The world loves puzzles. They are something on which to whet the mind and are usually solved in time, so one day the puzzle of the Thlinget Indians may be worked out.

Chapter III

TRIBAL RELATIONS

One cannot tell much about these people without first giving some idea of their tribal relations, for these relations are the most vital elements in their lives.

While it is true that most of the Indians of Alaska are Thlingets and that the different names applied to certain groups are names indicating village or locality solely, such as the Henyas around Klawock, the Stikeens at Wrangell on the Stikeen river, Chilkats at Haines, Kaskes at Kake, there are intertribal or clan groups which are the same in all localities, and these clans are often made up of still other family groups.

As nearly as I can ascertain, the Alaskan Indians believe that they were originally animals or birds or creatures of the sea; or rather, to express the idea in another way—they believe that the spirit which now manifests itself as a human being, originally bore the form of some animal, fish, or bird, but was able to take the form of man at will; and the perfect interchangeableness, the one with the other, as manifested in their thought and speech, is quite disconcerting to a white man.

Of all such creatures, the raven enters most largely into their life—not as a bird, but as a symbol of the most important group. An individual, what we would call a supernatural being, but which the natives called Yalth or other allied names, but which was typified by the raven, was credited with being the origin or creator of most that is important in their lives.

Those who have viewed the natives superficially have claimed that Yalth, or Raven was worshipped by them, but the mayor of the village, who has more than ordinary understanding of the white man's thought, explained to me one day in connection with the teachings of the missionaries,

"The natives have always known what the missionaries tried to tell us about God and Jesus Christ and the flood, only the missionaries didn't tell everything just right. That is why we didn't always believe all they told us. We never worshipped the raven, only one day an Indian man saw a bird that looked like Mr. Raven —that was what our people called the one the missionaries called Jesus—and said, 'that bird looks like Mr. Raven.' We didn't worship him, but we treated him well because of the one he looked like."

It is a very characteristic explanation and confirms the conviction that the Thlingets in their primitive state had no religious beliefs—a condition quite different from that found elsewhere among the North American Indians.

The white man who attempts to comprehend Thlinget psychology finds himself lost in the maze of their beliefs, but there never seems to be any sense of confusion or inconsistency in their own minds.

In their belief that they were the personification of the spirit of some bird, beast, or fish, or even of an inanimate object like a mountain, it was always the spirit of some long ago creature which was embodied.

The people were keen to note resemblances. They believed that all creatures understood human speech, so they would talk to anything they saw in nature, especially if it bore any resemblance to a human being, in the belief that there was a spirit in it; even the stone that tripped the hunter's feet was treated with respect, because it would not have tripped him but for the disgruntled spirit in it.

One of the things taught the children was the need of caution in speaking of animals, and to prove their point they would recount the experience of the chief's daughter who, while berrying with other native women, ridiculed bears. Suddenly bears appeared and killed all the women of the party save the chief's daughter. She was spared by the Bear Chief and became his wife, and to them was born a girl, half bear and half human. The child lived and grew and one day in her play she climbed a tree and was mistaken by Indian hunters for a bear, but she managed to make them understand she was human, so she was taken to the Indian village where she married and became the ancestor of the Bear Clan. Moral: if the Chief's daughter had not spoken disparagingly of bears, the other women would not have been killed.

Their ways of determining just which creature was their "patron saint," or was represented by them, were varied and infinite.

As a rule the origin was clouded in tradition or lost completely through succeeding generations, but if one among the ancestors of a family had escaped the pursuit of a bear by a great leap across a chasm, it was considered that the spirit of a frog must have dwelt within him, otherwise he could not have leaped so nimbly. In one case a man and his wife were hunting and heard something singing. After much searching they found a little frog in the stern of their canoe, and because the frog sang it was happy, so it must have been glad to be with them; thus the frog became the emblem or totem of that family and was carved on the house posts which blessed the family within. The same emblem when carved on the paddles of the clan gave power and insured safe journeying; carved on the horn or wooden spoons, it was a protection against poison (indigestion), etc. It was the clansman's charm—his talisman.

One clan claims the grizzly bear for its totem because it is tradition with them that one of their young men married a female grizzly; and one of the explanations of the eagle totem is that an eagle once upon a time rendered valuable aid to one of the clan, who in appreciation became an eagle; while the grampus, or killer-whale clan, which is a branch of the Eagles, took the grampus for its totem because one of the tribe made the first grampus that was made, by carving it out of yellow cedar.

Such explanations are almost as varied as the individuals who offer them, but there is always an authentic explanation which is accepted throughout the Indian population.

In earlier days the emblem or crest of a clan was marked by carving, painting or other representation upon the communal houses of the totemic group and on all the clan belongings; and today, though the Indians are supposed to have become civilized and christianized, the totem will appear on the marble tombstone placed on his grave.

The clan was like a modern college fraternity—an Eagle one place, or a Mink—an Eagle or Mink any place—and a house bearing a given totem was a place where anyone belonging to that totem, no matter how complete a stranger he might be, could walk in and be sure of a welcome.

I shall not forget the glow on the face of one of our natives when he explained to me in connection with an Indian visitor in the village, "He belong to my family—he Brown Bear like me."

They may not have the fraternity grip and password, but they have some sure means the white man knoweth not, of determining the simon-pure frater.

Of all the many clans found in the various localities, the Raven, or Crow clan is the most universal. It is found in every community and is represented in every family.

I had read in a book before coming up here, that it was an absolute tribal law that marriages could not take place between members of the same clan. The other day the storekeeper explained that his children did not belong to the same clan as himself, but to his wife's. She is a Raven and he an Eagle, but because the children belong to the mother's clan, according to their custom, his children were not Eagles, but Ravens. If his sisters had lived and married, which they didn't they being Eagles, their children would be the same and under tribal law, his children and theirs, own cousins, could marry.

Next to the Ravens in prevalence, are the Wolves and the Eagles. In some localities the Wolves hold second place. Here the Eagles outnumber the Wolves.

The tribes in the past were very clannish and no matter what act a member might commit, his tribe stood whole-heartedly behind him and would pay any penalty in his behalf that might be necessary, even life itself. Today the tribal affiliations are not as manifest, but they are still there and wield as great influence—a thing I daily discover in one way or another.

Formerly there was no native government except that wielded by the tribe or clan, but there were certain ideas which were universally entertained and which operated as law, the chief of these being that the tribe was responsible for anything and everything the individual might do. If he injured in any way, accidentally or wilfully the body, property, feelings, or a member of the family of another, that injury must infallibly be atoned for to the injured one's tribe. The same rule operated between the clans and families. If an Indian was murdered his murder must be atoned for by a life—not necessarily of the one who committed the crime, but by some one of rank in his clan equal in rank to that of the murdered person. If a woman killed a man, not the woman's life was forfeit, for she wasn't considered the equal of a man of her caste; but some man of her tribe of necessary rank must pay the penalty, and there was always someone who would unhesitatingly step forward to pay the debt.

A woman was killed during the early work of the missionaries in one of the villages in a drunken quarrel with her husband, and of course redress was demanded by her clan, but it was slow in forthcoming so war threatened. The missionary, in an effort to meet the situation, explained to the Indians that the white man's law placed the responsibility and penalty on the one who committed the act. The murderer said, "It is not right that I give my life for a woman—take my sister and kill her—that is justice." So it was—a man for a man—a woman for a woman—a chief for a chief and a slave for a slave. Even an eye must be of the same color and a tooth the same kind and size.

Life was not held very dear among them and it was never difficult to find some one willing to preserve the honor of his family at the expense of his own comfort or existence; but these people are thrifty and injured honor could always be appeased by commercial recompense, as in the case of a son who accidentally killed a father in another tribe. The tribe of the deceased demanded the life of the son or some one of the son's tribe. He was perfectly agreeable and stepped forward to present himself for execution, but the idea was broached that a liberal supply of blankets was worth more than a dead Indian, and the matter was finally adjusted on that basis.

Even if a Thlinget committed suicide, a thing which very rarely happens, some one else was considered responsible and redress was insisted upon, no matter how far-fetched might be the explanation. Opposition was never made on the grounds of the unreasonableness of the claim.

In one case a man attended the funeral of another of a different tribe and he was so grief-stricken that he literally drowned his sorrow in "hootch-i-noo," the native equivalent of whiskey. He failed to survive his grief. His clan demanded damages from the dead man's tribe because if the man hadn't died, their clansman would not have attended his funeral, and if he had not attended he would not have been so sad. Had he not been so sad he would not have drunk the "hootch," and if he had not drunk the hootch he would not have died: a perfectly reasonable and logical argument. Responsibility was accepted and recompense made by the injuring clan.

Of course these, to us, extreme cases are not evident today, but the principle is in operation just the same and is responsible for many a surprise to the white man. There can be no injury or loss to a Thlinget, intentional or otherwise, without redress and damages from some one, and claims are often made when least expected and not frequently long after the incident happened.

Fortunately we have been involved in no complications thus far, and such things are easily possible in school work; but that is probably due to the fact that Alma always stimulates such an interest in their work on the part of her pupils, that discipline is easy, and because the native children are the most earnest learners and best behaved pupils she has ever had. They come to school because they love to and not, as with so many white children, because they have to. That simplifies the work with them in some ways immensely.

The morning after we arrived one of the natives trundled our baggage up to the teacherage on a two-wheeled truck. I was relieved to have the question of its delivery so easily settled, for it had been intimated to me that the Thlingets were very averse to anything that suggested servitude, and I did not wish to insult any of the people among whom we had come to work, by asking him to work for us. The relief was short-lived, however, for I found myself facing a question of etiquette. Should I assume that the natural courtesy of the man, and his sense of gratitude that the benevolent Government had sent us up there, had prompted the act, and compensate him with a few carefully chosen words of appreciation, or should I run the risk of offending him by offering him money? I was puzzled. I wanted to make a good first impression, but there was no one to guide me, so I offered him half a dollar for wheeling the luggage twenty rods. He declined it and made me understand that he would be the grateful recipient of any old coat I might have brought with me. That emboldened me to place the coin in his hand while I explained that I had traveled light and was wearing my only coat. His hand closed over the money, but he repeated his request for the coat and sidled off. Later I learned that he was "nephew to a chief." That sounded important, but at the time it meant nothing to me. Afterwards I learned that it meant he was next in line to the chief—in other words—heir to a chief, and was the highest caste of anyone in the village.

If I made a faux pas he was forgiving, because he drifts in to see me frequently and has proved to be a most interesting character and a source of much information.

I understand there is none among the Thlingets today who knows more of their traditions, legends, lore; their songs and dances; their arts and crafts, than Peter Lawrence. He is a wise man among them and as "nephew to a chief" he looks at things in a large way and is willing to make allowances.

Chapter IV

A DAY OF REST

Unfamiliar experiences crowd along rapidly, and just now I find myself presiding over a justice court, as it were, for George Demmert one Sunday brought a young fellow named Gilbert Cook and his wife to see me. They wanted advice in connection with a controversy over an estate matter which was so complicated I have had great difficulty in gaining an understanding of the facts.

The next day the other party, Roy Williams, came to see me, and then Paul Davis, Roy's step-son. In the evening Roy came again with his wife, who couldn't speak a word of English and who is sister to Gilbert Cook, and mother to Paul Davis. Again George was interpreter.

Two natives, Jim Cook and Sam Davis, bought a gas boat called "The Age of Reason" from one of the canning companies of the West Coast for $6,000. $2,000 was to be paid down and the balance from the earnings of the boat.

Davis was married to a daughter of Cook's wife by a previous marriage and they had three children. He died the same year and the company took the boat back but when Roy Williams married Mrs. Davis and assumed support of the children, the company agreed to sell the boat to Cook and Williams for another $2,000 in cash and a mortgage of about $2500.

The Davis estate was settled and the court established the interest of the children in the boat. Then Jim Cook died and his stepson, Gilbert, brother of Mrs. Davis-Williams, undertook to carry on in his father's place. Roy had a boat of his own so he let Gilbert take charge of The Age of Reason. The latter appears to have promptly forgotten that anyone else had an interest in it and appropriated its earnings, paid off the mortgage and considered the boat his own.

The case illustrates the marital complications of the natives, for Mrs. Davis and the children are heirs of both estates; and it shows, except in the case of Gilbert, how loyal they are to one another. When I quizzed Paul Davis, the sixteen year old stepson of Roy, in my effort to learn the relations of one to another, he said of Roy, "He good father to us—I don't call step-father—I call him father. He can have the money."

During Roy's visit later he assured me, "I don't want money—

I take care of children, they my children—but money belongs to children—court says it does and tells me I must look after their money for them—that money send them to school—it's theirs."

As for Mrs. Williams, she told me through the interpreter that she didn't want any of the money from either of the estates, but the children should have their share of their father's property; while Gilbert's mother has urged him to be just to his nephews and nieces and pay them their share. He is modern, however, in his views and insists he is going to have it all. George has advised him to treat the children fairly but he says, "Gilbert, he say nothing —just turn and walk away." So the case has come to me as umpire.

Of course I know nothing of what may be in the background— there is a background for everything here—so I can only do as the court would do, consider the evident facts and try to get the parties together. But it interests me to see both parties friendly with George and trusting him to present their cases properly. It also interests me to see them willing to submit their case to me—each confident in the merits of his own case but without apparent bitterness towards the other. Roy is not disposed to be exacting, but he wants to see the case settled, for the boat is getting older each year and is depreciating rapidly: then the dispute is a source of discord in the community.

I have urged them both to come to a settlement. The Cook estate hasn't been probated and there is no doubt if it goes to probate the children's full interests will be recognized. In addition there will be the cost of the action to be met. Evidently Cook sees that for he came and told me that they had reached an agreement and wanted me to cable the lawyer at Ketchikan to call off the probate proceedings which were to be started. Next day Roy told me that Gilbert was to pay $500 the following October, but if the fishing season was not good he was to pay $300 but the following October another $300. So the matter was settled after about eight years of disagreement, and harmony prevails.

This has been the most involved problem they have brought to me, but it is only one of the many ways the people make use of me.

One day a young native came to borrow a mattock and shovel —they come to us for everything under the sun—and a lump rose in my throat as I got them for him because I knew he was Billy George and was going to dig a grave for their little baby which had died the night before.

Poor little thing! The nurse had told us soon after we came

The only street in the village of Klawock. Taken from the dock of the Klawock Commercial Company. The Presbyterian church and the "Manse" are the highest buildings in the distance. The schoolhouse is the large building at the left background, with the gable and one window of the teacherage visible. The mountains east of Klawock, looking across the tidal bay to where Klawock creek comes in.

Jumbo McFee, blind with cataracts on both eyes, but he traps and fishes and works like a moose, and runs an outboard motor boat.

The Government schoolhouse at Klawock, Alaska, maintained for the Thlinget Indian children of the village. The building at the right is the teachers' residence. Jumbo McFee, a blind native, is carrying blocks of wood up from the beach where trees have been sawed into blocks at low tide, for the use of the school.

School section of the village. Big building at the left is the town hall. Next, the schoolhouse and the teacherage.

Getting the town hall ready for the school and village Christmas program and the community Christmas tree. The entire roof was shingled in two days in rain and snow, by volunteer labor—as many as fifty men working at one time. The surface covered was over 7000 square feet.

The dedication of the new town hall at Klawock, Alaska. The great flag was presented by the Alaska Native Sisterhood to the village and is carried by them. The eagle carried by Mrs. Fred Williams and Mrs. Tom Adams was carved by Bob Asneal to be placed on the front of the hall as a totem representing the United States, to remind the people, in their own words, "that while the people of Klawock belong to many different tribes, they all belong to the one great tribe, the United States." The man at the right in light overcoat is the town mayor, R. J. Peratovich, known as "Bob." The woman in the fur coat at the opposite corner is his wife. The man nearest Bob in Salvation Army uniform and carrying a cane, is Captain William Benson. Next to him is Envoy Tecumseh Collins. The village band is playing in the background. Rain was falling.

At the close of the dedication of the new town hall built by the natives of Klawock. The band is on the steps, but the falling rain had scattered the crowd.

Andrew Wannamaker, wife, and adopted daughter, Elizabeth. Pastor of the native Presbyterian church at Klawock, Alaska, July, 1927.

A Thlinget babe and its father, Sam Thomas.

Peter Anniskett, a Thlinget Indian of Klawock, Alaska, hewing his dugout from a cedar log. The little adze with which the work is done is in his hands and is virtually the only tool used in the work. The canoe is about ready for spreading. It will be filled with water and redhot stones will be dropped in to heat the water to the boiling point. The hot water softens the wood, when the sides are carefully spread so as to give the right flare and are held in place by cross pieces which act as permanent braces.

Kelp loaded with fish eggs and drying in the sun.

A stone implement used by the early Thlingets as a pestle for crushing berries and fish eggs, in their preparation for food. Some think it is a wolf head, some a dog head, some a seal head. The Wolf clan is quite numerous in Klawock and among the Henya group of Thlingets, to which the people of Klawock largely belong, so it would seem quite possible that it is a Wolf totem. It seems, however, to antedate these people, for none of them are able to give information concerning it. The nurse paid five dollars for it.

Andrew Wells, the ice cream king of Klawock, and George Saunders. Little Mary Smith has just spent her nickel and Peter Anniskett's wife, who has taken to the woods more than once when her tempestuous spouse goes on a rampage, is in the left background.

Gulls rising from a raft of piles beside Bob's dock.

The gulls.

The gas boats, Pirate and the Radio, having made too big a haul with their seine, so that the fish are dying before they can be brailed out of the pond, have opened the seine and turned out a flood of the dead and dying, which illustrates the destructive wastefulness of the bait fishers.

Herring milling in a purse seine, about to be turned into Bob's bait trap.

Drying "fish eggs" on seaweed of another kind. The seaweed and fish eggs will be prepared and eaten together.

William Stuart, a Tsimpsian, holding spruce boughs loaded with herring roe.

Fish eggs (herring roe) on spruce boughs, drying on the porch of Fred Williams' house.

The gas boat, Gypsy III, aground at Canoe Pass. C. W. Kellogg, the owner, on the boat deck; Mrs. Kellogg and O.M. Salisbury on the gravel bar beside it.

Mrs. Salisbury by one of the totem poles on the bank of Klawock creek. The figure carved on the pole is the totem of the Mink clan.

The totem pole standing in Pioneer Square in the city of Seattle. It is a fine type of the legendary pole and originally stood on Tongas Island in Southeastern Alaska, but when the Indians moved their village the pole was left behind.

R. J. Peratovich, Mayor of Klawock, and his wife with the Salvation Army in front of their hall. Bob and his wife belong to the Presbyterian Church, but they were on the best of terms with the Salvation Army. When the Army made plans for a new hall, Bob donated forty dollars and his wife ten, which was so much appreciated that threatened opposition faded into nothingness at election time and he was reelected mayor.

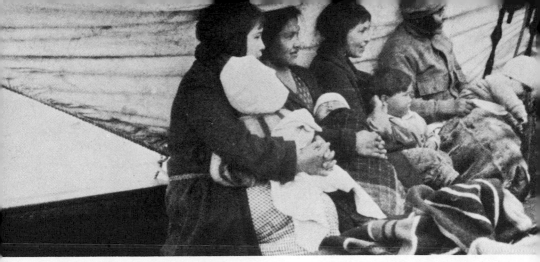

Indian mothers and their babes on their way to the "Hole-in-the-wall." A sail has been stretched so as to protect them from the fresh breeze that was blowing.

These are two gravestones standing near the teacherage. The one showing the bear is a totemic pole. The bear has a dancing hat on its head and a Killer Whale is on top of that. Of course it tells a story to the natives, but I never succeeded in learning what the story is. The other is commonplace, except that the inscription reads "Mary Ha-clan. Age 112 years."

The Indian village on the beach at the "Hole-in-the-wall" and the scow used as a store by the Klawock Commercial Company during the trolling season. Low tide.

The crowd watching the tug-o-war on the school ground on the Fourth of July. This is looking across the inlet towards Canoe Pass in the middle distance. The thin film of a cloud can be seen drifting through the pass which is around the point of timber at the right.

Peter Lawrence, the historian, starting the tricycle race on the Fourth of July.

that the baby was doomed. It had contacted "T.B." from an older child living in the same house—several families often live in the same house, and even in the same room—and while she has done all she could to relieve its suffering, she could not alter the result. She came in much excited one evening with the news that the baby was drunk with moonshine. The parents had been told that whiskey was good for such trouble and Billy had gone to Craig and got some. The ideas these people have of treating sickness are often startling.

Recently I went to the store to get some flavoring extract and Demmert found none on the shelf and that a case in the stock room had been opened and emptied.

Day before yesterday he brought Billy George to me with the information that Peter Dalton, the 21 year old school boy who lives in the same house with Billy, could account for the lemon extract. During our conversation he told me about getting the moonshine and giving a few drops in water to the baby, and he thought the baby was going to get well, but it didn't. His story did not sound quite so bad as the nurse's.

When I expressed my regret at the passing of the little one, he answered, "We have all got to go that way some time."

That may have been a repetition of the consolation some one had attempted to give him, or his recognition of the inevitable termination of mortal life. It is the second child they have lost though they are nothing but kids.

The day of the burial the funeral party boarded Gilbert Cook's boat, the Age of Reason, which is one of the larger boats, and with flag flying at half-mast, the boat glided down the bay in the beautiful setting of blue sky, forest-covered shores, and mellow sunlight to the burying ground on an island a mile or more distant, where so many have been laid away.

This afternoon Mrs. Konky Snook came to see about getting the money from some stock she holds in the store of the Klawock Commercial Company. Mrs. Snook has been educated outside somewhere and is much above the average in understanding, but she is steeped in sadness—and for cause.

I judge from what she told me and from what I have learned elsewhere, that her marriage with Snook was a love marriage—a rare thing among the natives—and he must have been a faithful, adoring, hard-working husband and father. Last February he died of "T.B." and had scarcely been carried over to the island when a cablegram was received telling of the death of the oldest daughter who was away to school, from the dread disease.

She likewise was carried over to the island; then the younger daughter passed in the same way. Three times the grim reaper visited that home within two months and left the wife and mother almost destitute, with two small children and an older boy her only possible help.

Her only resource was the money which her husband, in a period of prosperity, had invested in the stock of the store in his name, her name, and the names of each of the children. It had taken most of that to pay the funeral expenses and now she desires the rest in order that she may properly honor her dead with a tombstone and pay for the necessary feasting that should accompany its erection.

It was tragical to hear her tell her trouble in the low, soft-voiced, unemotional manner characteristic of the Indians, but she seemed almost overwhelmed with the burden of her woe. And the nurse says the other two children are doomed to go the same way. The younger, Jerry, a bright little lad of seven, is in school whenever his health permits, for he is eager to learn, but he is very frail.

In the afternoon John Darrow of the Salvation Army, came to ask me to copy for them in multiple on the typewriter a song which they wished to learn for their trip to the Salvation Army Congress soon to be held at Hoonah. These Indians are shrewd psychologists. They aren't up on the principles, but they are keen on the operation. John tried some on me—and it worked.

He has a little lad in Alma's room—a frail child—which is the apple of his eye. Possibly he really felt what he tried to express —possibly he simply desired to create an amiable attitude on my part—but Phillip had started in school and dropped out. He returned not long after Alma took charge of the primary room. John was liberal in his commendations of Phillip's teacher. For some reason he felt disapproval of the lad's first experience in school.

"No good!" he ejaculated. "Want good teachers for children. Thlingets can't read—don't know lots things—Thlingets got good eyes, see good!" and he pointed to his eyes.

"Thlingets got sharp ears, hear good!" and he pulled his aural lobes.

"Children come home—talk—father, mother listen— Thlingets can't read, don't know lots things—know good teachers."

These people are very psychic and are as sensitive to response in one another as a dog.

Well John had me helpless. I was completely disarmed, so I sat down and typed a dozen copies of the song for him.

Then Gilbert Cook and his wife came in—a social call this time—and stayed an hour. She is an intelligent girl and has been outside to school. For the first time we got her to talking and found her very interesting.

Eagle Horse and his little French wife and Carmel were the next callers and spent the entire evening with us.

As we finished our dinner of a venison roast, Bill Gardner, a Hyda Indian, came to the door with a goose which he had shot. "I brought you a geese," he had said, as he turned it over to me . . . The word "goose" is not mentioned by a Thlinget in polite society.

Chapter V

CASTE

The life of these people has undergone very radical changes in many respects during the last twenty-five to fifty years, but in spite of that, there are left-over influences that play a vital part in their lives today.

It is not easy for a white man to comprehend the present day social system of the Thlingets, because he knows absolutely nothing of what is going on beneath the surface, and little of what has gone before.

In the days before the advent of the whites, caste was the dominating element in the lives of these people, and that may still be true to a greater extent than we realize, although it is not evident to the casual observer.

The chief had the highest caste of all, but because rank depended chiefly on wealth, it was possible even for a freedman— one who had been a slave, but who had bought his freedom from his owner in some way—to become a sub-chief, if he could afford to build a house and give a potlatch. Wealth acquired and wisely manipulated could accomplish much with the Thlingets, just as it does with us today, and carry a man far; but influential as a chief might become, there was still an authority greater than his own— the power of totemic law. It settled all disputes; it passed on the eligibility of marriage; determined inheritance; settled the question of the number and rank of guests invited to feasts or pot- latches; designated what gifts should be given and to whom. The chief's voice was the first heard and carried much weight, but the final decision was reached in the totemic council.

Because rank was not a matter of birth, but of wealth and influence, the possibility existed with all of some day becoming a chief, just as our youth are led to believe that some day they may become president of the United States. A rise in rank was the sole ambition of the Thlinget, and his only interest in accumu- lating wealth was to that end. He was childishly fond of display and the aristocrats of a clan were easily identified. They were just as gluttonous and dirty, and smelled as vilely as the common herd but they had the manner. Their superiority could be seen in the dignity of their stride, the reserve of their manner and conserva- tism of speech, and in their assumption of authority.

There might be more than one chief in a tribal village; and there were clan or subchiefs among the clanal group, but this rank was not a matter of inheritance. A chief's son did not succeed him, for inheritance was not through the man, but through the woman's side of the family; so a chief's heirs were not his own children but the children of his sisters. His own children took the totem of his wife and only his sister's children were of his own clan.

Nor did the chief's rank entail upon any particular individual among his sister's children, but his successor would be chosen by the totemic group for his special fitness in wealth and other qualifications. No outsider can give definite and accurate information on these very complicated matters, for the understanding of the intricacies of the Thlinget mind is beyond him. He can only observe and listen and draw conclusions, which may have some measure of accuracy.

Among the Indians caste, which meant wealth, could cover a multitude of sins. A high-caste woman, even though she might be depraved, was respected and honored and was buried with pomp. As with us, caste had a powerful influence in the administering of justice. A low-caste woman would be awarded fifty blankets for the loss of an eye and her high-caste sister, four or five times as many for the loss of a finger; while the life of a chief was considered equivalent to ten or twelve ordinary men.

The chief was honored above all. He did no work nor any member of his family. The work was done by his slaves. He was supplied with game, and in all distributions of goods at feasts or potlatches, his was the largest share. No one else could build so large a house or erect a totem pole.

In the pre-white-man days the greatest element of wealth and evidence of rank, was the number of slaves possessed. The Thlingets were a warlike people in their native state and warring with their neighbors was both a favorite sport with them and a business. Their wars were sometimes punitive; a neighboring tribe may have raided their village or hunting or fishing preserves; possibly carried off a coveted maiden, or otherwise got on the wrong side of the fence. Frequently no excuse was needed other than that the young men were feeling their oats and needed exercise—also, how could they learn how to make war without practice?

The victorious party was always richer for the plunder accumulated—canoes, furs, weapons and captives who became the slaves of the captors.

In such cases it was a decided advantage to be a chief because in the division of slaves and plunder, the lion's share went to the lion, and the disposition of the rest was largely influenced by him.

If an individual showed social qualifications as a leader; if he distinguished himself in battle; or attained distinction as a mighty hunter, the way was open to improve his rank as fast as he was able to accumulate the means to build himself a house and hold the customary feasts which accompanied such an enterprise, and to round out the whole experience with a creditable potlatch.

The potlatch was an institution which was not merely a feast; it was more. If given at the completion of a house, or at the burial of the dead, or the carving of a totem pole and its erection, it afforded opportunity to pay those who had taken part in the work. In such cases the gift-giving was confined to those to whom pay was due, though others shared in the feasting.

Except in the case of a conspicuous chief, a potlatch was a village affair. The chief, however, who was known outside his immediate environs, might send invitations months in advance to individuals of rank in neighboring villages.

Because the potlatch was in the nature of a business obliga- tion in many instances, and because there was the underlying purpose of furthering one's social standing in the village, plans were usually very carefully made long in advance. A man would scrape and save for years and his family go without necessities in order to hoard up for the coveted potlatch; and during the great event he would lavishly give away all his property—his slaves, blankets, furs, canoes, weapons, and even his cooking utensils; and the old clothing would be distributed among those of low-caste. When it was over the family might be completely empover- ished, but oh, how proud they would be!

The value of what had been given away, if estimated in dollars and cents, would sometimes run as high as $10,000; but the in- creased standing of the family in the community amply compen- sated for any lack thereafter in worldly effects.

The giving was no haphazard affair. The Thlingets are shrewd business men and the distribution of gifts was cannily conducted. Not infrequently when a potlatch was contemplated, the man would distribute his property in advance among the leading citi- zens of the village, which would appear to be a lavish gesture; but inasmuch as etiquette required that the recipients should return the gift with generous interest shortly before the time set for the potlatch, it was an adroit method of swelling one's resources. Such maneuvering among us would arouse deep resentment, but with them it was accepted as part of the game and was religiously carried out by everyone involved. Pride was a strong trait with the Indians and no shame could equal that of obligations avoided. It was looked upon with the contempt bestowed on one who abrogates gambling debts among the whites.

The potlatch would extend over several days, or so long as the food supplies lasted for the feasting, which would be interspersed with dancing and with the accompanying singing; with the recounting of the valorous deeds of the host in war and in hunting; and the traditions and lore of the tribe, which would be narrated by the tribal historian, for there always were certain individuals who were authority on such matters and were adept at telling stories; and by intervals of work, if the potlatch was given in connection with the erection of a totem pole or the building of a house. The gift-giving was the culminating act and was performed with great ceremony. Hosts and guests arrayed themselves in ceremonial attire and the business was conducted much like a Christmas tree celebration with us. Everything was stacked in the center of the floor and clansmen, under the host's direction, would conduct the distribution. When the important gifts had been made, blankets and calico would be torn into strips or squares to make them go farther, and the old clothing would be divided among the lowly.

In the early days slaves were the most valued possessions and were distributed as gifts to those of highest rank; and at intervals during the prolonged affair, the host, with the nonchalance of a young scion of an American millionaire lighting his cigaret with a five dollar bill, would have the heads of some of his slaves bashed in with an axe of jade, just to show what a devil of a sport he was and that expense meant nothing to him. It is tradition among them that as many as 200 slaves have been killed at a single potlatch of a chief, and if the building of a house was the occasion for the event, a far-sighted and cautious chief would have a live slave buried under the corner posts of the house so that they might fend off any evilly disposed spirits.

Or course all such practices passed when the missionaries brought about the abolition of slavery.

The potlatch well illustrated the doctrine that "to him that hath shall be given," for who had the most, gave away the most, and received the most in return; and he who found himself destitute following such a spree, considered himself amply compensated by the increased deference shown him at ceremonials, by the seat of honor that was bestowed upon him at feasts, and the knowledge that at future potlatches he would be the recipient of still more generous gifts.

With some, a potlatch was never possible; with others it was the great event of a lifetime; while with a few it was an event which, if several times repeated, could cause a rapid rise in the social progress and resources of the climbers.

There was but one person in the Thlinget social register who out-ranked the chief—that was the medicine man, the Iht, or shaman, as he was variously called. His prominence came from the power he was supposed to wield over the individual. It would hardly do to call it a spiritual influence, but it was due to his supposed relations with the spirits which surrounded the Indian in his daily life and mixed in his affairs—particularly the evil or mischievous ones.

Naturally the social climber among these primitives was accompanied by jealousies and strife. Caste was the subject of debate and dispute at every fireside, and often the cause of feuds and war.

Of course all this is of the past, but we have found that a knowledge of it is important in aiding us to understand the people among whom we are living and working.

Those of high caste did not work, nor any member of the family: the slaves worked for them. Today there are no slaves, but that attitude towards menial labor persists. We were disposed at first to characterize certain individuals and families in the village as lazy, till we gained some insight into their social relations to the community and learned that they are high caste. One family in particular is poor as the traditional church mice, but there is a certain something—shall I call it the hackneyed "It"? about them that has led us to say, "There stalks the lordly Indian in all his pride," and I wish you could see the stalking. The woman has a dignity of bearing that is almost awesome. The sense of her superiority is strong within her and forces her fellow villagers to place the same valuation on her. We think of it as "bluff," but that is our opinion. The natives may accept them at their own valuation as the simon pure article. We would have to see into their minds in order to answer that question, and that is a thing no white man will ever do.

Her husband strides the street, splendidly physiqued, erect and commanding, genial in expression, stately in bearing; and to behold him is to suggest the stalking of a chieftan. Yet the young generation view him lightly. Two stalwart sons are the most perfect specimens of the Indian type among the young generation, but their mentality is not nearly as distinctive as that of numerous others, though they are steeped in the tradition and lore of the race. This family counts as nothing in the community, industrially. They do not produce, therefore they are poor; but they look down with disdain because of their caste, upon certain others who are a real power for the advancement and development of their people.

Today there seem to be two elements in the community—the older element, still dominated by the influence of age-old customs and traditions; and the younger generation—numerous ones of whom have been outside the community to the mission schools at Sitka, Haines, or elsewhere, or down to the Government Indian school at Chemawa in Oregon, which the Thlinget children have been allowed to attend. They, like the youth of the States, have thrown reverence for age to the winds, but they reveal an astounding mixture of primitive beliefs and twentieth century characteristics. They modernize very readily in many ways and show the same tendency to take the bit in their teeth and travel their own pace, as our own flaming youth who are furnishing us many problems.

Between the two elements stands a single individual—the mayor of the village, who in many ways is the most remarkable person in the community—a sport, as it were, among his people

Chapter VI

A HUNTING TRIP

I have been hunting—once—and I shall remember the experience. A young chap, a native, whose physiognomy would surely take a premium for its lack of beauty, told me he was going to Klawock Lake deer hunting the following Saturday and asked if I cared to go along. He promised to find me a firearm, which settled that point; when he also offered to furnish rubber boots, which he said would be necessary, the obstacles seemed removed so I grabbed at the opportunity, not knowing when I might have another. Now it is over I am glad that I went, but I would pass another similar opportunity by.

We would have to start before daylight on account of the tide. I didn't see what the tide had to do with deer hunting and Klawock Lake, but I was up at four o'clock. It hadn't rained for two or three days, but the sky was overcast, the wind blew, and rain threatened; so in the absence of rain-resistant clothing I fortified myself against exposure by putting on two or three of everything I had in the way of clothing—underwear, shirts, and socks. I still think I took wise precautions and don't know what else I could have done under the circumstances, but were I undertaking the enterprise again, I surely would do something different—or not go.

After loading myself with clothing till I could not bend readily, I lunched on cold venison, bread and a banana and waited till the men, Gardner and Joe Demmert, came along about five o'clock.

They had two shot guns and a Springfield rifle and were prepared for geese, ducks, deer or what have you? They turned the rifle over to me: I fancy because they thought there was less likelihood of their having use for it and it would be a convenient way of having it carried—and we started.

It was night, yet the darkness was not absolute, but because everything was unfamiliar to me, I simply followed their scarcely discernable forms the best I could—the three of us in Indian file. The plank street was slippery and slimy to my rubber boots, but it wasn't a circumstance to the slippery, slimy beach of jagged rock which we followed after we left the walk. They knew where they were going and probably followed a path, but I knew nothing and could see nothing, so I floundered along in the dark like one learning to skate and at times slipped badly into the background. When we returned that way by daylight I saw that we had followed the beach around a tide flat which separates the little island on which the village stands, from the main island.

It was easier going when we left the beach and struck into a trail that led through grassy swales—almost marshes—for some distance and then plunged into the timber which covered the banks of the tumbling creek we came to. I had heard that creek vociferating from the time we left the beach, but the swales led us away from the roaring clatter until the trail returned to the stream. By that time it was daylight so I could see the surroundings.

The boiling water of the stream as it tumbled down hill over the rocky channel, was still further disturbed by the plunging humpback salmon which were determined to go up stream or die in the attempt. The sight was alone worth the trip to see, although I could have dispensed with the smell of the carrion fish which lay along the banks until the ground was white. The salmon go as far upstream to spawn as they can get, and when they have functioned, they die and their bodies drift down stream to lodge along the banks where myriads of gulls, ravens and crows gorge themselves in a noisy, tempestuous struggle to "get while the getting is good"—quite suggestive of children at a church picnic.

Ducks—mallards and fish ducks—floated in the eddies, but we did no shooting because we wanted to bag the big game first.

We reached the lake where we had expected to find a boat but there was none there, so there was nothing to do but struggle through the tangle of windfalls and undergrowth that covered the steep sloping banks of the lake. By that time the boots I was wearing were weighing five pounds apiece, and I would have liked to peel off one of the layers of clothing I had on; but those Indians were ploughing along ahead of me so I floundered and stumbled along in the effort to keep them in sight. We climbed up and up between the mountains and got among the muskegs with their coffee-colored water standing among the bogs. It was another new experience for me to walk on that heavy mossy cushion in which I could see small wild cranberries growing, while up through it squeezed water, as though we were walking on a great sponge.

Joe picked little tri-lobed leaves and put them between his lips, making in some way a sound which marvelously reproduced the bleating of a fawn. Bill confessed that he himself could not do the trick, so he slipped the skin from an alder stem and contrived a deer-call of his own which, however, did not furnish the realistic touch of the other. Had there been any deer around they surely would have been in evidence, for the men told me a deer, hearing the call of a fawn, will walk right up to a hunter who is calling. None walked up to us. We were doing the walking.

The men pointed out a little plant which they said is called "Hudson Bay tea" and which is used by the natives as we use tea, when they are in the woods, but that was all the good it did. It was merely potential tea. I could have used the real thing just then.

The clouds hung low around the mountain tops; the wind blew and a cold rain started. Joe had wandered apart on business of his own, while Bill averred that the deer were up in the timber of the mountains beneath the clouds, and the way to get them was to go after them. He seemed to have confidence enough in his judgment to start up the mountain, so of course I followed, but by that time my boots weighed ten pounds apiece and I would have liked to peel off two of everything I had on, for perspiration had seeped up by capilarity to meet the rain which soaked down by gravity, till the twain had met. With less clothing I could not have been wetter and my temperature would not have been so high.

We didn't find the deer on the first mountain, so we climbed down and up another. I had read as a boy about the tenacity with which the Red man holds to the trail. I know something about it now from personal observation. Bill Gardner was out after deer, or to show the checacho how to hunt for deer, and he intended to make a thorough job of it. He did. The deer weren't on the other mountain either, so he decided we might as well go down again and get some ducks along the river. The idea appealed to me. I liked to hunt ducks almost as well as to hunt deer—sometimes, better. I had been walking over that spongy ground for hours, like a horse with the stringhalt, and I had a notion that the increasing weight of those boots would be offset in a measure if I carried them down hill instead of up.

I had thought the lake was beautiful when I first saw it—a long narrow ribbon of water winding around between crowding mountains, but I scarcely noticed it coming back—I was thinking only of the trail and its far end.

We reached the creek. My Indian assured me that there we would find ducks—possibly geese—maybe swans. I had never hunted ducks with a rifle, but I wasn't feeling a great deal of initiative, so I followed him—it seemed the logical thing to do—it was his hunting party. Again I admit that though I don't see how I could have done differently, yet if I were doing it over again, I would surely do otherwise. The creek banks were a terrible jungle. Big windfalls lay along the bank and by the time I had straddled over a few of them, unwittingly grasping handy supports of devil's club to steady myself, those massive boots weighed a quarter hundredweight each, and the perspiration which flowed into them added to the burden. The gulls and ravens swirled in noisy clouds above me—I had lost my guide. He was hunting ducks. I sat on a big log after dragging my feet over it, and watched an eagle skim the water and snatch a salmon from the boiling surface. Heartened a bit I started on, but the muscles which had been lifting those giant boots for ten long hours, began to cramp. I came to a big log and found my feet riveted to the ground. I couldn't go around the tree, nor under it, nor stay there, so I sat down on the big trunk and backed over it like a crab. With my feet once on top of the log I could push them off on the other side. There was nothing to do but go on, so I went, but had to watch the gulls and those black humps surging their way up the creek every time I came to a fallen tree. In between time I rested while I picked the hairlike needles of the devils club from my hands.

Bears had visited the creek and, raking the dying or dead fish out with their great paws, had tossed them deftly upon the bank where they feasted happily; while gravel bars and shelving banks were fringed with the putrid fish. Even my exhaustion could not rob me of an interest in what I was experiencing—nor of a desire to get into a less impressive atmosphere.

There is an end to everything, and there was to that struggle along the roaring creek. I found myself out of the jungle and following a path which took me past a tall totem pole topped with an eagle carved with outstretched wings; and though I knew I had been over the ground in the morning, it was all new to me, for I had not seen the trail I had traveled in the dark. But there was no beach, when I had gone as far as I could go. The tide was in and the slimy beach I had slid and slithered across was several feet under water with Klawock on an island beyond. I found my guide at the water's edge with no more ducks than deer, and after scouting about he found a boat which he thought would stay on top till we got across. It was a case of chancing it or waiting there in the wet and cold for six hours for the tide to go out. We made it. I bailed with a rubber boot and Bill paddled with a piece of board, and at last we landed.

I got home because I didn't have to lift those boots off the board walk—I could slide them along, but when I got in the house they fell off my feet.

I peeled off my sodden clothing and after a good rub-down, I stepped on the scales which stood in the bedroom—I weighed an even ten pounds less than I had the night before—then I rolled into bed to get the chill out of my body but could not sleep for the cramping of the muscles in my calves and thighs; but hot drink and food and a period of rest put me on my feet again—glad of the experience, since it was over. But listen, son, to the wisdom of a father: when you climb mountains don't wear rubber boots—at least, until you are accustomed to carrying them around; and unless you are hardened and in good condition, don't go hunting with an Indian.

Chapter VII

THANKSGIVING DAY

It is the night of Thanksgiving Day.

Of course we had to have school exercises yesterday. That was inevitable, and anything in the nature of a public entertainment is meat and drink to these people. We discovered that when we attempted to have an Armistice Day program at the schoolhouse on the night of November 11th. If anyone in town wasn't there, it must have been because they came and couldn't get in, for every seat available and possible, and every foot of standing room was full of men, women, children and babies and no more could even look in. We could hardly clear space enough for those who were to take part.

During the war Chief Eagle Horse, participated in the Liberty Loan drives in New York City. Much publicity was given to the manifestation at such time on the part of our dusky wards, of their patriotism and loyalty to the nation. He is a Thlinget Indian who has educated himself to a point where there is quite a gap between him and the mass of his people. He was a fine singer at that time and had toured various sections of the world in vaudeville with a troupe of Indian singers. Well, he is living here in Klawock, his boyhood home, with his beautiful little French wife. He says he has worn his voice out and has returned to live among his people.

He talked Armistice evening, as did I, and two of the young men who saw service—one in the Navy and the other in the Army—for the war touched even the natives of remote Alaska.

By rights we should have had our Thanksgiving exercises in the evening, but I felt unwilling to go through another such experience as that of Armistice Day night, so the exercises were held in the respective school rooms in the afternoon, with the idea of splitting up the audience. It was so thoroughly split up that only the Primary room had a real audience. Their program was quite a success, but otherwise the observance was something of a disappointment all around.

I had been asked by Andrew Wanamaker, the native pastor of the Presbyterian Church, to talk at the Thanksgiving service in the church this morning, and of course I consented, though I never felt more nonplussed as to what to talk about to an audience which would have to sit and listen to the sounds I made and then be told in their own tongue what it was all about. The problem was to keep within their experience and understanding, both in thought and speech, and I was not sure I could do that.

I had planned a little talk but when Mr. Wanamaker gave out the hymn I saw that it dealt with religious persecution and freedom from it. I am sorry that I cannot quote the passage which was my inspiration, but I was so intent on my train of thought that it did not fix itself in my mind, and I do not have one of the hymn books here. However, I explained about the coming of the first white men to America and that they came because they were not willing to be told they must all belong to the same church—that they must all be Salvation Army members or go to the Presbyterian or some other church—particularly some other church, and I told about their finding Indians occupying the country and how they became friends with them. I pointed out what the coming of white men to Alaska had meant to the natives . . . I was on ticklish ground there, for the white man's presence has not been an unmixed blessing to the Thlingets . . . and how they had learned about the white man's God and recognized in Him their own Ke-An-Kow— the "Great One over All."

I showed how, as the number of people increase in the world, it is necessary to have a Great Chief over all the people and that there must be law to protect the Thlingets as well as the white people, and it was something to be thankful for that we had that law and that we could be members of any church we pleased.

I pointed out how their own lives had changed—that now they lived in houses instead of bark sheds; that they no longer made war on their neighbors and owned slaves; that they owned gasboats instead of big canoes; and that their children were going to school and learning about things their parents had never dreamed about.

As I developed an idea Mr. Wanamaker would interpret it for them in Thlinget and they certainly listened earnestly.

When we came out of the church it seemed like a Thanksgiving Day down in the States, because instead of the customary rain, we stepped into flying snowflakes—the first we have seen— and the air was chill and the sky black and lowering.

We had invited the nurse and teachers and Eagle Horse, his wife and little Carmen, a native child who lives with them and who has taken a great fancy to me, to have Thanksgiving dinner with us; but no turkeys arrived on the mail boat, so in the end we pooled our resources and had a joint dinner. The girls furnished the venison, which had been presented to them by the natives, and Alma roasted it with dressing and made mince and pumpkin pies, while the nurse added a box of fresh vegetables sent up by her daughter, and candied fried sweet potatoes, prepared the cabbage, brussels sprouts, made fresh rolls and a jello dessert. It was a loaded board when everything was on the table and no dinner we have ever had down in the States was appreciated more than this Thanksgiving dinner in Alaska.

Following the dinner the teachers left by gasboat for a dance at Craig, our nearest neighbor, but Eagle Horse and his wife and Carmen stayed.

Carmen is such a dear little chick. Her parents both have white blood and she is quite fair and brown-haired, instead of black. She is only five, but she will sit still as a mouse—as still as all Indian children sit—never teasing, never fidgetting, never wanting to go home.

Early in the evening word came to the nurse that Mrs. Billy Benson was in a serious condition from a heart attack, and she hurried off. Eagle Horse, who is a nephew through some connection, went with her.

Later I went down with him to look in on the community dinner in Bob's Hall. I had wondered in the morning just what Thanksgiving Day meant to the natives, and I don't know now, but I do know this much, that it is a chance for a feast for them and they make use of it. The hall was so packed that we had difficulty in squeezing in where we could look on for a few minutes from the balcony. The tables, two of them, ran the length of the hall and were groaning with the weight of the food, while in spite of the fact that we were full of dinner of our own, it looked so tempting that we could have sat down and attempted to do it justice.

There was extended speech-making and it would be impossible to say which enjoyed it the most, the talkers or the listeners. The Thlingets love to talk in public and do it as easily and naturally as they sing. Of course most of it was unintelligible to me, though I could catch something of the drift of the talk through the interpolation of English words where they had none of their own to serve the purpose, but it was hugely enjoyed by those who understood, and the constant laughter at quips and stories at some one's expense, showed the keenness of the Thlinget sense of humor.

But after all I am still a little hazy as to whether Thanksgiving

Day has been seized upon as an opportunity for a traditional feast, or whether it is merely an accompaniment of a ceremonial event introduced by the white man.

There is another thing not clear to me. Everyone was not present at the feast in Bob's Hall, nor were we invited to be present. I wonder whether they felt diffident about asking us, or whether they would have felt restraint had we been there. I also wonder whether Eagle Horse was supposed to be present and was not because of our invitation, or whether he did not belong in that crowd. I did not see the Demmert people in evidence. Possibly it was only a Peratovich clan affair. There are so many things we do not understand about these people, or rather, so few things we do understand.

Chapter VIII

VILLAGE GOVERNMENT

Just now I am amused and interested by the political organization of the village. A mayor and a judge, councilmen and marshals sound like an anachronism in an Indian hamlet, but they have them and to the natives, they are the real thing. I haven't had either time or opportunity, because part of almost every day, in addition to my multitudinous duties, is given up to individuals of the community and their troubles, to dig into the whereforeness of the village organization. I would say at a guess though, that the white man's political organization was undoubtedly initiated by the missionaries in order to separate the natives from their barbaric customs; and was encouraged and fostered by the Government, when it finally turned attention to its wards in the great new territory of Alaska.

The village of Klawock is located on a Government reservation, so there is no private ownership of land here. Much of the village was here before the reservation—the Government took it over "as was," so the building of houses was entirely haphazard and promiscuous. A house was built how, when, and where the individual felt disposed. The points of compass meant nothing to the builders—the sole consideration being proximity to the beach and availability of drinking water, and of the two the beach was the more important. It was largely the source of their living and it also constituted their sewage system, though as such we would consider it a failure, because the tide brought as much as it carried away. In the early days the beaches were strewn with the carcasses of dead dogs, the decaying remains of fish, seals, sea lions, the bones of deer and other wild animals, and the bones of slaughtered or otherwise deceased slaves, who were never given burial but were cast into the sea for time, bird scavengers, and the waves to dispose of.

The missionaries in the course of time modified the situation somewhat, for the human bones and remains are no longer seen, but on warm days our noses reveal that there is still something to be hoped for.

But I had a call from the village judge today and that is what I started to tell about.

A fisherman, in hip rubber boots and oilskins, for it happened to be raining as usual—gaunt, actually cadaverous. I asked myself if he was one of the numerous "T.B." cases the nurse has told us about; but however that may be, he is father to a large litter of children and husband to a buxom brunette wife who has babies as a cat has kittens and with the same regularity. His name is Maxfield Dalton and I think he understood me less than I understood him—but he managed to reveal that at one time when the West Coast had experienced a bonanza fishing season, some enterprising white man had visited the village and "sold" him, and undoubtedly many others, to the idea of investing his savings in one of the white man's gilded dreams. The details are unimportant: the results were per usual; but the thing that interested me as a bit of Indian psychology, was the fact that contrary to the white man's custom of keeping everything in his own name, Maxfield had invested a certain amount for himself, the same for his dusky wife, and as much for each member of his extensive family, regardless of age. The aggregate was considerable and all a loss. I had to send him out into the sudsing rain two or three times, though the distance was less than twenty rods, to round up all the papers he possessed and such correspondence as had stayed by him, before I could get any comprehension of what it was all about. He had labored, as is usually the case in such matters, under the impression that he could recover his money, but the numerous exceptions and provisions had carefully guarded against any such possibility. He is simply "out of luck." I wrote a letter for him which he signed —he could do that—but that was all I could do for the Judge.

I have found that the Judge is a real personality in the community and takes his position seriously according to his lights. One day one of the men sent his daughter, a school girl, to tell me that he had shot a deer and would let me have a quarter of venison. We were without meat. There was none to be had, so the news had an encouraging sound, but I hesitated, because of my official position, to violate the letter of the game laws. I was reassured later by the man himself, who said he had sold the other quarter to the Judge. Afterwards, when I came to understand the extent to which the Judge's larder was usually supplied with fresh meat, I suspected it was simply my neighbor's way of making me feel I was among friends. The venison cost us $2.00 and nothing ever tasted better—except more of the same. A canned diet can get very monotonous.

It has puzzled me somewhat to know under what code Judge

Dalton administers justice, and I cannot point to the basis of it all, though I can see that he was strong on previous court decisions— his own, of course. As a matter of fact he can only handle cases when the penalty does not exceed a fine of $25 or a jail sentence in the local "hoosegow," which is a smoke house. If the prisoner escapes through the smokehole, that is so much responsibility escaped, an escaped prisoner does not have to be fed. Nevertheless, the Judge is judicial in his decisions, which are not questioned by the villagers, and he insists that the proper procedure shall be followed. On written complaint, which he cannot read, one of the marshals, is rounded up and the arrest is made. The Judge has the complaint explained and sentence is pronounced. There is never any question of the guilt. Half of the fine goes to the Judge for his trouble, and what gets by the marshals goes into the village treasury, if use isn't found for it before it gets there.

The other limb of the law is represented by the marshals, of which there were three when we came to the village.

I shall have to stop here to explain that there are really but two families in the village: the Peratovich family, and the Demmert family. The Eagle and the Raven clans are represented, of course, in each, but otherwise there is strong rivalry between them. They occupy different sections of the village and each has its conspicuous leader; but in order to preserve some semblance of harmony, political patronage has to be distributed, so I learned one day through the talk of school children, that three more marshals had been appointed by the village council; and a cautious question or two, these people are very sensitive to curiosity, elicited the information that a feeling had been current that the political pap was not otherwise sufficiently distributed. A village of 400 souls with six marshals is well marshaled.

But the big figure of the village is the mayor, and he really is a big figure. I consider him one of the most remarkable men I have known.

Robert J. Peratovich, whom everyone knows as "Bob," at the time he reached young manhood, was a primitive Thlinget Indian. Unquestionably there is white blood in his veins, I have never learned just where it came in; but if the name indicates anything, it dates back to the Russian occupation.

Bob was primitive but he was different and one day appeared before the missionary, David Waggener, who labored early, long and faithfully for the Presbyterian Board of Missions, with a dusky maiden and wished to be married in the white man's way. He was married and set to work to learn the Boston man's language. and the white man's ways, and the extent to which he has succeeded is a marvel to me.

He is probably forty-five or fifty years old—short and heavy set, with regular features and thick hair not as black as is usual with the Thlingets. He speaks with an accent and does not always phrase his thoughts quite as we would, but he is careful and surprisingly successful in his choice of words, and very clear in his understanding.

He early started a little store and when the native co-operative store was organized under the guidance of David Waggener and later, the Bureau of Education, it was at first decided to put him in charge and he was to turn in his own business on account, but complications arose and he decided to operate for himself and has been doing that ever since. His little store, under shrewd management, prospered and has developed into a large general store which must do quite a volume of business annually. In time he started a salmon cannery which he has operated for a number of years to much advantage of himself and his fellow villagers.

In connection with his growing interests he visited Ketchikan and Seattle and became intensely interested and keenly observant of the white man's ways, and returned to his native village to put into practice the things he learned. His mind has shown a power to comprehend and absorb that which is new, to an extent far in advance of the rest of his people. He is one of the "sports" who is possessed by an urge—who reaches in his vision much ahead of his time.

When Bob saw the electric lights of Seattle, he wanted Klawock to have electric lights, so he bought a Diesel engine and had it installed in a shed back of his store; set the necessary poles and had the wire strung for the incandescent street lights. He found no difficulty about installing lights in the natives' homes. Electric lights were fine! But when he sought to collect compensation for them once or twice a year, that was a different matter and he found it necessary to become hard-boiled—no pay, no lights. That was all right. They didn't like to pay for what was used and gone; neither did they like to pay for what they had not yet received; in other words, they just didn't like to pay at all. They had as much light without them as they had ever had: What was good enough for their ancestors was good enough for them, so they let it go at that. But that wasn't progress and Bob was all for progress, so he continued to operate the street lights at his own expense, shipping in fuel oil from Ketchikan by the barrel, until the tankers began to make the West Coast for the cannery trade. Sometimes, if the village had money, he got some pay. Sometimes he didn't.

When we arrived the Diesel engine had broken down, so the village was unlighted, but Bob is back from the south and the Diesel chugs again. The lights come on at dark and burn until Bob goes to bed, which is when he gets ready, but the nights when clansmen are sitting up with the dead, lights burn all night.

Bob's store grew. His cannery helped it to grow. He gave credit to his clan, and sometimes others, and bought their fish during the trolling season and shipped them to the fresh fish market at Ketchikan or Seattle. Those who owed him worked for him during the salmon runs and he collected their store bills. It was a profitable arrangement all around. It insured profitable customers for his store, and credit for them when they needed it, and guaranteed him fish and fishermen for his cannery—and them a market for their labor when the need was mutual. Bob's success has been a great advantage to the village. He built a public hall on piles beside the shore end of his dock and on his return from one of his trips to Seattle, he brought a moving picture outfit, so Klawock is modern to the extent of possessing a movie theater where the "movies" can be seen on Wednesday and Saturday nights— when the Diesel is in working order, and when the mail boat has brought fresh films.

The Klawock Commercial Company is largely owned by the other family, and it also has to give credit, but having no cannery, is without the means of collecting store accounts; consequently the stockholders are eating up their stock and it is supposed to be my problem to keep a business going which is selling on credit and consuming its capital, because when the accounts of the stockholders reach the value of the stock they hold, they say, "You can have my stock to pay the account." It's some job I have.

But to return to the Mayor. I have told you about the problem of water supply and that we are having to use rain water from the roofs, or coffee-colored spring water which seeps down the hillsides through decaying organic matter. The morning after our arrival I searched out the mayor for conference on the subject and found him on the eve of his annual trip to Seattle.

To secure water for his cannery he had gone up in the hills

and tapped a pocket or small pond of water and brought it down in wooden pipes. He had endeavored in the past to interest the Government in a water system for the village, but Uncle Sam had been more fertile in objections to the plans suggested than it had been in constructive ideas, so this aggressive, go-getting Thlinget Indian, working on the principle that the Lord helps those who help themselves, went ahead and got water himself. I would like to know all the details of the experience—the financing, the planning, and the work, but I have been able to catch only occasional glimpses of the inside. The fact remains that Bob bought four inch wooden pipe in Seattle, shipped it to Klawock on a freighter, had it packed up through the jungle of the mountainside by his workmen, and got it laid; but in tapping the lake a ledge of rock was encountered running directly across the path of the pipeline like a dam, with its top two or three feet below the level of the lake. One of the men on the job had been out to school and learned something about the siphon. He assured Bob that it would be foolish to cut through that rock rim when a pipe could be laid and the water siphoned over the rim. Why not make use of the white man's knowledge? The pipe was laid, but the water failed to flow. Not so good! The white man didn't know so much after all. A day came, however, when the lake filled with melting snow and rain and lo! water came bubbling and boiling down through the pipe and all the village came to see. Not so bad after all! The water was wet and cold and pure—fine while it lasted—but it doesn't rain all the time on Prince of Wales Island, and the snow on the mountains melts, so a time comes each year when the water in the pipeline gurgles and splutters—and stops running.

Bob didn't tell me that in my interview, but he did tell that for the sake of aiding the Government of the United States, he was willing it should tap his pipeline and carry a supply of wholesome water to the school grounds in order that the teachers might have water and the children not have to drink from the rain barrels. All the United States need do would be to furnish the necessary pipe, which could be shipped up on the same freighter with the winter stock for the store.

Nothing could better illustrate that this man is in advance of his race, than this action on his part, for giving, without receiving more in return, is not good Thlinget practice.

I transmitted the information to the Bureau of Education office in Seattle, and the worthy mayor interviewed the Seattle office in person. The Government gratefully accepted the generosity of its ward and we have been promised the pipe, but I doubt if it will reach us in time to get it into the ground before winter prevents.

The mayor helped me estimate the pipe and equipment needed, and the cost of laying the pipe; but knowing more now than I did at the time, I realize that he figured on what it would cost him to get the pipe into the ground, but not what it would cost Uncle Sam. I find there is quite a difference and that the allowance made for labor will hardly lay the pipe on the ground. However, more time is coming and it will be something to have the pipe here ready for laying. Also I have learned that Bob's water doesn't run all winter, and when the flow is once interrupted, it runs no more until the lake level rises again to the hump of the siphon and the white man's knowledge begins to work again. Bob says however, that he is going to blast through that rock rim and lay larger pipe, and I think he will. His greatest handicap in the progress which he craves is the lack of know-how.

Chapter IX

THE LANGUAGE

The Thlingets have no written language and of course, no alphabet, so if one wishes to put on paper anything they say, it is necessary to spell it phonetically with our alphabet. That is difficult to do because they have sounds we cannot make or represent, and they do not use a number of our sounds.

The designs used on the baskets which they weave, and on their ceremonial robes, and the carvings on their totem poles, express certain crude ideas, but they can only be read by those who already know what they mean . . . they cannot be considered as writing. They are merely records or reminders of events or ideas which have been transmitted orally from generation to generation, and serve the same purpose as the string we tie around a finger to remind us of something we must not forget. The Thlingets seem to have made no attempt to transmit ideas pictorially as have the Indians of the States.

When one comes to understand what a meager and restricted life the natives have lived on their rocky island beaches, between the mountains and the sea, it is evident that they would not have an extensive language. Their experience was too limited. Their contacts were with objects of the sea, the mountains, and the forests, so their language would naturally be largely one of names, and their expressed thoughts largely comparisons of new experiences with old. It is already very clear to us that their language is wholly inadequate to express much in the way of abstract thought, or to communicate fine distinctions or shades of meaning; and probably it is both cause and effect that their very limited thought has made an elaborate language unnecessary.

I could not comprehend at first some of the difficulty some of the young people, who speak American freely, have seemed to have in translating or interpreting their own thoughts, until a young fellow said to me one day, "I don't know how to tell it to you, because I know of no words in your language to use." Often very funny mistakes are made by those acting as interpreters, but I am gaining a little insight into the reasons for it. For one thing, there is no gender in their language. "We nearly lost one of our young men," the mayor told me yesterday, when I dropped into his store on an errand, "she was skating and broke through the ice, but some boys pulled him out and now she is all right." Such errors in gender are very common among the natives of the older generation.

Then I understand that their nouns are followed by adjectives, and the verb, which is most often implied, comes last and is preceded by the adverbs. Articles, prepositions, and conjunctions are conspicuous by their absence. Of course to me—not knowing their language—this is apparent in their attempts to talk mine, as when expressing disapproval of a youth of the village one said, "Him no good! Heart too much high down," meaning that he was conceited; and when the nurse asked an old lady to whom she rendered medical aid, how she felt that morning, the reply was "Itten bit haf much," which carried the idea that she didn't feel so badly as the day before.

We have had much trouble in school in properly identifying children, for they would tell that certain children bearing different surnames were their brother or sister, when we did not think that could be the case. As a result I have begun to make a record of all family history that comes to my attention.

One stands as much chance of getting information from a clam as from these people, if he goes after it; but if he shows no apparent interest, but uses his ears instead of tongue, they will spill the most surprising and intimate information and enjoy doing it. As a result my record is rather staggering in the nature of some of the data, but it is illuminating and helps us to straighten out some otherwise inexplicable things. As an illustration, there is a little chap in Alma's room who goes by the name of Oscar Demmert and who the census of last year shows is the son of James Demmert; but in taking the census recently of school children, one of the teachers found him living with an old couple, Kokash Demmert and his wife whom the child called father and mother, and who proved to be the parents of James Demmert—more or less. Later "Judge" Maxfield Dalton told me that Oscar was his son, but his command of my language did not permit him to explain the paradox. Eventually the nurse came to my rescue and by piecing together fragments of information she accumulated with what I already had, we have learned that Oscar Demmert was born Oscar Dalton, by a wife of Maxfield's who died. Maxfield of course, married again and his older daughter married James Demmert. Because the Judge's new wife was having children of her own, Oscar's sister and her husband adopted the lad; so his sister became his mother; but she died and James married another sister, according to ancient custom. That sister was made Oscar's aunt by the first marriage, and his mother by the second. Such a combination of sister, aunt and mother all in one, would naturally complicate relations, but Oscar preferred his grandfather to both his father and foster father, and spent most of his time with them and called them father and mother—so what is a poor teacher to do?

This is a typical illustration of the complications with which we have to struggle; but to add to them, it seems that in the Thlinget language the word "La," mother, is applied not only to the actual mother, but to the mother's mother, the mother's sisters, and to all the women of her clan and generation, and the term "sister" is equally broad in its application, which explains some of the things we have puzzled over.

The mother's brothers, and all the men of that clan are "uncles," while the term grandparents is applied only to the older generation on the mother's side.

One day several of Alma's little pupils were in our quarters and I asked their names. There were Annie Collins, Tecumseh's little granddaughter, though he called her daughter; Mary Smith, whose father is white; Jane Roberts, and several others.

"She's my sister," explained Mary Smith of Jane Roberts.

I looked at Alma in surprise, and she looked at me.

"They're cousins," Alma said. Both of us concluded the children didn't understand what "sister" meant, but later I learned that girl cousins on the mother's side are called sisters among the Thlingets.

We are making no effort to learn the Indian language—we are here to teach them ours—but it makes it difficult to get proper results when the native tongue is always talked at home. I have urged with the people, whenever I have had a chance to talk to them in public, that they should help their children to learn the American language by making them talk it at home, and I make this argument with them; that the Thlingets are few and the whites many; that they cannot expect the whites to learn the Thlinget language, so the natives should learn the language of the whites if they wish to sell their fish to them, buy their gasboats from them, and associate with them. The mayor sees the importance of it and he translates to those who do not understand me, and emphasizes the force of the argument in his own way. I wish I could understand him. His argument is probably much more interesting than mine.

But though I make no effort to learn the Indian language,

I am interested in learning about it. Because of the very restricted life they lead, their language is very simple and very meager. The words are usually monosyllables or, when grouped, each syllable has a separate significance. And their names usually refer to some animal, generally the totemic animal of the clan, as "Dish-ta" —frog sitting in the road.

Their experiences are so largely connected with the sea, the the mountains and forests, that every new experienc is expressed in terms of what they know. We think their language is figurative and poetic. It is to us, but it is their only mode of expressing their ideas to one another.

I think by quoting part of one of their legends, I can illustrate how the Indians instruct their children by means of their legends, and teach them not to speak unkindly of animals.

As translated literally the story runs:

"town—was long—in the middle of it—was lived—chief— his daughter—berries liked to pick—for berries—with them she went—her father's slaves with—on it she stepped—grizzly bear's dung—way up in the woods—while berrying—so she said to— grizzly bear's dung—'Always feet down to—they went—asses wide.' "

In intelligible English:

"A chief lived in the middle of a very long town. His daughter was fond of picking berries. Once she went for berries with her father's slaves and while picking far up in the woods, she stepped upon some grizzly bear's dung. 'They always leave things under people's feet, those wide asses,' " she said.

There is no rcfinement among primitives. If they have any-thing to tell, they tell it. There is no way for them to beat around the bush or imply or suggest. Their language permits only direct speech. For that reason there is no modesty or immodesty about their speech and some of their plain talk to the nurse would make a sensitive white man's skin creep.

Limited as their language is they always manage to express themselves in their own tongue to one another, even though the same expression may be used in various different connections.

But of more interest to us than their language, which we do not understand, is their speech, which we have to listen to. They make much use of aspirant or breathing sounds very hard or impossible for us to produce; and gutturals, like the Germans; while they use several "k" sounds which we do not have at all and which give their speech a clucking sound quite unlike anything

I have heard before. They speak deliberately and their voices are very low, doubtless due to so much use of the aspirants. When the native speaks he does it with lips apart as when we make the sound "aah," and by using the inside muscles of the throat and the base of the tongue, in a way which the peculiar formation of their throat makes possible. The lips are used very little, but the tongue a great deal, and because of the breathing and guttural nature of their voices, they not only lack volume, but are pitched very low. Even the women's and children's voices are pitched so low as to sound like men's. When the Thlinget woman actually sings soprano pitched with an instrument, her voice is not particularly pleasing, but when pitched to suit herself it is rich and musical.

In talking the people make use of sounds which the white man's throat is not formed to make. To imitate them in a measure he must talk with his mouth nearly shut and with little use of the lips and teeth.

The older Indians seem unable to pronounce consonant sounds which bring the lips together. "P" and "B" are not used at all in native speech; "M" is used occasionally; "L" is not used when it should be, but "N" is apt to take its place. When my roly-poly friend, Tecumseh Collins, would talk to me about "Langen" I was greatly mystified and it was some time before I realized he was talking about Wrangell. The Rev. S. Hall Young, in his autobiography, "Hall Young of Alaska," in commenting on that limitation, told that they never could pronounce "Mr. Young" except as "Wisle Yuy." "F" and "R" are also sounds which they do not use much, but they have several distinct "K" sounds, and the consonants D, G, H, N, Q, T, W, and X are used a great deal.

Their limited vocabulary and their contact with people from the outside world in later years, have been responsible for the introduction of many of our words into their speech and the coining of new words to meet new experiences, as when on their first experience with ice cream, they called it "frozen grease"; and gave lima beans a name that suggests fat found in a moose; and Quaker Oats a name, because of its resemblance to the seeds of the wild celery. In the same way they often nickname one another for some peculiarity.

Of course the language has been handed down orally from generation to generation—probably for hundreds of years—and the younger generation does not understand many of the words used by their grandparents. One of the school boys told me one day that he had three different native names and one day his grandmother called him by another name and he didn't know she was talking to him because he had forgotten what it meant.

We do not get their native names in school, nor as a rule, do we know the natives by their Indian names. In their contact with the whites all natives have accumulated names by which they are generally known. When the salmon canneries came to Alaska and began to employ Indian fishermen and workmen, the time-keepers would give each one some name to designate him and that name in time was accepted by the native. It was quite incomprehensible to me at first that in a family claiming to be brothers and sisters, each would have a different surname. I have found that to be due in part, to the reason just given; and in part, to the fact that they often had only a mother or father in common, and the father wasn't always a native.

An old lady lives near us who is the mother of Fred Thomas and Tom Adams, but whom I have heard called "Mrs. Jackson," "Mrs. Cook," "Mrs. Jack," and "Mrs. Cook-Jack." On inquiry I learned that her husband, or at least the last one, was put on a payroll at one time as "Jack." Later he worked as a cook and to distinguish him from other Jacks, he was called "Cook Jack." The other names were used according to people's tastes and served their purpose in designating that particular woman. I never did learn her native name, nor any of the other names she doubtless had in the course of her life.

I understand that all Thlinget proper names have a meaning, as "Ska-wat-klon" (big woman), and "Ka-uh-ish," (father of the morning). Further, names applied to persons are carried down from generation to generation. There seems to be some belief of reincarnation involved, but I have not been able to get a definite enough understanding of it to attempt to explain it, except that when a child is expected it is hoped that it will resemble some particular individual who has gone beyond, and if that resemblance is detected, the child will be given the name of that individual and the belief is held that the spirit of that one has returned to dwell in the child. The unwillingness of the natives to punish their children seems to have some connection with this belief.

Surnames were not used in the early days. The totem of the clan identified the family, and the smaller groups living in the big communal houses were generally indicated by some description of the house or family. For instance: the Henya clan to which the natives of Klawock largely belong, originally lived in Tuxican,

68

which I think I have explained, was their winter home; so people of Tuxican were known as "the winter people"—people of the "winter town." Sukwan was known as "grassy town"; Kasaan, as "pretty town"; and Klinkwan, as "town where people get things at low tide."

The Raven group was the main group of the Henyas, but as the result of a quarrel between families living in a community house, one part seceded and built a house of its own of poles and bark, and became known as "barkhouse people." Another group were the "martin people," and still another, the "human foot people."

It would be fascinating could we know the origin and history connected with such names as: "Copper plate house"; "Steel house," with its chief, "Wounded goose flopping around"; "Lively herring house"; "Rock house," with its chief, "Raven crying everywhere"; "Iceberg house," chief, "Saved a captured man"; "House on point," chief, "Copper green color of frog"; "House that carries a big load and is bent over with its weight," chief, "Boneless frog"; "Halibut house," chief, "Wolf wailing around a person"; "House with two doors," chief, "Eagle going around a dead thing and making a noise"; and so on indefinitely.

Individuals were given names for some particular reason; for instance, a boy might be called by a name that means "whistles like a bird." Later in his childhood a bear pursues him and he becomes known as "Boy chased by a bear." One of the girls in the Primary room whose name on the roster is Vivian, is known as "Kay-ish-tik" (picking something up) in the native tongue; and a boy enrolled as Embert, grandson of "Kewpie" Collins, is "Kla-oosh," which means seaweed.

When a man becomes a father the syllable "ish" (father) was added to the child's name. If the boy's name is "Hult-zoo," the father is called "Hult-zoo-ish" (father of Hult-zoo). That was illustrated above in the name "Ka-uh-ish" (father of the morning).

Chapter X

I WONDER

Every time I turn around I run into something I don't understand.

We have a Delco lighting plant in the basement of the schoolhouse which furnishes us with light — sometimes. This is my first contact with one, so when I learned from one of the teachers that a white man named Joe Yester, living in the village, was going away and that he was the only one who knew anything about it and could repair it, I hastened to get hold of him to learn all possible about its tricks and ways.

I found him an intelligent fellow. He told me that he and his wife were going down to the States to live. They have three children and are going to take the two babies, but though he wanted to take the oldest girl too, and educate her, his wife's family wouldn't allow it, so they would have to leave her behind. He showed so much distress over it that I looked at him in astonishment and asked, "What has your wife's family got to say about what you do with your own children?"

"Everything, in this damned country," he answered, with much bitterness.

I didn't understand, but I hesitated to appear inquisitive by asking questions.

Well, Joe has gone and the little five-year-old child has been left behind — little Emily. She is a bright little chick and due to her white father, is much lighter than the usual run of natives, but she didn't get her father's blue eyes.

The nurse has illuminated the matter somewhat for me. In the first place, Joe and his Thlinget wife aren't married. He is a, so-called, "squaw-man" — a white man living with an Indian wife — and while he wants to marry the girl, she doesn't care for it — considers that they are sufficiently married already — and why not? What constitutes marriage in the eyes of civilization is purely an arbitrary matter and not a decree of nature; but this isn't civilization up here — it's betwixt and between, and in the old days marriage with the Thlingets consisted of living together.

The sister of Joe's wife is a blind girl, but she is about to bear her third fatherless baby. She lives with her parents and they are raising the children, as they are going to raise little Emily Yester. Of course I know nothing of the particulars, but I suppose that the clans involved have come to some satisfactory adjustment over the children. That is the way things are done among the Thlingets and there are never any abandoned waifs among them.

If we can believe reports, there are few girls in the village old enough, and the Indian girls mature early, who have not experienced motherhood. No disgrace seems to be attached to the experience, and little inconvenience, for either the girls' mothers take charge of the babies, or they are given a home by others of the clan.

There is a young fellow here, son of one of the men with whom I have contracted to get wood out for the school, who married a young Hydah girl. He is only a boy—seventeen-years-old—and she is but a girl. They speak different languages and while she is an intelligent girl, she is ostracized by the women of the village because she is not a Thlinget. The boy, who is handsome and makes a splendid impression, is brutal in the extreme to her—beats her and we have learned that he pushed her off the boat the other day, in the effort to get rid of her but someone fished her out.

The boy came the other day looking for the nurse and said his wife's baby was coming, but "she couldn't get no furder wid it." The nurse went at once to render assistance and found the girl sitting on an old mattress in a corner of a small one-room cabin, lighted by a lantern and heated with a small sheet-iron stove. The only furniture in the room was an iron bedstead from which the mattress had been taken, and a table. The room was dirty and foul and a pile of filthy rags lay in one corner, while around the room, squatted a dozen or more women and girls with their backs to the wall—filling the room to the limit. An old Indian midwife seemed in command of the situation and appeared to be brewing some concoction on the stove while she kept up a steady babble. All the black eyes in the room looked slyly askance at the nurse, but no one said a word or otherwise paid heed to her. The nurse gave them tit-for-tat and went directly to the girl, sitting with frightened eyes and at the mercy of the women whose talk was unintelligible to her.

The situation was too much for the nurse. There was no basis on which she could work under such conditions, so she returned to the teacherage and fixed a bed in the room over ours, and despite the silent hostility of the native women and the surly obstruction of the midwife, brought the girl and the boy and put them to bed, for the girl's hour was not yet.

In the morning all was quiet overhead and when the nurse went to investigate, she found the pair had softly slipped out and taken to cover, like the wild things they are.

Bad as conditions are now accompanying motherhood, the nurse says they were infinitely worse in the earlier days, for when a woman approached her time, she was considered unclean and was driven out of doors where she had to remain, regardless of weather conditions, until the child was born. If everything did not go right, the poor things were doped up with the most inconceivably filthy and revolting concoctions of spiders, burned hair, and anything else disgusting that could be thought of. There are those among the whites today who believe that medicine has no "kick" unless it is nasty to take. Possibly that is a throw-back to the primitive days of their progenitors.

When the babe was born the woman was taken to a shed or outhouse and kept for ten days before being allowed to enter the house. The babe was washed and well greased with seal oil and wrapped in the skin of some animal—fur side in—or in a blanket, padded with soft moss. It was unwrapped but once a day and the moss padding changed. If the child was disposed to cry too loudly or too long, it was held under water to teach it to be still.

We have marvelled ever since we have been here at the behavior of the children. Little Carmel Demmert, who lives with Eagle Horse and his wife, is a demure little five-year-old who has taken quite a fancy to me, like Queenie, the dog, for some reason and comes to visit me. She will sit quietly and talk with that soft low voice of hers about the things her bright little eyes see, and very few things escape them; but in the presence of older people she is silent as a little bug and will sit in a chair by the hour, with an occasional squirm, but never a chirp. I wonder if she had the water treatment as a babe.

But why should these Indian children, little creatures of the wild as they are, be different? I had thought of the traditional stoicism of the Indians and sought to explain it that way, but when we heard of the "water cure" we comprehended that it was a matter of training, rather than of instinct. Even at that there is cause for wonder. Thlinget children are unrestrained. Parents never say "don't" or "No! No." They seem to be allowed the same latitude of activity as young puppies—possibly that is because there are no piano legs to be hacked, no furniture to be scratched or marred by playthings, none of the fripperies of civilization to be pulled down and broken. But since that is so, isn't it remarkable that any course of treatment can restrain their natural activity?

Another suggestion comes to mind: May it not be a manifestation of that instinct of wild life which causes a fawn to lie curled up in the brush for hours at a time, virtually motionless, even if almost stepped upon; or the young partridges to squat motionless at an alarm from the mother, until a reassuring cluck tells them the danger has passed?

Another thing we don't understand of the many, is the instinct these native men seem to have concerning the weather. We had a period of several days of perfect weather—blue sky with fleecy clouds, rippling water, amber sunshine, and gentle, balmy breezes —and there was no reason why it should not last, so far as I could see, except that perfect weather never lasts; but when I went to the store I fell in with one of the fishermen.

"Weather fine!" he said. "Going to change—snow tomorrow." I looked at the cloudless sky and at him.

"What makes you think so?" I asked.

He grinned: "Thlingets know—he can tell," was the answer.

The next day dawned just like the others and conditions remained unchanged.

"Thlinget doesn't always know," I assured myself, but at midafternoon the sky changed and at dusk snow was flying. How did he know twenty-four hours ahead? I can't tell you.

Eagle Horse says the natives judge the probable severity of the coming winter by the conduct of the snails—those big slimy things —some of them as big as my finger and six inches long. They go into the ground for cold weather, but they are still kicking around (to step on one gives the sensation of stepping on a cat's tail), which is assumed to indicate a mild winter.

Jumbo McFee was one of my early acquaintances, for the school was about out of wood when we came and when I undertook to secure more, I was sent to Jumbo. He is a moose of a man— not so tall as I, but with a frame that in itself is indicative of great strength. But Jumbo is blind—has cataracts on both eyes and says he is only faintly conscious of the difference between darkness and light. Well Jumbo McFee and his partner, George Anniskett, mutually made a contract with me to supply 60 ricks of wood—part fir—part cedar, and some hemlock. I have bought wood before, but this was a new experience. They have no roads in this country—no draft animals of any nature—no means of transportation save by water, so the blind man and his partner had to locate their timber—dead trees—on the shore of some rocky island and close enough to the water to be got into it at high tide with a minimum of effort. That was not easy to do for the natives have been robbing the shore lines of available fuel for no one can tell how long.

They found their trees a matter of two days distant, cut them and got the logs into the water—blind Jumbo pulling his end of the crosscut saw and swinging his axe to trim the fallen trees. They had to wait several days for favorable weather to tow the logs in, but they beached them eventually below the school grounds where they sawed them into sixteen inch blocks at low tide; and then I saw why Fred McFee was called "Jumbo." Blind as he was, he would get those great blocks two feet and more in diameter, on the back of his neck, looking like Atlas upholding the world, and would plod his way up the steep hillside and dump his load at the top, close to the building. It would have been a job for a giant who could see, but how could a blind man do it?

How does Jumbo run his boat with its outboard motor—which he does?

How does he seine for trout at the rapids on Klawock Creek —which he does? for I sent for his annual Government permit for him. And how does a blind man trap for fur in the winter time— which he does? and they tell me he is one of the most skillful trappers in the village. I daily marvel at what I see that patient, gentle, soft-voiced, genial man do—the hardest and most per- sistant worker in the town—and confess to myself that is possible for mortal frailties to be compensated for by spiritual guidance. There is no other possible explanation: but that does not make the matter plain.

I don't understand something else. I asked Jumbo one day if he was married.

"No, not married," he answered, in his soft voice—"Friend die—friend say, 'Jumbo, you have my wife—I give you money— my things—' so I do. No, I not married—good friend he die—I do what he say."

What did he mean when he said he wasn't married, though he has a wife? I am still puzzling over that. Maybe some day I shall know.

Then there is George Anniskett, his partner on the wood

contract. George is a younger man—Jumbo is 49. George is very active in the Salvation Army—so active that he left us hung up for our wood supply while he went to the Hoonah Congress of the Salvation Army. He needed the money, but he came to me to see if he could go.

"I play in band," he confided, "I play anything. I best player in band—band need me—Salvation Army need me too—I go, but I come back."

He did both things; but it is a fact that he can play any instrument they have in the band. Now how can he, an Indian not yet out of the primitive state, who has had no instruction, who reads music as so many specks on a page, manifest the skill and understanding he does? It is beyond me, unless it is instinct. But he is not alone. The same is true of others, though possibly not in the same degree.

But before leaving Jumbo and George, I am going to say that the word of both of the men is as good as a Government bond; both have the instincts of gentlemen, and Jumbo is very much of a philosopher, although if he were to hear me say that he wouldn't know what kind of a name I was calling him.

Daily we get new glimpses into this strange Thlinget psychology. There is always something to arouse our interest and keep us puzzling.

Chapter XI

SCHOOL

Alma generally prefers to work with older pupils and was supposed to take the upper grades. She started with them and soon had her room busy as a beehive, but I found the work with the little ones was going in anything but a satisfactory way, so I asked her and the Primary teacher to change places; and Alma is having the most novel experience of her life with the little ones. For a while she was in despair. She had about forty of the little black-eyed bugs and they simply would not stay put, but while she was turning around they would flow all over the landscape.

Soon after she took charge I wanted to know just how many pupils she had and their names, for the records were badly mixed. One morning she undertook to get the information for me and carefully counted all the noses and got their names as well as she could get them from the timid little things, then took up the work of the day. By recess time she had a feeling that the large room was fuller than it had been, so she counted noses again and found that eight had slipped in on her while she was teaching. Word was evidently circulating through the village that there was a real teacher in the Primary room and the children who had not been there before were sifting in. She had not seen a single one of them enter and could not imagine how even an Indian child could have been so adroit as to get in without attracting her attention. She gets so absorbed in her work that I can see how it would be possible for the children to slip in unnoticed; but it was laughable.

They are the oddest little jinks imaginable. They speak their native language at home and of course they have very little of our language to go on, so she is at her wits' end sometimes to get her ideas across to them.

In the beginning, all the dusky little faces looked alike to her and she couldn't keep them in their seats; but she has them now where she can with some confidence expect to find them twice in the same place, and she is getting much attached to them. When she opens school she has the pupils line up against the front blackboard—the boys in a row on one side, and the girls in another on the other side; then Jackson Sookum and Rosabella go down the lines respectively, carefully inspecting the hands, ears and necks of each child for dirt, and looking to see if the hair is well combed. Jackson starts first and reports:

"Johnny, hiss face, hiss hands clean. Jerry, hiss ears dirty," and so on down the line. Then Rosabella very carefully looks over the girls and all who do not come up to the standard are sent downstairs to the clinic where the nurse puts them through the washing machine; but after the first day very few needed to be sent down.

The voices of the children are very soft and low and they enunciate almost to the extreme, while they give a hissing sound to the final "s" which makes their speech rather fascinating to listen to.

As a further elucidation of the situation, I should add that after the inspection Alma takes a roll of soft toilet paper, Rosabella takes an empty chalk box, and they go down the lines to wipe noses, and they do it in a very conscientious manner. Then they march to the music of a portable phonograph which we brought with us, and sing—every last one of them sings—as easily and truly as birds; but I catch myself looking around for the men because I hear voices that are pitched as deeply as a man's. Only children are present, however.

The voices are not those we are accustomed to with children: The girls' are pitched much the same as the boys' in singing, and the boys' voices do not change when they get older, as with us. It is no trouble to get the children to sing—no urging of bashful ones, no scolding at those afraid to try. They sing the way a fish swims. It is their nature and it helps greatly in the work.

We have over one hundred enrolled in the school and they run from six years to twenty-two, and in all that number there is none who is vicious and maliciously troublesome. Of course there are disciplinary problems, but they especially need to be treated with wisdom and sympathy. The children cannot be handled as white children would be handled. They are keenly sensitive to ridicule and when shamed are taciturn and stubborn as the traditional Indian; but there is always some way of dealing with them if one is kind and seeks to understand.

One of the greatest problems at all ages is to prevent them from studying out loud. They do it unconsciously and while the softness of their voices mitigates the trouble somewhat, when they are busy there will be a steady low hum like that of a swarm of bees; and it is natural for them to get up and move about, as for any wild animal to follow its inclinations. It is really intriguing to work with such unformed minds, but though primitive in their development and expression, in no respect are they deficient in power, except in a few sub-normal cases and they are found as well among the children of the white race; and their ignorance of everything beyond their simple lives leaves them with an active interest in everything new and a burning desire to learn.

In some directions they show surprisingly proficiency. They take to writing as they do to singing, and instead of the penmanship work being the usual drudgery which children abominate, that period is one of the happiest of the day for them, and they write beautifully.

They also love to spell and become excellent spellers; and they love contests of any kind, but they do not make good readers, probably because they are learning in a language which is not native to them and because theirs is not a written language. The whole idea of getting thought from a printed page is a novel one to the race.

They are good at simple arithmetic work and enjoy it, but the text-books used are a handicap because the examples deal with things entirely out of the experience of these children who have never seen a horse, cow, sheep, or pig, except in pictures—who do not know what wheatfields, pastures, highways, or fences are like, (the only fences in their experience being old herring nets supported on frames and used to keep chickens out of their little gardens). Their life deals with fish and products of the sea; with canoes, gasboats, salmon fishing; with wild game, water fowl and things that grow in the wilderness, so their learning would be greatly aided if they could deal with familiar subject matter instead of that entirely outside their daily lives.

I have been having a class in, so-called, General Science, and have been astonished at the difficulties I have met in explaining comparatively simple matters. I tried one day to explain what happens when wood burns, and every time I used a word or expression I had to explain what I meant, and in turn explain my explanations. I never had comprehended before how much understanding of our environment is born with us, until I came in contact with those reared in an environment different in almost every respect. But they had something to tell me. I learned from them that the crackling and snapping of burning wood is due to spirits in the wood. That was something they knew which I didn't, so they had something on me and it delighted them.

But I must tell you about Rosabella. She is nine years old

and has been in the beginners' class for two years, and Alma was assured that she was a perfect dunce—that in all that time she had learned nothing—couldn't read nor write nor do any number work. She has seemed hopeless and has been the despair of all her teachers. Alma easily identified her the first day she had the room, by her size; but she assured me a child with Rosabella's eyes couldn't be stupid. If she hadn't learned there must be some explanation, but as the days passed she could find none and admitted she was baffled. It seemed impossible to teach the child a thing. She couldn't read and couldn't figure and didn't seem to care if she couldn't. Throughout the day she would sit idly in her seat, but her gazelle-like eyes were always busy and seemed to see everything that transpired. She was interested in everything but her work, and in one respect was a decided nuisance. She was always talking. To be sure it was in that soft, low monotone hardly loud enough to be heard, yet which arrested the consciousness and when combined with the same thing from many others, gathered volume. In exasperation one day, after repeatedly quieting the child, Alma called her forward and told her if she couldn't keep still she would have to fix her so she couldn't talk, so she took a strip of clean writing paper, spread some library paste on it and stuck it across the child's lips. Then she stood her in a corner with her back to the school. The other children were wide-eyed and solemn but never made a sound. There was none of the snickering one would have heard under similar circumstances with white children, and Rosabella took the discipline in all seriousness. After a time Alma noticed that the paper was not sticking well, but Rosabella would conscientiously press it back in place each time when it loosened. Becoming absorbed in her work, she forgot about the child standing in the corner with a piece of paper over her mouth, until she heard a low monotone and little brown hands were raised and soft voices said, "Rosabella iss talking— she iss talking," and she was.

"Why are you talking?" Alma asked her sharply.

"The paper—it came off—I lost it," she answered and seemed to feel that that explained everything.

It was true. The paste had dried and the slip of paper had floated away out of the child's reach, so Alma dodged the issue by dismissing school, for noon-time had come; but she was in despair at her helplessness, when she came to lunch. She wouldn't admit that the child couldn't be taught, but she did admit that she didn't know how to teach her.

She decided to have a talk with the mother, so after school one day she went down to the end of the plank street and along a footpath that took over windfalls and through salmon-berry brush and wild celery, to a log cabin at the edge of the timber where she had been told the Williamses lived. When she reached the open door she saw Rosabella swinging her baby brother in a blanket hammock swung between the corners of the room, and she asked the little girl if her mother was home.

"In there." She pointed to the adjoining room. Alma stepped to the doorway and saw Mrs. Williams rocking back and forth in a chair. She looked at her, but said nothing, so Alma introduced herself and found a seat on a big chest.

"I don't know what to do about Rosabella," she told the mother. "She is a big girl—too big to be in the first grade, but she can't even read and doesn't try to learn."

"Yess, Rosabella, she fool—go to school two-three years— she learn nothing—she can't read—she no good," was the placid answer.

Alma sat where she saw the child in the adjoining room minister efficiently to the little one and then feed it with a spoon.

"Is Rosabella much help to you?" she asked.

"Yess—she help—she take care baby—she play with Freddy —she get food to eat—she help lot—Rosabella don't know any- thing—she no good," Mrs. Williams calmly answered, without interrupting her rocking.

The conversation seemed to end there so Alma withdrew, no wiser than before. No, not quite that, for she marvelled that a child who could be so capable at home should be "no good" at school.

"That child has a handle somewhere," she told me, "and I'm going to find it," but she couldn't.

One Saturday morning when it was a little dryer than usual, for it rains most of the time, she was following a footpath that led up into the brush and heard children's voices. She cautiously peeked through the bushes and saw several little girls sitting on a log in an open spot. They began to chant a song which she had often heard sung by the Salvation Army, and who should be lead- ing the singing but "stupid Rosabella"? The song ended and Rosabella announced:

"Let us pray." She closed her eyes, lifted her face towards the sky, and began;

"O good Ke-an-kow, we are your children. We do many bad

things. We don't study our lessons. We talk in school. We make teacher sorry. O Ke-an-kow, be good to your children and make them good. Amen! Now let us sing 'Nearer My God to Thee,' then Sister Katasi will tell us about her sins," and Rosabella led off in the song.

Convulsed with amusement, Alma slipped away and when she recounted the experience she added:

"That was my stupid Rosabella, who in two years hasn't learned to read, and isn't learning now. What do you think of her?"

I dropped into her room several days later when I heard something going on, and found that she was exercising the restless little creatures by having them march and take free gymnastics to the music of the phonograph, and whom did she have acting as major-domo but Rosabella? Catching my eye she glanced significantly at the child and smiled, so I knew she was busy with some scheming. That night at supper she told me she had found the handle.

"That child is a born leader. She is head and shoulders above the other children in the room in alertness and intelligence. If that child doesn't learn it is because she doesn't want to, and I'm going to make her want to. You watch!" she told me.

One day she had occasion to leave the room while the class of little ones were doing some busy-work, so she told Rosabella to help any that needed help while she was gone. When she returned there sat Rosabella at Alma's desk, ruler in hand. She was not only in charge of the class, but she had taken charge of the entire room. Alma concealed her amusement, which wasn't lessened at recess time when little Jane Roberts sidled up and confided:

"Rosabella make Jimmy John read. She whack him when he don't—whack him like that" and she hit herself on the side of the head.

A few nights later she said again that she had found Rosabella's handle. She had told the school that day that it wouldn't do to have a leader who didn't learn and who wouldn't study. They all looked at Rosabella—so she was going to pick out a new leader—one who could read as well as lead. She saw Rosabella stiffen up in her seat and while Alma was hearing the chart class recite, she said the child's eyes were glued on the chart and she could see her lips repeating the words. Then she got her book from her desk and apparently was hunting up the same words in that. She was a busy child the rest of the day. A fire had been kindled at last.

After the children had marched from the room at the close of school, dusky Rosabella came softly, slowly back into the room and up to where Alma sat at her desk.

"Teacher," she breathed, "I know those letters—I can read—I know those words." And she did!

"Rosabella, that's fine!" Alma told her. "Take your book home and show your father and mother that you are learning to read. It will make them happy. But Rosabella, you must learn to read better than the other children. You know a leader is always one who does things best—just like a chief."

"Yes ma'am," she answered, and slipped from the room as softly as she had come, but Alma heard her feet fly down the steps and rattle the board walk as she sped home.

Later Rosabella came into the store and sat quietly across the table from me, looking at me with her limpid black eyes as though something were on her mind.

"When I get big my father going to send me to Seattle," she finally breathed in her soft, barely audible voice, "I'm going to be a teacher, like Mrs. Salisbury."

Chapter XII

TECUMSEH COLLINS

There is at least one character in this village who has a real sense of humor, and not only has he a sense of humor, but he himself is a humorist. He is my friend, Tecumseh Collins. I know he is my friend because he sees me often and there is always something he is willing I should do for him. One would have to be hard boiled indeed who could refuse to respond to his jovial disposition.

Peter Lawrence, the "nephew of a chief," was my first Thlinget acquaintance. Eagle Horse and his wife were our next acquaintances; then Bill Gardner, the physiography of whose face is truly Alaskan in its ruggedness; and then came Tecumseh Collins.

Bright and early on a sunshiny morning there was a thump on our kitchen door and in burst as merry a sunbeam as ever entered our kitchen. So roly-poly was he that when I asked him to sit down I wondered just how he would go to work to do it.

"Tecumseh Collins!" he introduced himself by thumping on his drum-like chest, and proceeded to tell me that he was "Envoy Collins, Salvation Army," which I understood—and more, which I didn't understand, except that I got the idea that he has recently been promoted to his rank of Envoy. Probably we were the only ones in town who didn't know it, so he had hastened to let us in on the secret. I do not know what the official duties of an Envoy of the Salvation Army may be, but of course there is a possibility that he was greeting us in an official capacity—"giving us the key to the city," as it were: an official "gladhander." Whatever the motive that brought him, his welcome was genuine and acceptable.

I have gathered in the course of time, that Tecumseh is something of a capitalist. He is a shrewd business man—the material of which bank presidents and directors are made, for he is always more willing to let some one else's money work for him than his own. I know because I have had business relations with him and got the worst of it.

The impression I gained at first, one which he evidently desired I should have, was that he was a poor fisherman who had been unable to catch any fish, therefore he had no money. So far as I now understand the situation, his main business is avoiding work, which keeps him pretty busy; and he fills up the rest of his time in the interests of the Salvation Army, of which he is a most happy and enthusiastic member. And no one is more conscious of his place in the community than he, when he is dressed in his Army uniform.

There was to be a convention of the Salvation Army units of Southeastern Alaska, or a "Congress," as they call it, at Hoonah on Chichagof Island, where my predecessor and his wife, who labored here two years, are now stationed; and Tecumseh was exceedingly busy over that and I found myself materially involved in his plans.

The Thlingets dearly love to get something for nothing—particularly from the whites—possibly because they can never get across with anything of the kind among themselves. They seem to feel that all that can be gotten from the other fellow is clear gain—a trait a little more universal with them than with us. Tecumseh's poverty is an illustration, I had sympathetically paid a Montgomery Ward bill for him that came through the mail C.O.D. before I was informed that he had lots of money.

Two boats were going, the Wm. T. Kelly and the Age of Reason. A cabin was improvised on the open deck of the larger boat with old lumber, and a diplomatic visit from Envoy Collins revealed to me that unless I furnished it, there would not be enough roofing paper to cover it. I saw the point and was impaled, which wreathed Tecumseh's face in additional smiles. Another formal call resulted in my being given the privilege of furnishing some stovepipe from the school supplies because, I was assured, there was none elsewhere in the village. I furnished it, but there was.

As a final evidence of the high esteem in which I was held and the confidence they placed in me generally, they formally conferred upon me the honor of supplying a sack of soft coal in order that there might be some means of keeping the hands of the dusky ladies warm, while on so worthy an excursion. I furnished it. The coal was there for the educational welfare of the village, and was the spiritual welfare any less important? I took the chance.

The day they were to start in order to reach Hoonah in proper season turned out to be election day. The Alaskan Indians have been enfranchised and they exercise their rights to a man, through the influence of the Alaska Native Brotherhood; so they delayed their departure so as to vote, but at eleven o'clock they got away.

The two boats were tightly grappled together side by side—

the women on one, in their extemporized cabin, and the men on the other, with a little shanty fixed on the deck for sleeping purposes. It was their intention to make the trip that way unless stormy weather prevented. There were fully twenty-five in the party—men, women, and two school girls—all in their quaint uniforms. The American flag was run up to the masthead—a nice big, worthwhile flag—while the Salvation Army banner was held extended by men on top of the cabin. The band played and Captain Benson of the Salvation Army offered a prayer for a safe journey. The boats swung around and headed out of the inlet in a fog on their long trip up Chatham Strait.

It was an inspiring sight to see them chugging down the bay, waving their banners and singing hymns. I thought of our Pilgrim Fathers leaving England for their long trip into the unknown, and the spirit that prompted them to cross the Atlantic. Here was the same desire to worship God according to their understanding.

I had a vacation from Tecumseh for a fortnight, but one night when the Prince of Wales was discharging cargo at the dock and I was down for the mail, the sound of a band playing came across the water and around the red light, in the beautiful moonlight, came the Salvation Army delegation, safely returned from Hoonah. The Prince of Wales cast off, her Diesel engine pulsing efficiently, swung around and slipped swiftly out of the inlet through the glittering ripples stirred by the gas boats. Still lashed together as when they left, all singing who weren't playing in the band, they swung up to the float and unloaded—as tired and as happy as we would have been in their places. I was glad to see them back and felt a warming of my heart at their enthusiasm.

Tecumseh called the next day to report and it made one feel pleased with the world to see his happiness.

The Thlingets are inordinately fond of children. They marry very young and the women bear as many children as they can, while childless couples adopt children. There are no homeless orphans among the Thlingets, for there are always some who are willing and eager to adopt every surplus child. The children are given as much consideration as though they were grown people and the parents exercise very little restraint over them. They are very tractable children however, not at all obstreperous, as one would expect them to be with such an absence of discipline. Their parents take them everywhere and one sees among these people something never seen among the Indians of the States—the men carrying the babies around, and proud as peacocks too.

To illustrate their indulgence with the children, the nurse told us one day of seeing a small boy haggling with a knife at a warm cake the mother had just taken from the oven and dumped on the table. Imagine the emotion of a white mother under similar circumstances!

"Don't use that dull knife," said the Thlinget mother, "Get a sharp one and cut straight." The child went on cutting.

One morning Tecumseh came to me before school with the nearest to a long face his physiognomy would permit. He has two boys in school—Johnnie and Embert, and a girl, Annie, and all are just as interesting as he. They are the children of a son, dead from T.B. Johnnie is the picture of his "kewpie" grandfather, but they are both as full of irrepressible spirits as Tecumseh himself.

"Misl Commission," he couldn't pronounce my name and couldn't say "superintendent," but he knew the United States Commissioner at Craig represented the Government and so did I; things equal to the same thing were equal to each other in his judgment, so I was a "commissioner." He could pronounce that.

"Embert—Johnnie no help grandmother—no bring wood—no help—you whip—make good boys." He was very earnest about it and deeply concerned and had come to me because I seemed to be a "cure-all." It certainly was a case of "passing the buck," but it well illustrated the attitude of the natives towards children. There were things the children should do—the influence of the old days when the individual's acts were ruled by tradition and general sentiment, have passed. The new generation is feeling its oats and the old timers don't know what to do about it. I wonder if a Thlinget parent ever has whipped a child. They sometimes bat them about under sudden impulse, but to whip a child in cold blood, as he wanted me to do, I think is impossible for them.

I couldn't enter into a discussion with him of the ethics of my whipping his children for him: he wouldn't have comprehended in the least, so I told him I would see the boys. I rounded them up when they came to school and gave them a talk that impressed them, coming from the "Big Man," which the children call me, and which relates not to my size, as I first supposed, but to my position of seeming authority in the village. Even if they did not understand it all, they sensed a "kick" back of it which they respected and the next time I saw Tecumseh his face was dimpling with smiles again.

There are few unmarried women. Marriages used to be decided by a clan council, and an old widow would be married to a young boy or a girl to an old man. If the old one died, then the youngster was permitted a young mate. In accordance with that practice, Tecumseh, as a young man, had been married to a woman of much experience. She had been very much of a stepper herself, so far as husbands formal and informal, were concerned and has a large progeny as a result, but she continued to live after her marriage to young Tecumseh, and values him so highly that she feels wholly unwilling to share him with anyone else, although she does not hesitate to tell how much finer some of her husbands have been than he—particularly the white ones.

"Old Tecumseh" hasn't always been old, and knowing him now, I imagine he was quite some boy as a young fellow, although no reports have come through of his philandering. His marriage was one of those ordained affairs, for she is much older than he, but she wanted no question or uncertainty concerning her proprietorship and was very jealous of him and fearful of designs on his chastity on the part of other women. I would not be surprised if there had been danger. He is a very winsome boy.

Her jealousy became quite annoying to Tecumseh—jealousy is apt to have that effect—so in his native innocence he devised a plan for breaking her of her fussiness. When a good chance offered he rolled up blankets in the semblance of the human form and placed the roll in his bed with a pair of women's shoes protruding at the bottom; then crawled under the blankets with his enamorata (their beds are made on the floor). Mrs. Tecumseh, gum-shoeing around with her suspicions, peered through the window at the form in his arms and the feminine shoes revealed, and went into a brainstorm. She battered the door open and rushing to the bed, dragged the blankets back, prepared to brain the hussy.

It worked. She was never allowed to forget the incident by her appreciative neighbors.

Old Mrs. Collins may have controlled outward manifestations of her jealousy after she caught her husband "loving up" the rolled bedding, but it was there in her heart and on an occasion when the old lady was ill, she assured Tecumseh she was going to die and then he could marry the young wife he had waited so long for. The old boy had a notion she was "spoofing" him, so when she persisted in her mournful, self-sacrificing strain, he flopped down on his knees and besought the Lord that since she was now resigned and ready to slip the leashes of this earth, she might be taken speedily and relieve him of the long and patient waiting for the promised young and beautiful wife. *The old Skeesiks!*

The heart stimulant was more immediate in its action than Tecumseh had contemplated and before he could properly taper off his prayer, she was out from under the blankets and belaboring him so enthusiastically the neighbors had to rush in to save his life; and just to spite him, she has continued to live, until now when he gets his young wife, she will have an old man for a husband and will be waiting for him to die.

Chapter XIII

THE TOWN HALL

The *biggest* thing in Klawock is the Town Hall. The school-house is a good sized building for a small Indian village, but standing back of the schoolhouse and looking as though it had backed into the jungle of windfalls and rankly growing undergrowth, so that its front steps could debouche upon the playground, has stood the beginning of a town hall. It was one of the first things we noticed. It couldn't escape notice it was so huge and uncouth. It was framed and the walls were sided, while a dozen rafters had been raised to place before the work stopped; and the weathered condition of the lumber looked as though it had stood some time as it is. I paced the dimensions one day and found it measured 60 by 80 feet, and the walls were twenty feet high. A rough floor had been partly laid over the joists and the shingles for the roof were stacked upon it; but when the workmen ran out of rafters the work had to stop because no more were available.

In this day of diminishing lumber supply, 20 foot stuff is quite unusual, but they were using 40 foot 2 by 6's for the rafters of the building and had to ship them in from Ketchikan on the big freighters which make the West Coast occasionally during the summer season. They were too long for the mail boat to carry.

My first tour of inspection after our arrival had taken me over to it and I marvelled that the villagers should attempt such an enterprise on so extensive a scale. Thereafter it loomed as a great ghost, visible whenever we stepped out of doors—a shadow of a disappointed hope—for I doubted if it would ever be completed. I didn't know my Indians.

We have been preparing a Christmas program, for we learned early that the Klawock Christmas celebration is the big event of the year for the West Coast, and that oftentimes entire villages will come over to share in the event if the weather conditions are favorable; but I supposed it would have to be in Bob's Hall, although I could not see how such a gathering as has been foretold could possibly get under its roof. When the Mayor returned on the Cordova our "Klawock Daily Bulletin," the nurse, who in her contact with the natives gathers a great deal of current news, announced, "They are going to finish the hall for Christmas,"

It did not seem possible that they could do it, but one morning ten days ago, there was great activity and much noise and the old, loose, decayed planking of the *city street* was ripped up and new planking laid. A host were at work in various crews—the young men carrying the new planks from Bob's dock where it had been unloaded from the Cordova, and the older men ripping out the old, laying and spiking down the new.

That was the first step. Next thing I knew the "Disappointed hope" was alive with men one morning and hammer and saw were going noisily. Judge Dalton was the boss for the day and the crowd of men surely got action. The great forty foot rafters all had to be carried up from the dock, be measured, cut and raised into place; but I was astonished at the speed and certainty with which they worked. In a week's time the rafters were up, the roof boards on, and the roof half shingled; while another crew worked inside under the direction of Johnnie Skan, laying the rough floor flooring in preparation for the fir floor, and building a big stage.

The weather had turned bad and rain and snow alternated, making the work on the roof very dangerous. I had been asked to lend the bigger boys in order to hurry the outside work, and the Mayor had issued an edict that every able-bodied man who did not report for work would be arrested and fined. They do things that way here, and as fines seem to carry considerable "kick" with them in the eyes of the natives, everyone was out, even some of the high caste stalkers who ordinarily are too proud to work; but judging from my observations, the presence of the latter had no material bearing on the progress of the work. Of course the Mayor wasn't there. He was the man behind the gun.

Inside, the activity was just as pronounced, but not so dangerous. Rain and snow had sifted in through the unshingled half of the roof and soaked the old floor and the new lumber, but the work went ahead nevertheless. Johnnie Skan had blocked out a great stage across one end and proudly asked my opinion of it. His stage was to be four feet above the floor—these people love to do things in a large way—and I advised against it as unnecessarily high. Others agreed with me. But John was father of the idea, and being his idea it was all right, so the four foot stage was built.

Today the "Klawock Daily" was scooped, for after our noon lunch I heard the band playing and saw a crowd assembling down on the new planking in front of Bob's Hall. Something was going to happen, so I seized a camera and started for the playground just as the populace marched up from the street. It was dark and stormy, with misting rain and floating snowflakes, and the temperature was a little above 40 degrees. The ground was wet and soggy, but it is a natural condition which no one heeds. The shingling had been finished in the forenoon.

As I reached the playground the procession entered also, led by the Salvation Army band in uniform. The mayor followed and the officers of the Salvation Army — Captain Billy Benson, Envoy Tecumseh Collins, and Sergeant Major Peter Anniskett— and the rank and file, men and women, all in uniform. Two of the Alaska Native Sisterhood followed carrying the life-size carved figure of a bald eagle; and by others carrying stretched between them a great American flag, 12 by 20 feet. Still others of the Sisterhood carried the fruit, candy and pop which are the essential features of every native celebration.

They stopped while I photographed the scene and then entered the hall, after first nailing the eagle to the front of the building above the door. Inside, the big room was damp and chilly from the wet lumber, and dark because the window openings were boarded up, but there was more band playing. The mayor then made a long speech which he loves to do. The great flag which had been carried by the women was hung on the wall behind the stage and was formally presented to the village for Tom Adams, the donor, by the Sisterhood. I greatly regretted my inability to understand what was said, because I am certain it would have been very interesting, for the whole ceremony seemed to be one that meant a great deal to them.

Later in the day I prepared an account of the ceremony for Captain Benson to send in to the Salvation Army official paper— he dictating the ideas and I phrasing them.

I questioned him about the significance of the eagle—whether it represented the totem of the Eagle clan, or otherwise. Captain Benson is an impressive figure — tall, erect, dignified, typically Indian in appearance, but handicapped by a physical infirmity which compels him to walk with a cane; and with an impediment in his speech, rare among the natives. To meet that handicap he speaks slowly and deliberately and the stammering really adds impressiveness to what he says. He answered my questions:

"All Thlingets have totem—some belong Raven—some Eagle — some Wolf — some Bear — all have totem — all in same clan brothers. United States great tribe — greater than any tribe — greater than all tribes — Eagle totem of United States. Bob Asneal make that eagle—he make it for Klawock. Natives nail that eagle on town hall they built so all Thlingets know they all belong to biggest tribe of all—United States. Flag totem of United States too—Of every bodys—all brothers with same totem."

That experience sent a thrill through me that I shall not forget. These people may lack the intellectual advancement which we boast, but they have a spiritual insight and response which we can envy. All the complications of civilized life are the result of human whims and notions which tend to magnify the greatness of man and minimize the allness of our Creator, The Indian is always conscious of a power greater than his own. He gets crooked notions concerning the nature of that power, but he never loses his awe of it, nor his belief in it.

Benson explained further concerning the participation of the women and their presentation of the flag:

"Thlinget men belong to Alaska Native Brotherhood—they work for all Thlinget Indians. Alaska Native Sisterhood Thlingets too—work for women—for men too—for Thlinget children—for all Thlingets. They belong big tribe United States too—Eagle their totem too—Bob Asneal make eagle for Klawock. Tom Adams give flag—Native Sisterhood happy to give them to village for Tom Adams and Bob Asneal."

These dusky "heathen" up here are far more spiritual-minded, considering their understanding, and are much closer to their Creator than ourselves, with all our intelligence. They can't argue on how many angels can dance on the point of a needle, nor on the doctrine of atonement, nor on the merits of baptismal emersion; but Alma finds the children wonderfully sensitive and conscious of the spiritual ideas in Tennyson's Holy Grail and other similar literature they study in their classes—far more so than any white children she has ever had. She has found that to be true among the adults also. She saw the wife of Billy Benson, whom the nurse considered on her death bed, gasp out her conviction that the good Ke-an-kow, the Great Spirit over All, was a good God and was not responsible for her suffering, so it couldn't be real—and she proved it to the marvel of all.

The story of Lois Chuck, a young matron of the village, and the church organist, which has come to us, further illustrates their comprehension of God.

Lois Gunyah, for that was her name before she was married,

had longed to play the organ from the earliest time she could remember. It had seemed such a wonderful thing to her that when the fingers pressed the keys and the feet worked the pedals, sounds could come forth which filled her with a consciousness of the "Good Ke-an-kow"; and she had carried the resolution in her heart that one day she would be able to make God's music herself. There was no one to teach her how to make the sweet music come forth, so the years passed without her attaining her greatest ambition.

One day she overheard some of the older people telling that Metah, who played the church organ, was going to be married to a young native of Craig, an adjoining village, and would go there to live, so she could no longer be their organist.

"Who play organ then?" she heard her father ask the minister and other officers of the church who were holding a meeting one evening at her home, for Bill Gunyah was one of the deacons of the church. No one could answer the question for there seemed to be no one else who could play the organ. The desire to serve her people in that way seemed to possess the girl so overwhelmingly that she fled out into the starlit night, and with eyes uplifted, besought the good Ke-an-kow that her fingers might be guided on the keys of the organ. A falling star streaked its way across the sky and to the Indian girl that was a sign that God had heard her prayer. She re-entered the house confident that her plea would be granted and told the worried deacons that she would play the organ for them. They were thunderstruck, for they knew no one had ever taught her to play it, but she told them she had prayed to God and she knew in her heart the prayer would be answered because He had given her a sign. They, in their turn, knowing the all-power of the God they worshipped, accepted her assurance and went to their homes happy that their need had been met. It *was* met, for Lois played the organ for the hymns after Metah left, and is still the church organist, although now she is the mother of a robust babe. We see no fault to find with her playing and there is no one in the village who does not believe that God guided her fingers in those early days of her service.

But I have gotten away from the event of the day!

Of course the feast followed the oratory, as it always does, though it was a rather damp, chilly feast in the dark hall and was limited to the fruit and candy brought by the Sisterhood. It was symbolical, rather than substantial.

The mayor told me this evening that this was not the real dedication of the hall, but merely in the nature of a preliminary house-warming, anticipatory of the Christmas celebration, and that the big, honest-to-goodness affair would take place New Year's eve. There are rumors that the Thlingets are going to put on a big dance, and because Bob is deeply prejudiced as a good church member, against the white man's dancing, I have a notion it will be an old time Indian dance and will be well worth seeing.

Chapter XIV

CHRISTMAS

We understood, of course, that the school would be expected to have a Christmas program. The natives dearly love anything and everything in the nature of entertainment. It is the orthodox thing to do anyway, but we had not been here long before we realized that the Christmas celebration was no ordinary event in Klawock. The people talked about it and smacked their lips over it as they do about "fish-egg-time," consequently I was alert to get all the light on the subject I could. I couldn't quite see why a school program and a Christmas tree should be such a tremendous event to the natives, but after we saw the way the village turned out for our Armistice Day and Thanksgiving Day programs we knew what to expect. Everything they can look at and listen to is worth while with them, and why shouldn't it be so when they have no books, magazines, or papers to entertain them, because they cannot read; and no place to go because there is nothing to see.

I early assured the mayor that we would have an entertainment Christmas Eve, and he in turn told me that the village would have a Christmas tree and they would complete the town hall so the doings could be held there, although there was no provision for heating it. That situation was finally met by my installing three decrepit stoves from the schoolhouse basement, and the men produced a fourth made from a big gasoline drum. We ran the stovepipe through the boarded windows and had an excuse for a heating plant.

Opera chairs were supplied by supporting planks on blocks of wood from the school wood pile.

All the day before Christmas we kept the stoves stoked with wood beyond the point of safety, and by night the chill was off the great barn.

A twenty foot spruce tree had been brought in from one of the islands—as beautiful a tree as ever graced Christmas Eve— and was mounted on the stage, where it was bedecked with gay and glittering ornaments and the customary strings of popcorn. All the afternoon people were bringing packages which were hung upon the tree or piled beneath it. Others hung borrowed gasoline lamps, arranged the seats, cleared up the carpenters' litter, and helped get everything ready, while in the midst of all the turmoil, but before they started work on the tree, the teachers struggled to go through a rehearsal of the program, which hadn't been possible before in the hall because of the cold. The hall was a very busy place and the focus of every villager's thought.

The band was there of course and Eagle Horse had drilled a Christmas Chorus, while there was much school singing because there is nothing the Thlinget children like to do better than to sing.

The lights, the music, the great dazzling tree, and the stacked packages put all the pep and enthusiasm into the children the occasion demanded so that Alma said afterwards, "All my worry was for nothing. I didn't know my children."

It was very fortunate considering our inadequate heating arrangements, that the weather, which had been rather bad for several days, took on the Christmas spirit and lightly froze the soggy ground and sprinkled it white with a thin covering of snow, while the wind died down and the temperature stood about at freezing.

The crowd began to gather early and came in families — father, mother, children and babies—and all the unattached of the village, but the visitors from outside were few because of the stormy sea surrounding our island. The school children were seated on the big platform, while Bob Peratovich, the mayor, and the minister, Andrew Wanamaker, had seats of honor there also. When at last the village seemed fully assembled, we started the evening's entertainment.

When I asked the mayor how much time the school might have for their share of the evening, he replied:

"Mr. Superintendent, the peoples of Klawock have come here to see and listen to their children—we always like to do that—we have all night and nothing else to do. The longer it lasts, the better we'll like it."

That was reassuring. It was more than reassuring when we saw the complete lack of self-consciousness manifested by the children, they surely did their best. If they forgot their pieces, they backed up and started over again until they accomplished their purpose. I've never seen white children fight their way through lapses of memory as those children did.

The time and pains some of the mothers had devoted to their children's costumes were very evident, and the mother of the little six-year-old, black-eyed boy who was to be a miniature Santa Claus, had copied a Saint Nic's suit from a Sears, Roebuck

& Co. catalogue and had made a very finished costume. The tad came down the chimney with his pack on his back and made a great hit. In fact, everything was a hit with the audience—even those who could not make themselves heard above the rustling noise of the crowd, were given all the applause they could have asked for; and such little mishaps as the tumbling of someone off the high stage, and the collapse of the improvised wings, were hugely enjoyed.

One of the most effective features of the evening was a play consisting of a Civil War romance represented by a series of living pictures in frames, from which each character stepped in turn to enact his part and the hero and heroine came to life as present-day characters. It had seemed very doubtful that these boys and girls of a primitive life could enter into the spirit and portray the emotions of those from a life so entirely outside their experience, but again all doubt was set at rest, for the simplicity of their hearts gave them power to portray the old-fashioned love scene in a way that could hardly have been equaled by the self-conscious and sophisticated sons and daughters of the so-called, civilized whites. That is especially surprising because love, as a mating emotion, has not entered much into the lives of the Thlingets. Marriage with them has not been a sentimental mating, but a matter of tribal arrangement. But we are always being surprised here!

The school's share of the evening's doings closed with the singing of "Holy Night."

We had started a little after eight with a prayer by the minister, the usual speech by the mayor and with singing by the school. The program took about two hours; a concert by the band, led by Frank Peratovich, who had been leader of a navy band during his war service, followed; the chorus took another half hour. By that time the crowd was getting well tuned up for the big event, when suddenly there was noise at the rear of the hall—the big doors were thrown open and in pranced six reindeer drawing a Klondike sled loaded with bundles. A white whiskered, red clad Santa Claus accompanied the sled and cracked his long whip over the prancing reindeer, which were men covered with blankets and with deer's antlers lashed to their heads. It took the house by storm.

My opportunity to slip into the background had arrived, so I found a seat on a plank near Eagle Horse and his wife, and little Carmen snuggled up to me and slipped her hand into mine. When the reindeer and their sled came in she simply gasped her wonderment, but I felt her little hand grip mine. She was motionless, but all eyes. She finally whispered to me, "Why do they shake their heads like that?," they were rattling their antlers together, "And look! They have feet like men!" but such unimportant anachronisms as men's feet on reindeer, affected her not in the least. She accepted the reindeer for what they appeared to be and was thrilled.

The sled was unloaded, Santa swung his pack to his back— a crack of the long whip, as it snaked over their heads, sent the reindeer clattering through the door, then he turned to the crowd and with the help of several volunteers proceeded to distribute the packages in his sack. When it was empty he climbed to the stage and attacked the heaped up bundles under the tree, and I have never before seen so many at a Christmas tree.

People were packed in the hall thick as herring in the inlet, and everyone was laughing and telling stories and having a good time. Little Carmen sat with her tightly clenched fist tucked into my hand, but she scarcely moved or uttered a sound, though her eyes were seeing everything. When one of the children would be given a present I could feel her little body stiffen, but she said nothing, and I began to keenly regret I had been so engrossed in the Christmas preparation as to forget about her. Just as I was beginning to feel very uncomfortable, one of the men handed her a little box. It seemed to be the realization to her of something too good to be true, and she sat holding the box tightly clasped in both hands like one in a trance of delight. When Eagle Horse asked her why she didn't see what was inside, she opened the box and the sight of the string of red beads broke the spell and loosed her tongue.

"Oh look, Marthe!" she cried to Eagle Horse's wife, "I got something after all!"

It gave me a pang to realize how the little self-contained Indian girl had been suffering as she beheld her mates receiving gifts and nothing came her way. Hugging her package, she sat through the rest of the evening, and I do not know whether she was happy and content with what she had, or felt neglected because she did not receive more. I do not think jealousy was in her heart, but she certainly furnished an illustration of Indian fortitude.

Still the distribution went on with more men taking a hand,

and it was one o'clock before the last of the over 3000 packages had been distributed to their owners. Then the crowd began to scatter. Baskets and baby carriages were loaded with the gifts as families started home; while some even had to get washtubs to carry their bundles in. It was a Christmas we won't forget, but it has left us wondering, as usual—wondering whether the gift-giving we had witnessed was a celebration introduced by the whites, or an indulgence of one of their primeval customs and was in fact, a modified potlatch.

Chapter XV

RELIGION

This is a beautiful night in January, the full moon hangs in the sky and its reflection glistens from the gently rippling water of the cove. The sea lions are floundering and splashing on the other side of the channel, but are in the shadow of the wooded ridge, so we see nothing except the ripples which come running to our beach; while from the spruce and hemlocks on the ridge behind the schoolhouse, which loom black in the soft light, comes at intervals the "Whoo-who-whooo" of a big owl, answered by his mate in a slightly different pitch a little distance away.

At such times—under such conditions—the spirit of nature enters into one's being and fills one with feelings which cannot be expressed.

It may be that we are especially responsive tonight because we have just returned from a Salvation Army meeting. We go as frequently as we find opportunity, both because it gives them great pleasure and encouragement to have us show our sympathy and interest, and because we derive inspiration ourselves, even though we sit and listen to the unintelligible clucking of their guttural speech.

It is an impressive thing to witness the spiritual unfolding of primitive people. I spoke a moment ago of the "spirit of nature" entering one's soul. Of course it is simply a "tuning in" on God, and the same thing is experienced in the presence of these people when they too are "tuning in on God."

Before the advent of the white men, the Thlinget had no religious manifestations. The early missionaries found no evidence of a belief in a supreme being. They had no "Great Spirit," like the Indians of the States. They believed in *spirits*—particularly, evil spirits; they believed spirits were everywhere and in everything, but that was not a religious belief. They believed in the immortality of man, in a measure, and that belief had many interesting manifestations; they believed in re-incarnation; they had many interpretations of death; and they had among their legends many that closely parallel Biblical tales, so that when the missionaries told them, for instance, the story of the flood, it was an old story to them. The mayor told us one day, when we were making the trip to the "Hole in the Wall" on his boat, the Dubrovnik.

"When the missionaries come they talk to us about the flood, but they don't tell the truth. We know all about flood before missionaries come—they don't tell it to us right—not the way we know it happened. That's why we don't believe all the things they talk to us." They preferred to believe their own authorities— just as we do.

I had that brought home to us recently. One evening one of Bob's half brothers and his wife came in. She had been away to school and seemed quite above the average in her understanding. He looked intelligent, but confessed that when he was sent down to Chemawa, the Government Indian school in Oregon, he couldn't learn anything so he came back home. Well, the subject of thunder and lightning came up and George asked me: "What is thunder?"

It was rather a poser, because I knew he would have no comprehension of the scientific explanation, so I stalled while I tried to decide how to tell him so he could understand. He didn't wait for an answer, however.

"I ask sailor—he tell me something"; he said. "I ask preacher, he tell me God make thunder; I ask teacher, he tell me something different; everybody tell something else—nobody know. When Indian medicine man asked, he know—he always tell same thing. He say Thunderbird make thunder—all medicine man say Thunderbird make thunder, so I know they right—white man don't know."

I said nothing: he had a unanimous verdict behind him. My opinion would have been simply that of another white man who didn't know.

I didn't quiz George about the thunderbird—I suspect I may have curbed my curiosity more than has really been necessary, but Charlie Chuck, son of one of the high caste stalkers, who is an inexhaustible source of interesting information, says that the thunder which is sometimes heard at a distance, is caused by the thunderbird. It seems that the thunderbird considers the whale a special delicacy, and when it gets hungry it goes out and catches one, and it is the flapping of its wings we hear. It is a fierce bird— of course it would have to be to catch and eat whales—and when it is in pursuit of its sustenance the fire that flashes from its gleaming eyes causes the lightning we see, or rather, it is the winking of the baleful eyes which causes the flickering flashes.

Charlie says the thunderbird is so big that it carries a lake on its back and when even a single quill moves it sets the waves rolling in the lake until the water splashes over the edges and reaches the earth in a spray which we call rain.

He says the thunderbird lives on the top of a high mountain, he has pointed out the mountain itself whose top I can see in the distance. George, however, said the mountain is over near Juneau, but they agree entirely on the essential facts—that it catches whales and eats them. As proof of that they say that whenever the thunder stops they know the bird has caught its whale and has carried it back to the mountaintop. They assure me that anyone going to the top of the mountain can see the bones of whales that have been carried there. It would be an interesting excursion to climb the mountain some day and confirm the report. Of course the important thing would be to find just the right mountain.

Charlie says the bird has been seen three different times, but because, when people look at it, it makes them sick, those who saw it, one of whom was an old woman who fell down and kicked her arms and feet around, wouldn't look at it, so no one can tell just exactly what it looks like. Another man came very near seeing it. One day there was a terrific flash of light that blinded him and when he could see again, there was the great thunderbird sitting astride a mountain top, but he was afraid so he didn't look. The third time a Thlinget saw a whale in a tree top and there were marks on it he knew were claw marks, which proved the thunderbird had left it there.

It seems the thunderbird is a rather sensitive creature and is quite jealous of its reputation, so the story is current among the Indians that one day long ago, when the sailors of a Russian ship were ridiculing the idea of there being so large a bird, there was a great flashing of light and they heard the rushing sound of the bird's wings. Suddenly the ship was picked up out of the water, but the bird's claws slipped and the ship dropped back again on the sea with a tremendous splash. After that the Russian sailors were very careful in what they said about the thunderbird, and Charlie says all the Indians know they can't afford to take chances.

It is worth this trip to Alaska just to have found out how thunder is made, and to learn the habits of so remarkable a bird; however, I have taken Charlie's story with a little seasoning because mistakes creep in when anything is told over many times orally; besides, the mountain Charlie pointed out is the one I understand Bob to say was the "Mount Ararat" of the flood, or the Thlinget tradition. He says it was there the native canoe was stranded when all the world was covered with water, and the people landed there and lived until the water went away.

But strange as it may seem with such a background, these people have an amazing comprehension of the spiritual idea of God. It is as though they had at last found a key to many things that have mystified them in their primitive life.

While their greater faith in their own legends and traditions often were serious obstacles in the work of the missionaries, the ideas represented were at the same time a preparation for a new understanding. For instance, they had a mythical character which was in some instances known as "Yalth," which they translate as "Raven," who was born of a virgin who conceived by drinking at a fountain in which a spirit had hidden in the form of a pine needle. Yalth was all powerful and a world benefactor through bringing light and brightness to a world immersed in darkness. But Yalth wasn't worshipped. He was simply believed in as a spirit that had wielded great power and influence and who had done much for the Thlingets.

When the missionaries undertook to teach the natives about Jesus Christ, they said at once:

"We know about him—he Yalth." But the missionaries were off in some of their facts.

The Indians very readily grasp the idea of an all-powerful, Divine Mind that rules the world; but they become a little clouded in spots in making their application of that idea.

When the missionaries first went into Alaska in the '70's, they found a deplorable condition, due to contact of the natives with the white riff-raff who found their way to Alaska as sailors, soldiers, prospectors, fishermen, and explorers. Disease in its worst form was widespread and it is very manifest today.

A mission was maintained here in Klawock by the Presbyterians for many years—ever since David Waggener brought a bride to Klawock from the south and undertook to convey the white man's idea of God to the dusky natives. I would judge from all I have learned, that Mr. Waggener and his wife were exceptionally gifted for such work, in the rare wisdom and intelligence with which they labored.

Contemporaneous with our going to Klawock, a young native preacher educated at the Sheldon Jackson School at Sitka, with his wife, was sent to carry on the work in the village and they are accomplishing far more through their understanding of their people, than most white men could hope to do. Because the

Christian Endeavor of the church has been allowed virtually to become the church, and because it has allowed some of the practices of the Salvation Army to slip in.

Alma and I sat and listened one Sunday to a very learned doctrinal sermon preached to a small congregation of natives, by a doctor missionary who had been laboring earnestly and strenuously among the Eskimos of the Arctic Region. It was the kind of sermon one familiar with the Scotland of Barrie and Jan McLaren, would expect to hear from a Scotch Presbyterian; but such a sermon to preach to the Thlinget Indians! I doubt if a single word was understood by the listeners, except the word "God," and more of the audience would have understood that had the native term, "Ke-an-kow" been used instead. Its argument was too finely drawn to interest even us, or to appeal to our intelligence or arouse spiritual reaction, so it surely didn't mean a thing to the patient listeners who sat like so many solemn owls throughout the service.

The Christian Endeavor, however, is a human, vital, breathing organization, unhampered by doctrines; and Andrew Wanamaker, the native pastor, through it, is stirring the very souls of these people.

I do not know when the Salvation Army entered the field. It would undoubtedly be an interesting story, if one could know the inside of it, but I sincerely believe that its coming has been a tremendously fine thing for the natives of Alaska, because it is wonderfully adapted to reaching such people. They have their own methods of appeal and approach. Where the church attempts to reach the natives through intellectual channels, the Salvation Army begins in a rudimentary way, in a rudimentary civilization, to develop the idea of God and of man's relation to Divine Love. That they are grasping the idea was recently shown us in an interesting way. We have a big, man-sized boy in school who, with bad company, has acquired a reputation for stealing and has been involved in a very serious case. Through some adroit work on the part of George, the store manager, and under the pressure I was able to exert as representative of the "Big Chief" at Washington, responsibility was definitely located. One day Maxfield Dalton, the "Judge," came to me and confided that the people felt the influence of the young fellows involved was a destructive one in the village and they wished to take action that would protect the community, so they desired my assistance in laying the matter before the United States Commissioner at Craig. It was decided that I was to go over with others in Maxfield's boat on the following Wednesday.

Wednesday came, but Maxfield didn't, though I learned he had made the contemplated trip to Craig. It was all right with me; however, I wondered at their change of heart, but I have occasion to wonder about a good many things and this was just one thing more.

A week later John Darrow, an active Salvation Army man, came to me and explained. Mr. Wanamaker and the Christian Endeavor had been holding revival meetings and on Sunday night several young and old of the village had been actively interested and had been drawn into the fold, among them Peter, the man-sized schoolboy.

John told me: "They say they wicked—they steal—they lie—do wrong things—they sorry—they turn their minds round—be good Clistens." Of course everyone was enthused. Daily papers aren't needed in Klawock. What is known by one, is quickly known by all—except ourselves.

It seems big Peter, with the slant eyes and complexion of an oriental, is an orphan and has long been the ward of the Salvation Army, which has clothed him, seen that he had a place to spread his blanket, and food to eat, and in other ways been a father to him. When they learned by their native wireless that Peter had got "ligion" at the C. E. they gathered him into their arms as a father would, with the hearty approval of the native pastor. Peter pledged himself with them to watch his step, steal and lie no more, to attend school faithfully and strive to profit thereby. He also agreed with them that this should be his last chance and if he broke his pledge they were to go ahead with their contemplated action before the Commissioner.

So that was the reason why Maxfield Dalton had gone to Craig without me on that Wednesday.

"Now we going to talk to other boys," John added, "Maybe they get sorry too—be good boys. We try."

Who can say they do not know the meaning of brotherly love? "Ke-an-kow," (Ke—high, an—power, kow—great chief: the Great one over All) is a real force in their lives, but they interpret God and His teachings in the light of their experience and understanding. We all do the same or there would not be the many sects and cults.

Some one has said, "When nature is grandest, imagination

is most active and the spirit of investigation keenest." Alaska is a country of grandeur. Its expanses of water, the rockbound shores covered with dark forests, its mountains and glaciers, turbulent streams, its tides, storms, thunder and lightning, make a deep impression on the native mind and bring home to him a consciousness of power far surpassing his own. He quickly grasps the idea of a "Great One over All," but he adapts that idea to his conditions and his surroundings. We have been shocked at the promiscous parentage of the children of the village, as it is revealed to the nurse from time to time; but the customs and practices of the generations behind them exert a tremendous influence upon them which will require generations yet to come to outgrow.

It would not be right to call these Indians immoral, any more than to call the natives of Africa or other remote localities the same. The whites who have corrupted them were immoral, but rather are the natives *unmoral,* according to our standards. They have had their own, which in the past were more rigidly enforced than has been the case with us. Intimacy between members of the same totem was punished promptly by a near member of the same clan, who strangled the woman: as usual, the woman paid. But relations between members of different totems was another matter. If discovered, there was occasion for financial adjustment by the man's clan—otherwise there was no offense. And relations with the white men who came up from below, were quite acceptable because children by a white father were highly prized.

I was told recently concerning one of the young matrons of the village, that a young man of her own clan had clambered to her room with the aid of a ladder and her brother, learning he was there, was persuaded only with the greatest difficulty from killing her in the presence of her paramour; and the reason for the persuasion was not from any feeling of mercy, for she had committed the most heinous offense against tribal law and should pay the price, but from fear of the white man's law which seemed fussy about such matters and was disposed to meddle with native administration of justice.

Only recently we learned the particulars, via the nurse and some of her sources of information, concerning a situation that had a portion of the village very stirred up. In the absence of the husband of one of the native women, his wife and one of his brothers, who was also a husband, found favor in one another's sight with consequence quite common under such conditions. It was public knowledge and the husband on his return, was deeply resentful, but towards his wife—not his brother. When the nurse asked her informant what the husband would do to his brother, she was answered in surprise, "He do nothing—man his brother—brothers don't count."

Wives take exception to such conduct on the part of their husbands, yet not on what we would consider moral grounds, but because of a jealous unwillingness to share personal property with another.

The point I want to make of all this is that these people grasp something of the spirit of Christianity and make application according to their light; and yet, in spite of their earnestness and religious enthusiasm, they may be guilty of committing freely what we look upon as the grossest sin, because they are still people not very far removed from the primitive condition of animals whose actions are controlled solely by inclination.

In the old days the diversion of the natives was war, feasting, carousing and dancing. Hunting and fishing was their business. Civilization has robbed them of their oldtime pleasures. War is no longer possible; the old potlatch, which often lasted for days, has been put out of business by the missionaries, while the wild orgy of dancing which enthralled the natives, has gone the way of the potlatch. Life, compared to the old days of yore, must seem tame and innocuous to them.

They have their phonographs and Klawock has a movie theater which shows twice a week, but otherwise they find their diversion in their religion, and they put into their services, particularly in the Salvation Army, all the verve and enthusiasm that used to go into their dances, but the band instruments take the place of the tom-tom.

Chapter XVI

THE WOMEN

Very few of the women can be called handsome and none of them are pretty, but some of the children are beautiful—as wild things are beautiful. Of the old women of the passing generation almost all would answer the description of the traditional squaw —shriveled and wrinkled with age; bent and misshapen from hard work, and often crippled in the hips from the ancient practice of the midwives of dislocating a girl babe's hips to facilitate child-bearing later; hair in a little grizzled wisp of a pigtail down the back; clad in rags and tatters. Their interest in life has passed and they linger on like the last leaf to the tree, as in the case of old Mary Ha-Clan, whose gravestone which stands outside her door waiting to be put to use, credits her with being 112 years old. I've never been able to ascertain whether that is an estimated or an anticipated one. Forming my own judgment from appearances, I would say that it is a figure which has not been brought down to date. She is living—can move about, but looks hardly human and lives most of the time on her blankets on the floor. What an interesting tale her life-history would reveal.

The next generation of women are solid and stolid. Some have elements of attractiveness about them, but frequent child-bearing and hearty eating make them shapeless and heavy. Some of them have bobbed their hair and look better for not having the stringy locks hanging about their faces. They are easy-going and indulgent and enjoy their comfort, but with rare exceptions cannot be accused of showing beauty. There are two sisters, however, one the wife of a white man and mother of a family of positively brilliant children, who would thrill an artist because of their remarkable Madonna-like type. Both have heavy heads of hair which they wear in big loose coils in the nape of the neck; finely shaped heads gracefully set on their shoulders and with lines that blend into the harmony of their profiles; large, liquid black eyes, and the full bosoms of the perfect mother. We admire them greatly and they live up to their type, for they are very fine mothers and home-makers. The youth of the village are a different proposition—especially those who have been outside to school, and some of them, with their modern dress, snappy haircuts and vivacity are beauties of a type.

As a rule the women are lighter colored than the men, although they too, become several shades darker under the summer sun. The girls often have rosy cheeks and those who have been outside enjoy drugstore complexions. Alma, who is more observing than I about such matters, says many of them have small and beautifully formed hands and feet; and sometimes, as young women, they have finely formed, curvy bodies. The girls are lithe and virile, but are too heavily boned to remain slender long, and with their early maturing soon become heavy and dumpy.

The situation of the women among the early Thlingets was an anomoly, for while they were not considered the equal of men, they were the only parent the children had—the father didn't count. A woman could not be a chief, but it was possible for her to have as much influence as one in the councils of the clan, and for her to exercise more in the settling of family affairs. Aunts on the maternal side, there were not others, had, and still have, the authority of a mother over the children and are regarded as mothers and are so called by the children. If the mother died and there was an available sister, or even the daughter of a sister, the clan supplied her to the widower for a wife, and she became the mother in fact to the children. If a mother was not found for them in that way, they were automatically taken over by the maternal grandmother or aunts, and the father's responsibility towards them just as automatically came to an end. Often, if occasion arises, one or more of the children in a family may be adopted by a sister and reared, yet a mother's affection is very strong.

One of the women of the village told Alma one day that she had five small children and had been trying to work in a cannery and take care of the children too, when her sister came to visit her from Sitka. Her sister saw what a struggle she was having to care for the children and work also, so she offered to take one of the children back with her until such a time as the affairs of the family should be in better shape. The mother finally consented to let one of them go and it was decided that the next to the youngest should be the one. New dresses were got for her and everything was made ready for the going, even to packing things in a satchel and taking them over to where the sister was staying.

The woman said, "My sister make me promise to behave when the parting came. The boat was to leave at midnight. Sister brought the baby over at supper time and we didn't say goodbye, so I got through all right; but after everyone else had gone to bed I sat and watched the hands of the clock move around towards twelve. 'I'll go over and take a last look at baby before she goes,' I told myself. I found them all ready and so happy. Everything was all right and I said goodbye and went to the door. Then I did wrong thing—I looked back—and it was all off. I just couldn't give up my baby and I took her back home with me. My sister was terribly mad at me."

In the early days of the missionaries the blanket was the dress of both the men and the women. Today they wear the garments of civilization, but the women are apt to be quite indifferent to personal appearance, and to the appearance of the home inside, although outside they are much more particular.

In the primitive days the ears and noses of the women were pierced and labrets were worn as a sign of rank. Bars of silver were worn in the nose and often several pairs of earrings in the ears, while heavy bracelets of silver decorated the arms.

They painted in those days too, but the standards of beauty differed from those of the present, and whale oil and soot took the place in their toilets of cold cream and rouge.

The labrets and nose ornaments and the collections of earrings have passed into history, but the native bracelets hammered from silver dollars or copper—rarely gold—and engraved by hand, are still in vogue and are much coveted and highly paid for by tourists. Some of them are very old and have come down through several generations.

I think I have already explained that women's rights prevail in Alaska. This is undoubtedly due to the totemic descent through the women, although that really does not explain much. Anyway, women are "it" among the Thlingets, and their standing and importance often is superior to that of the husband. There is such a case here now, where old Mrs. Demmert seems to wield an influence that is almost supreme throughout her family; while old Kokash, the present spouse, cuts little figure. That may be because he happens to be the only survivor of several. All the children she has born are hers and belong to her clan, while he is merely one of the incidental fathers and no relation to the children. I wish as a matter of information, that we might know all the whys and wherefores, but even the nurse has not acquired that, although much gossip has reached her ears.

A father is considered of so little consequence in the Thlinget scheme of things that the children are considered no relation of his and in the event of family strife, would have to fight against him.

It was the mother and her clan who determined the marriage of the sons and daughters, without reference to the father; and while wives are supposed to look after the welfare of their husbands, in case of trouble, they "went home to mother," like their white sisters.

Women were often the tyrannical members of the family and the men were as apt to bear the marks of family disagreement, as their wives, and in addition to being the provider for the family, they were often made to cook their own meals and wash their own clothes, which they enjoyed no more than we do. Such is life, regardless of color.

Of course conditions are changing rapidly with the natives, so the old practices are being modified.

The women are great gossips and they are no more particular about facts than the gossips of the white race. No daily paper is needed in an Indian village. As much misinformation is in circulation at all times as used to ebb and flow through the army camps during the war; but whether false or true, it is always interesting, and is often the cause of quarrels between families and feuds between clans, with resulting claims for damages.

The modern young Thlinget woman lacks the disposition to work of her progenitor and, like the girl with the decaying fish-head behind her kitchen door, prefers to feed on cheap magazine literature, and to "strut her stuff" on the plank walk. Not infrequently her husband has to look out for himself, while she spends the money he earns. The women are very stubborn and cannot be coaxed or forced to do domestic work. It savors of slavery to them, for in the old days only the slaves worked. They would make very poor servants because they will not take orders or follow instructions; but there is no such thing as a hired servant in an Indian village.

The nurse had an experience which showed her the futility of expecting anything of that nature. She wanted to change quarters for the summer and move from her upstairs rooms to those of the teachers at the rear of the teacherage, so she told two girls she would pay them if they would move her effects. She discovered before the job was done that she had given the girls the treat of their lives, for, ignoring all instructions, they devoted themselves to examining minutely everything she possessed. They tried on her clothing, strutted around in her gloves and hats, searched through all receptacles, read letters, and in every way enjoyed themselves. When all was over and the nurse found herself in the midst of confusion confounded, with only such things there as it had pleased the girls to move, she concluded she would have been better off without them; but the girls asked fifty cents an hour each, for their services. She paid them enough and sent them off, but they didn't want to go—they were having too good a time. One of them ended the day by returning later and saying, "I come stay with you." And she did—until she felt disposed to go elsewhere. She enjoyed herself fully, sleeping till she got ready to get up, and eating so long as food was in sight. Her appreciation was all the nurse got out of the experience, except some acquired wisdom.

It was expected of women that they would be mothers of many children, and that attitude still prevails. A barren wife is not in an enviable position, so childless couples adopt children and have even been known to try to secure foundlings from Seattle. Because of desire and love for children, waifs and strays are never known among the natives.

Maturity is reached early among the Indians and in former times when that period was reached, the girls were sequestered for from four months to a year. Frequently they were confined in pits dug under the houses, so small that their occupants could neither stand up nor lie down in comfort. The darkness was absolute—the dampness what might be expected, and often they were deprived of clothing and were improperly fed. They were approached only at night and only by women. That any of them should have survived the exposure and torturing loneliness, seems inconceivable and bespeaks the vitality and hardihood of primitive people. Probably many did not survive. When the ordeal was over the girl was considered a woman and ready for marriage, and announcement was made to that effect by the mother or aunts and machinery set in motion to find her a husband. From that time it became improper for a girl and her brothers to be together in the same room unless other members of the family were present. Even after the girl was married it would have been improper for her brother to make her a present. If he felt any disposition in that direction, he could make the present to her husband, but not to her. Neither was it proper for a girl to look a male member of the family in the face. When together in the presence of others they either turned their backs to their brothers and father, or looked in some other direction. You see they had their ideas of etiquette and lived up to them very rigidly. All that of course, is now past history, but we had a surprise not a great while ago.

Alma has a girl in the upper room who is an excellent pupil and a fine singer. She is lighter in color than the average Thlinget and has brown hair instead of the usual black, showing the presence of white blood somewhere along the line—on the father's side probably. She has been greatly interested in her school work and has made good progress, but one day Alma expressed surprise to me at the lassitude and dreaminess of the child—said she had to prod her continually to keep her at work, and that she would sit with her eyes fastened on one of the older boys who had a seat at a table in front of the school, as a hypnotized bird gazes at a snake. He appeared to deliberately hold her gaze, but she was completely unconscious of what she was doing. It would take a sharp word from Alma to rouse her and she would start as though suddenly brought out of some spell.

One day the nurse told us that the girl had come down to the clinic with a look of terror in her eyes, but had hung around wordless, though she appeared to have something on her mind. At last she dropped her head on her arms on the table and began to cry and sobbed out, "I can't go to school any more. My mother is going to shut me up."

We looked at the nurse aghast, not understanding the meaning of such a thing.

"Why! She is one of the best students and hardest workers in the room," Alma exclaimed, "but she hasn't seemed quite herself of late. She sits and stares at Willie as though she were in a trance."

"There you are!" exclaimed the nurse. "That explains it. According to native practice she is approaching the marriageable age."

Then we understood, for we remembered the nurse had told us about the early practice of sequestering girls approaching womanhood.

We were horrified at the thought of such a fate for her, but so long as she continued in school there was nothing for us to do. She did not leave. Evidently there had been obstruction somewhere to carrying out the old practice. Possibly it had come from her handsome brother who had been out to school; possibly it came from the white blood in her father's veins; maybe it came from the Salvation Army, whose members had been baptized. It would be interesting to know.

Another practice of those far-off days was that of eliminating deformed or abnormal babes by stuffing their mouths with moss so they couldn't cry and abandoning them in the woods to die from exposure or by the wild animals of the wilderness. It sounds barbarous to us and yet, there is a question whether they in the end are not more humane than ourselves who do everything we can to prolong a life, even though it may mean long years of suffering and imbecility for the one, and heartache and trouble for others.

Only recently a badly malformed child came into the world in one of the village homes, but was reported to the nurse to have suffocated in the night, and she never learned what disposal was made of it. It was not given a funeral, that is certain, but simply faded out of the picture. However the life may have terminated, the nurse says it was a mercy all around that it did end.

The babies here are not bound on boards, as is the case among the Indians of the States, but it is still universal for new born babes to be tightly swathed like a papoose of the States, and kept that way for a year or more. When well wrapped they can be stood in a corner anywhere, they are so stiff. The nurse is making a strenuous effort to educate the women out of the practice, for she holds it responsible for hip trouble among the Indians, and the relatively weak development of the legs, as compared with the rest of the body. She has been able to influence two or three young mothers to give their babies the freedom they need, in spite of the strenuous opposition of the native midwives. A little girl of the village, when she saw one of these babies kicking around and playing with its toes, exclaimed in surprise, "Our baby always cries if she isn't wrapped up tight. Why doesn't yours?" Even babies can acquire habits.

The Thlinget babies are bouncers when they come into the world and grow at a rate that seems remarkable to us; but rapid growth and early maturity seems to be characteristic of the less advanced races. The babies are cute little beady-eyed brown things and are dearly loved by the other children of the family, and by no one more than by their unimportant, ignored fathers.

The modern mothers mentioned have fine baby carriages for their little ones. The mail order catalogues familiarize the people with everything in use in civilized surroundings, and the long plank walk makes use of the baby cabs possible. Whatever the merchants in the States may think of the mail order houses, they are a godsend to the people in the remote corners, and their great catalogues are a valuable text-book and a real source of education to the people.

It astonished us greatly when we arrived, to see how well and modernly dressed the children and young people were, for we had expected to see the natives still wearing blankets and living under the old primitive conditions. Instead we found a strange and interesting mixture of yesterday and today. The treatment the babies get is that of the Indian yesterday. Many white mothers, however, who wear themselves out chasing the creeping, toddling little busy-bodies and preventing them from having everything loose upon the floor, may see some redeeming features in the Thlinget method of baby culture.

The older children of the family are very good to the little ones and look after them well, but they are more easily cared for than our own, because a baby tightly swathed is pretty well established wherever it may be placed.

The mothers, in their care of them, have no bashful modesty, but bare their breasts and nurse their babies wherever they happen to be and regardless of who is around, while the young children in warm weather run around as nature clad them. For that matter, the absence of architectural secrecy prevailing at the present time among the women of the "civilized" races, fits nicely into the scheme of things with the Thlingets, and white men have become as hardened as their dusky brothers to meeting whatever sight may greet their eyes, without too acute embarassment.

Many of the women have become excellent cooks, as their living conditions have changed, and no better white bread can be made than that baked, and sold at 15 cents a loaf, by Mrs. Billy Benson, one of the older generation; or by Bessie Peratovich, a matron of the new school.

The native cooks are especially adept at cake making, but much of their home cooking is done in connection with their oldtime sea foods, and with the oils which they love, but which do not appeal to us.

Chapter XVII

HOME LIFE

The Alaskan Indians are fisherfolk. Their hunting is supplementary to their fishing, which has made it possible to have more definitely established places of residence. In their native state the Thlingets had no furniture in their homes. They led a life close to the ground in more ways than one: they sat on the ground, slept on the ground, and ate on the ground, for it was the practice for all who ate at the common board to squat in a circle around the pot in which the food was prepared and all eat from the same dish. The unwillingness of the natives to wash dishes was not responsible for the practice—they had no dishes to wash. Cooking utensils were not plentiful, and as for knives and forks, they knew no such things. Fingers and teeth served every purpose, just as they did with our ancestors a few hundred years ago.

The life of the early Thlingets centered wholly around the maintaining of existence. The only work necessary was that involved in securing food, gathering fuel and providing dwelling places, all of which was accomplished in the easiest way possible. The life of the primitive was not dissimilar from that of the wild animal and had not many more problems. Today, contact with the outside world has brought about many changes and greatly increased their needs. They are no longer clad in skins and blankets, but even here on the "West Coast," where they see less of the white man, all but the old folks dress well and quite up-to-date, and there is demand for all sorts of things which they did not formerly use.

Today an Indian village is made up of houses, like a white man's town, but one would hardly be justified in saying it looked like one, because shingled houses, decorative painting, lawns, and other trimmings of civilization are not all caught in the same breath. Neither can one assume that because they live in houses, they have found need for all the things we put in ours. People who can be comfortable squatting on their haunches, as the older ones among the natives are prone to do, have no real need for chairs, so many of the simpler homes have none or few. Tables come nearer to being a necessity now that they have come to use dishes and the customary tools of civilization, and they will be found everywhere; but beds, like the chairs, are not vital, and while most homes have at least one; those used to it can roll up in a blanket and be as comfortable as on a bed, so that is still the way a great many of them sleep, particularly the children.

Some families have taken to the ways of the outside world more readily than others, and such homes are well furnished and comfortable from our standpoint; while innovations are gradually creeping into all. A liberal percentage contain phonographs, two or three have radios and one or two pianos.

In the same way the houses are gradually changing and there are several quite modern looking bungalows in the village, though the interiors are usually disappointing, for the younger generation of girls cannot be accused of a fondness for work. Bill Peterson, the chap I described to you as having the aspect of a Thlinget, but a white man's mentality, was talking with me one day when a dusky maiden who looks as though she had black blood in her veins, though the hair doesn't show it, sauntered past us with a Japanese parasol jauntily held on her shoulder. "See her putting on airs!" growled Bill. "Struts like a crow on the beach. She forgets she was born in a smokehouse." And he went on to tell about a young matron: said that he had that morning gone into her house, and such a place! The bed wasn't made, dishes weren't washed, all kinds of things littered the furniture and the floor and she was stretched on the dirty bed reading the love stories of a cheap magazine.

"The place smelled like hell!" he exclaimed in disgust, which showed white blood, because the natives have no profanity in their own language and do not take to it naturally.

"Why don't you clean up this dirty hole?" he asked her, "Instead of lying there reading stuff that don't do you any good?"

He told me the stench was so fierce that he rooted around until he found a putrid salmon head behind the kitchen door. He kicked it outdoors, grabbed her magazine away from her, and told her to get busy and dig out the hole. Yet that same young woman and many others, dress effectively when they appear on the street, and with their trimly bobbed heads, appear to be anything but savages.

Natural conditions greatly influence the lives of the people. Because they depend almost entirely upon fishing for the money they need, they govern their lives by the habits of the sea, consequently they do not have set periods for work but have to labor when tides and weather conditions are favorable. I have told you how they get their fuel at considerable distance from the village and tow the logs home, where they anchor them on the beach to be cut up at low tide. It is quite common for us to waken on moonlight nights and hear the crosscut saws going down on the beach at ebb tide. They eat and sleep when they please, or when opportunity offers—eat what they can lay their hands on, and sleep in their clothing on the floor rolled up in a blanket.

The time was when cleanliness was unknown to the natives, but while their housekeeping leaves much to be desired as a rule, and in many ways their lives are quite unsanitary, personally the people are reasonably clean, which is attested by the lines full of freshly washed clothing. The absence of water for washing, except what is caught in the rain barrels, must handicap them, as it does us, and like us, they are apt to make prompt use of a rainstorm which has freshly filled the barrels. The older generation who grew up without other furniture than the ground—if they use tubs at all, place them on the ground and squat beside them to rub the clothes on a washboard. Before the advent of the tools of civilization, the natives accomplished such washing as they did by immersing their blankets in the nearest flowing stream, or in sea water if fresh water was not at hand, where they trod the dirt out with their feet, in lieu of the white man's washing machine.

One thing we can say of these people in Klawock—they are free from vermin as a rule, and those who are not, are looked at askance. One of the men, Sam Thomas, who had a white father and has a very fine mother who shows the influence of her white husband, has told me of an experience he had with "cooties" in his younger days. He had hired out on a boat to carry fish to Prince Rupert, and soon became infested with the vermin carried by the other men. They stopped at the village of Metlakahtla on the way, where they were so hospitably welcomed that the residents wanted to take them into their homes. Sam was ashamed of his condition, though the other men were not at all disturbed by their pestiferous company, so he would not leave the boat, hoping in that way to escape attention; but the Metlakahtla Indians could not be put off so easily, so a couple went down and compelled Sam to go home with them.

"And what made the matter worse," Sam said, "was that they insisted in putting me into their own bed. I would rather have been shot than sleep in their bed in my condition, but there was no one who would have done the shooting in that hospitable town. I always feel uncomfortable when I think of the awakening those kind people must have had after I left."

He had been promised another job on his return and he resolved to go to it clean, so he bought several suits of underwear and new clothing, and when he reached his native village he put his new underwear and clothes, a kettle and a camp outfit into his canoe and paddled off to an island where he made camp beside a running stream of water. There he put his kettle over a fire, peeled off his clothing and threw it on the fire, then bathed in the sea, scouring himself with sand, and put on clean underwear. For a week he stayed there, changing to fresh underwear several times a day and putting that removed into the kettle to boil. At last, convinced that he had freed himself from his disgrace, he clad himself in his new clothing and returned home a self-respecting young man once more.

In their primitive days, the women did most of the work not done by slaves, while the men hunted, fished, trapped, and made war on their neighbors.

Basket and mat weaving was work that took a great deal of time, for the materials used—long-stemmed grasses, spruce roots, and the long inside fibers of cedar bark, had to be laboriously gathered and prepared for use. The spruce roots used were of a special variety. They were charred carefully over a fire, were then soaked in water and drawn through a split stick stuck upright in the ground, to remove the soft outer bark. Then they were tied in bundles and allowed to dry till in good condition to split. The splitting was tedious and painstaking work, for the roots were split into the center part, which was the finest and was used for decorative work; the side or portions, used for the body of the basket; and the outer portions, which were discarded.

The colors used for dyeing or staining, also had to be prepared. The red they used was made from certain berries, and by soaking alder bark in some alkaline solution; yellow was made from a lichen known as deer moss, which hangs from the trees in swampy places in festoons like Florida moss, and is a valuable food for the deer when the snow is crusted so they can travel on it and other food is scarce; purple was made from blueberries; a greenish-blue from an alkaline solution of copper ore, which they had to travel far to get; and black from a black mud found around sulphur springs, boiled with hemlock bark, and from a black straw found at the bottom of certain lakes.

The skill of the women in weaving baskets was surprising, and the work was much more important in those days than today, because in the absence of the utensils of present day life, they had to improvise their own. Bowls were carved from wood, and spoons also, but mostly they used nature's implements. There was a variety of weaves in use. Some baskets were loosely woven and were used for straining the eulikon and herring oil. Others were so closely woven as to hold water and they were used for cooking by dropping red hot stones into their contents. Water could be boiled in them and meat cooked by the same process.

They had patterns and decorative designs which were characteristic of Thlinget work, and today the baskets are in great demand by tourists who visit Alaska, and who pay surprising prices for them. The weaving industry, however, is rapidly passing with the old generation. The girls of the later days have no inclination to acquire the skill or do the hard work involved. They would rather work in the salmon canneries.

The old women, in addition to their basket weaving, wove mats from the cedar bark, which served as rugs, wall coverings, and the many purposes to which the modern Indian puts canvas.

The women today are good sewers, but in those days they had to use bone needles and grass or root fibers for thread. Today they use modern sewing materials and are very skillful in their work. Sewing machines are in many homes, but the older women prefer the hand power machines, which they put on the floor before them as they squat on the ground. I went into the home of George Nelson one day—a new cottage and the kind a white man would live in—and there stood a new modern machine of a good make, but Mrs. Nelson, who sat cross-legged on the floor in the midst of her work making a dress for little Elizabeth, had a hand machine on the floor before her. Mrs. Nelson is highly skilled in all the arts of the primitive Thlinget — I might say, the *most* highly skilled—for her work is the finest of the village.

The women of the Thlinget home are in no respect inferior to the men, except that men are considered worth more, on a commercial basis, than women. They shared in the clanal councils and often dominated them; and while they were sometimes brutally treated, they often were perfectly capable of taking care of themselves and left the signs of battle on their mates. Today they handle the money and the men turn over their earnings to their wives as a matter of course.

I was much puzzled when Fred Thomas told me one day about his marrying a woman from further north who turned out to be "not so good as she should have been." Fred had had a good fishing season and turned all his earnings, some $1300 over to his wife, and both wife and money promptly disappeared.

"Aw right," Fred told me, "She gone with man—no see her two years—no one keep house for me—no one take care my boy— aw right—she no good."

The thing that puzzled me was the philosophical view he took of the disappearance of his money. He seemed to look upon it as an act of fate—what was, was, and that was that. Since then I have come to understand that in giving her his money he was fulfilling an age-old custom or Thlinget law-of-habit. If she failed to live up to her totemic obligations, why should he worry? In earlier days her clan would have had to make up the defalcation and pay a round compensation for lacerated feelings to boot.

To one who sees the homes of the natives for the first time, an impression is given of abject poverty, for they are so destitute of those features which enter into our lives and are considered necessities. But the situation is not as it appears. If the homes are bare of furniture it is because they do not feel the need of it. They will not have to create things as they go along, but can merely study the mail order catalogues and take and use what has already been created for us. There are indications right here of progress in that direction and a story the nurse has brought in concerning one of the young men who went down to the Indian school at Chemawa, in Oregon, has amused us. He felt the appeal of a dusky maiden from the Flathead Indian Reservation in Montana, who attended the school, and went home with her with the intention of marrying her. He came away in deep disgust—said he, "I couldn't marry her—her people lived and dressed just like Indians—not like white people at all—too dirty!"

On the whole, considering how short a time the Thlingets have been in contact with the conditions and appurtenances of civilized life, we feel that they have gone far and rapidly.

Chapter XVIII

OCCUPATIONS

Always the Indian villages of Alaska fringe the rocky shores and edge the salt water. If the sea and all that goes with it were taken away from the Thlingets, there would be little left in life for them. A few do labor in the lumber camps and some work in the various mines, but such labor does not appeal to them. Their time in the past has always been at their own disposal and it seems next to impossible for them to adapt themselves to the white man's servitude. They are their own bosses and do not have to punch time clocks when they fish. They have always worked with the tides and the winds, so to continue, is natural to them.

The herring run, which precedes the halibut fishing, offers some employment to the natives in seining for bait; the herring being frozen and kept in cold storage for the later fishing; and during the summer in certain localities, they seine for the herring salteries, where the most suitable in size are salted and packed in barrels, and the others are turned into oil and fertilizer. The labor in the plants themselves is largely brought up from below for the season by the packing companies, and consists of Japanese, Filipino and other cheap labor. The natives are used in getting the raw material.

The salmon fishing is the great support of the Alaska Indians, who find employment seining, tending traps and running the gas boats. The *King* salmon, also called the *Tyee,* which means king in the Chinook jargon, and also the *Chinook,* are largely caught by trolling, and as that precedes the run of the other species, it fills the gap between the early halibut season and the later canning season. The early king salmon are largely absorbed by the fresh fish market and bring excellent prices.

The commercial species used by the canneries, the sockeye, humpback, dog and coho, enter the Alaskan streams usually in the order named and then is when the really hard work of the natives occurs. In good seasons they earn enough to carry them through the rest of the year. Everyone works—the women and children in the canneries in various capacities, and the men largely outside, and it is intense work, because when the boats come in with their loads the fish have to be run through the mill and packed in their tin jackets as speedily as possible.

Trapping is the only winter occupation available for the Indians, but when prices are good some of them make very good money; but for the most of them the winter season is a period of relaxation, when they are not hunting or rustling their year's supply of wood.

The Thlingets are not a commercially inclined people, although they are sharp at driving bargains when bartering, and dearly love to get the advantage of the whites. In the early days they obtained property, not by earning it, but through warfare; by inheritance; or through compensation for claims for physical or mental injury supposed to have been suffered from their fellows. The natives seem to have no appreciation of the power of money to work for them, and will hoard and cache their accumulations rather than invest them in any way. Occasionally one sees an exception to that, as in the case of Bob Peratovich, who seems to have the capitalistic instinct; and of Charlie Demmert, whose leanings are towards industrial effort, which is especially rare in a native. Bob likes to buy and sell; Charlie, on the other hand, has no interest in that, but he has a strong urge to do things. He has a saw mill and a very modern and well-appointed salmon cannery, where he turns out a pack that is in excellent standing with the buyers.

As a rule the natives own little property of any value except their gasboats, which they usually buy from someone of the canning companies, paying for them from their earnings. In the primitive days the wealth of a Thlinget was hoarded for the potlatch, which was depended upon to materially advance his standing among his fellows, but he had little other motive for accumulating. Today the potlatch is banned, but he needs money for other things.

There is no bank in Klawock, and while the two native canneries and the Klawock Commercial Company, bank either in Ketchikan or Seattle, I know of no individual native who carries a bank account, so there must be considerable money hidden one way or another in the village, because no matter how hard up an individual may appear to be, there is always money forthcoming on occasion.

The Thlingets are surprisingly adept with their hands and become excellent carpenters. I marvel when I look at the big town hall that they should be able to plan and erect such a structure when they have known the use of tools for so short a time and have had no practical training.

There are several excellent boat-builders in the village, which is not surprising, because they were canoe builders before the white men came to their shores. One gasboat has been cut in two this winter and lengthened ten feet; while a new boat has been built and a second is under construction.

Their big war canoes were remarkable specimens of skillful work, with their carved prows bearing the totemic emblems of the clans to which they belonged. Some were 40 to 50 feet long, with a spread of six feet and would hold fifty or sixty people. They were usually made from yellow cedar and were always hewn from a single great log. The canoes were very light for their size and resistant to decay, but they were frail and not durable because of sun-checking and splitting. When in use the occupants would drench the shells with sea water frequently to protect them from the sun, and when not in use they were kept covered with fir boughs, rank marsh grass, or later, with canvas. Only because Alaska is a land of cloudy and leaky skies in those regions occupied by the Thlingets, was it possible to use them at all.

The native canoes or dugouts, in the village at the present time are sun-split and checked, and require constant calking and repairing, but they are beautiful things to see on the water, for their lines are fine and they ride high and gracefully as a swan.

Peter Anniskett, one of the most typical of the early type of Thlingets—tall, straight, beautifully proportioned and dignified, towed in a cedar log a while ago and rolled it above the tide line near his house, where giant skunk cabbages grow higher than his head, and started to hew out a canoe. It has interested me greatly to watch his work. I am sorry that I did not see the beginning of it when he blocked it out, but it was already roughly shaped before I realized what was going on, and he was digging at the inside. Aside from the rough work done with a sharp axe, his only tool was a small adze kept keenly sharp, with which he shaved off a chip here and another there, with wonderfully deft strokes and with an accurate eye for symmetry and balance. It was a pleasure to watch the work progress as the canoe came out of the log, like a sculptured figure from a block of marble; but as he seemed to approach the completion of the hollowing out, I was surprised to see the canoe gradually lose its beauty and the shell show a tendency to curl in at the edges, which I realized was due to the drying out of the wood.

The next stage in its construction was to fill it with water, then heat stones red hot and drop them in until the water boiled. The hot water softened the wood and made it easily manipulated. Cross pieces or braces were crowded carefully in between the edges until they were gradually forced back to give the sides the desired flare. This required careful handling to avoid splitting from too rapid and unequal pressure, but it was done in a masterly way and when the skiff was placed upon the water it floated as lightly and as perfectly balanced as an eggshell. The finishing touches were put on with sandpaper, but in the pre-sandpaper days the rough, harsh skin of the dogfish or shark was used for the purpose.

The braces are a permanent feature of the boat and when the canoe is equipped with oars, as is now often the case, they are used as seats for the occupants; but in those other days when the paddle was the only means of propulsion, the Indian squatted on his knees on the bottom. The woman was an important member of the crew and did the steering on her knees in the bow.

Canoe-making was something everyone could not do, but those who were expert at it were kept well occupied. The big canoes often brought as high as five hundred dollars, when dollars came to be an article of exchange with the Indians. Today most of the native-made boats are built like the white man's boats, of strips of thin or over-lapping boards in what is known as a clinker construction. I paid $50.00 for a good secondhand clinker-built boat in the winter, and imagine it would take much more than that to buy Peter Anniskett's canoe. It would be a matter of sentiment with him—confidence in the superiority of the old native construction, and loyalty to tradition; but for myself, in spite of the beauty of its lines and the grace with which it skims the water with its prow high in the air and the stern, with its occupant, riding the ripples in approved Indian fashion, I much prefer the modern boat, for the Thlinget canoe is as temperamental a creature as its birchbark sister of the States.

In the time that was, the carving of the totem poles was an established occupation among the Thlingets, that called for an artistic temperament and a natural aptitude, combined with poetical inspiration and imagination; but when the missionaries came to Alaska and secured a strong foothold, the totem pole passed out, although there is no question that in the recesses of the hearts of the older generation, it is still strongly entrenched. Only recently the mayor told me he had proposed to the leaders of the village that they salvage their poles from their abandoned village at Tuxikan and erect them in Klawock. I commended his idea because it would make a most interesting and picturesque feature of the village to have those unique and historical symbols of a past life standing along Klawock's solitary street, backed by the fir and hemlock covered ridge behind. It surely would be an attraction that would draw the ubiquitous tourist and, sad as it would be to experience their intrusion, it would diversify the occupations of the natives and help to make them less dependent upon the erratic fish industry. It would give the natives who are still adept at fashioning the buckskin and sealskin moccasins, at making the decorative beadwork, and at carving miniature figures from the soft red and yellow cedar, a market for the products of their handicraft; while Jimmie Staney, the crippled barber, could readily sell at good prices the native bracelets he hammers out of silver dollars and engraves so finely. But the fishing season is on and nothing interests them now but that.

There was a time when they hunted the fur-seal, the valuable sea otter, the mink and land otter, foxes, wolves and other fur-bearing animals and bartered their skins, but the hunting of the fur-seal is no longer their privilege, and the sea otter is nearly extinct. Trapping for mink, martin, and other bearers of fur however, still helps many Thlingets over hard winters, and this year the prices have been good and many pelts have been brought in.

While the Thlingets manifest little disposition to a commercial life, there is a growing inclination to dabble in business and there are nearly a dozen little shops in the homes of natives where they sell candy, pop, fruit and knick-knacks; and besides the two larger stores, there is the Roberts store, also general on a small scale, which is run by the fine and canny wife of the "blue-eyed Thlinget"; the Benson bakery, with its sidelines, where we buy the whitest and fluffiest of white man's bread; while Peter Anniskett, who has one of the little pop and candy shops, has talked with me about putting in a small stock of groceries. He is a stockholder in the native co-operative store, but like so many of our own people today, self-interest outweighs public spirit. He is the "hard-boiled egg" of the community and is something of a Bolshevik, in that in the past he has always been "agin the Government" and its representatives. His daughter, Rose, a well-developed girl of fifteen or thereabouts, has her full complement of thorns and the teachers have not found work with her in school an unalloyed pleasure. It has been necessary for me on occasion to take drastic action, even to forbidding her return to school until adjustment had been made. Quite to my surprise I found both father and mother took no serious objection to my action and they told me:

"She go back tomorrow." She did, and toed the scratch so far as was in the power of that stiff-necked family to do such a thing. They are very high caste and it is difficult for them to bow their heads to anyone. It did not occur to me at the time, but I have wondered since whether it might not have been their old totemic law of compensation for offense that worked in our favor.

I was still more surprised when the old rip-snorting meat-eater, who had a brainstorm two or three days ago that drove his family scattering for cover like a frightened brood of partridges, stalked into the house this afternoon. He opened the interview by asking for the nurse because, he said, Delphine, the little girl, was sick; then he sat down to talk to me. I wish I could have understood all that he told me, but that was impossible because he not only got the cart before the horse in his conversation, but they often ran away together and left me in a cloud of dust, wondering just where the whole shebang had gone. But I gathered that he and a number of others, do not like the way the co-operative store is being run. Evidently he represents a following who would like to see some dividends and who entertain the idea that I can help them bring that about. If I will stay in the village they will stay in the store. If I do not, he implied that they intend to abandon ship. He talked about two or three different parties, but I haven't the slightest idea what he was trying to tell about them, although he seemed to approve them; and finally he confided to me his ambition. He has been making a little money with the little store in his home—said he had been sick and started the store so his family would have something to support them if he died, and he thinks a larger store should make larger money—you see the commercial idea is germinating.

My first impulse was to discourage the establishment of another store, but the explanation of his reason checked me. I kept still and listened, for I sensed something out of the ordinary in the air. The future of widows and orphans has never been a problem with the Thlingets because, according to their practice, a young husband was always promptly found as a provider, but evidently Peter sees changing conditions and is shrewd enough to realize that the old customs are liable to prove undependable insurance for the future.

Many surprises come to those who work with primitive people. It is most interesting that my canoe maker, who periodically chases his family into the woods or to the homes of others of the clan for protection during his rampages, and who has held most persistently and arrogantly to the old traditions of his race, should be the first to manifest the white man's concern for the welfare of his much abused dependents, and take special measures for their protection should they be left behind.

He talked about his little business and said they were going over to the "Hole in the Wall" for the trolling season, to run a little store there, and when he returns he wants to order his stock. I helped him make up a list of what he would find most saleable, and while he has large ideas, I induced him to make drastic cuts in his quantities—advised him to buy little and often—and framed a cable order for him to the wholesale house with whom he wants to deal.

I have no idea what the outcome may be. It will doubtless depend largely on his financial success at the Hole in the Wall this spring. Nevertheless, I have had my surprise.

Beyond what I have mentioned, I can see no way in which the natives of Klawock can broaden their field of activities, and if the salmon-canning season turns out no better than it now promises to be, what can save them from starvation? I know of but one thing—the size of the poke they may have hidden away. I hope it is a generous one.

Chapter XIX

FOOD

Tecumseh Collins has told me often about "fish-egg-time," with a rolling of the eyes and a smacking of the lips that left me in no doubt as to what it meant to him, but the time is approaching and he awaits it with glee. In the meantime Tecumseh has lived on smoked fish as a substitute—smoked herring, smoked salmon, and smoked "what have you?" until he has assumed not merely the contour of a herring barrel, but all of its suggested savor. In other words, Tecumseh smells, not like a smoked herring, but like many of them. It may linger about his clothing, but one has the feeling that it has entered into his being, as the spruce hen takes on the flavor of the spruce buds on which it feeds.

To be in the presence of a Thlinget is to think of fish. Fishing is their business and fish are their life and sustenance.

One of the sights which interested me, and I may as well frankly admit it, disgusted Alma, when we took our first walk around the village, was that of salmon drying in the sun and it wasn't a sight that tempted my appetite, but I have seen food prepared under primitive conditions before so it did not disturb me as it did her.

That first week we had beautiful weather and it was a valuable week to the natives. During the fall the Indians are active, like the squirrels down in the States, in storing up food for the winter, and the running salmon offer a splendid opportunity. I suppose they do not do it earlier because they don't have to, and possibly because the fish do not spoil so quickly in the fall. Anyway, they were at it when we appeared on the scene, and all along the street were to be seen strips of salmon strung on poles and suspended to dry. The sun and heat of the fires drew out the oil; the smoke and dust darkened the flesh; and the swarms of flies filled the air with a buzzing like that of a hive of bees.

Nature originally furnished the Indians with all their food, and still furnishes a large portion of it; and nature was called upon to help in its preparation.

Of course their contact with the whites has brought many changes into their lives, and the Indians of today are using our flour and sugar, tea and coffee, fresh bread, butter and lard, and canned goods in great variety; but in the early days they had their substitutes derived from nature for most of these, which were much more valuable as foods for them than our own products; and they retain their passionate fondness for them and make great use of them.

In the primitive state they had no flour, for they engaged in no agriculture of any nature. Wild honey was their sole source of sweetness; they made a beverage from a plant now called Hudson Bay tea; whale, seal and fish oils, bear and other fats served the purpose of butter and lard; various sea weeds, wild celery, the pulp of spruce and hemlock bark and various roots, were their vegetables; while the many varieties of edible berries which abound in Alaska, furnished them their fruit.

Someone has said of the Alaska Indians that when the tide goes out the table is set for them, and that comes very near to being the situation, because there are very few things found in the sea which the Thlingets do not turn to account. Besides the fish, seaweed, and seals, they consider crabs a great delicacy and clams, mussels, devil fish, sea grubs (most repulsive looking things), cockles, and an endless assortment of other creatures, are all items on their menu card; while the abalone, which can only be secured in certain localities at extremely low tide, is one of choicest tidbits of all.

Just as the natives used to talk to the spirits supposed to dwell in the salmon they wanted to entice into their traps, so when hunting mussels on the beach at low tide, they would address the spirits in the mussels and seek to placate them so they would not cause sickness when eaten. They didn't have our rule that oysters should only be eaten in those months with names containing the letter "R," but they had learned that there were certain times when shellfish should not be eaten. So when they dug for the clams, which work their way down deep into the sand of the beach, leaving only their long telescopic ducts to connect them with the surface, but drawing them down on the slightest disturbance, the orthodox thing to say was," Don't go down so fast. You'll hit your mother-in-law in the face," which I suspect was a sly bit of humor on their part, because the mother-in-law with them, as with us, was no negligible element in their lives. It also illustrated the extent to which they credited everything possessing life, with personality and with being the dwelling place of spirits which must be treated respectfully, if they were to escape their displeasure and avoid unfortunate consequences.

Should a clam digger cut his foot on a sharp shell, it would be because in some way he had lacerated the spirit's feelings.

The seaweeds of certain varieties are more popular with the natives than shredded wheat or corn flakes among ourselves. Kelp, that remarkable broad-leafed sea plant, which is very rich in iodine and other elements that are supposed to be good for what ails you, is an especially choice article of food and is put to many uses. They dry it in the sun, flavor it with the juice of cockles or other shellfish, and pack it in the modern five-gallon oil can, where it is pressed in square cakes about an inch thick. A layer of hemlock twigs is added and another layer of kelp until the can is full. The twigs keep the kelp separated and lend a flavor which the Indians relish. When the can has been filled, stones are piled on it to compact the contents. The cakes are taken out daily to dry in the sun and harden, but at sundown they are again carefully packed under pressure. This is continued until the seaweed is properly cured, when it will keep its sweetness and flavor for months. It is eaten, of course, with oil.

The seaweed bearing the herring roe—the "fish-egg" delicacy, is treated in much the same way. Fresh seaweed, salmon eggs, berries and oil may all be cooked together in a pot. In the early days the pot consisted of a closely woven basket made of spruce rootlets, and the cooking was done by dropping redhot stones into the contents. When it was cooked, the family squatted around the vessel on the floor, each helping himself with a wooden or horn spoon. The spoons were graded in size according to the age and importance of the owner, and were emptied at a gulp, regardless of size. They were unfamiliar with the modern etiquette of soup eating.

The salmon roe was a more substantial article of diet than herring eggs, though possibly not so great a delicacy. They were eaten raw or were dried in cakes for winter use. When dried with seaweed or by themselves, they were prepared for use by being pounded in hollowed stones with stone pestles, as the Indians of the States were accustomed to make meal from their maize. The pestles were shaped for the purpose and were worked into various forms. The nurse has one which is undeniably the head of some animal—we cannot decide what and the natives have called it variously a wolfhead, doghead and sealhead. It looks most like the latter to me. It is of dark gray granite and is a surprisingly good piece of work.

When thoroughly pulverized the eggs were mixed with water

or with oil to make a thick cream. Sometimes the roe was boiled with sorrel which gave a tartness, and were made into cakes to be eaten with fish, seal, or other oils. The oils of the natives' larder served the same use as the mayonnaise of the modern white man's home.

Fish and other meats were boiled in the same way or were roasted on a stick stuck in the ground before a fire. Of course today most of the cooking, except in camp, is done on the white man's stove. The salmon head, when mellowed or ripened by being buried in the ground for a period of time, was eaten raw and was considered a wonderfully choice bit although the smell would rival that of our limburger cheese. The smell of cooking herring was said to be mild compared with it. The salmon roe is mellowed also before being prepared for winter use, and I think the ripening process must be a rather common one with the people, because one of the natives attempted to explain to me one day, how fine the halibut heads became when they had been buried in the ground for a while. I had not heard about the ripening process at the time, so I failed to comprehend the significance of what he was telling me, but had I understood, I am confident I still would have preferred to put mine through the frying pan over a hot fire.

As for the salmon themselves, the king and silver are largely caught with a hook and line and are eaten fresh; while the hump-back and dog varieties are caught in shallow water with a gaff or net. They run later in the season and seem to be most generally cured for winter use by the natives. They were still running when we reached Klawock, but their humps, which develop at spawning time, were taking on the relative proportions of those of the American bison.

Halibut are most commonly used fresh, for they can be caught the year round.

The wild celery, which grows on every side and which looks like a squash vine trying to be a bush, is peeled and eaten raw, much as we eat rhubarb or sugar cane; but it also is pressed in cakes with fish eggs and preserved for winter use.

Use is also made of the wild rice which is found in some localities and which formerly gave them their nearest approach to our flour when pulverized with their stone pestles. In fact, there is nothing which nature supplies in this country, and she is generous, that can be used by man, which the natives do not turn to account.

Wild berries are exceedingly plentiful in season. I have been told there are over thirty varieties.

If anything is safe to eat, it is a certainty that the Thlingets have found it out and have put it to some use, regardless of its taste.

Huckleberries are a much-prized fruit, are gathered in great quantities and are pressed into cakes, like the seaweed, and dried, and furnish a tart relish which is generally flavored with the smoke of the wood fires used in drying them. A little additional flavor of such a nature is quite inconsequential to the natives. He likes variety.

In the muskegs small red berries grow which Bill Gardner called to my attention the day we went hunting, and told me were wild cranberries. Maybe they were, but it cannot be proved by me, for they didn't taste like the cranberries I have eaten, although they were certainly acid. However, they grow like cranberries and under similar conditions. The Indians make generous use of them—put them up in oil, or dry and press them into cakes with seaweed or salmon or herring eggs.

The salmon berries, which are possibly the most plentiful of all, and the most easily obtained, are a very great favorite. The bush grows as rank as tropical vegetation. The blossom is a pretty pink, while the immature fruit is orange or salmon-colored, turns a bright red as it ripens, and ends up by looking very much like the deep wine-colored fruit of the red raspberry, although larger and longer. The fruit when ripe is very soft and juicy— quite squashy—but very seedy and often quite large.

Blackberries and red raspberries do finely here, but I have not learned whether they are indigenous to the soil, or have been introduced. The strawberry thrives also and is found in most of the gardens of the natives, but the fruit does not take on the vivid coloring of the berries grown further south where the sunlight is stronger and there is more of it; nor is it so finely flavored, if what we have sampled is typical.

Various garden vegetables have been introduced and have been adopted into the dietary of the Thlingets, such as potatoes, carrots, turnips, peas and cabbage.

What little soil is found on the rocky islands is apt to be acid from the decaying vegetable matter and is antagonistic to many things; but the native instinct, or possibly a tip from the white man, has helped them to meet the situation in a measure, for those who have small strawberry beds have brought in broken clam shells which they find in profusion on some distant beach, and have spread them on the ground to furnish the lime which the soil lacks.

Most of the families have found little areas of suitable soil on the surrounding islands and there they grow their potatoes and other vegetables.

Some of the people had told me that peas grow wild here. It sounded rather surprising, but the time Alma and I walked around the island, we ran across such a patch in the tangled grass above the beach, bearing green pods, and we realized that they had escaped from cultivation in one-time garden patches and were continuing their existence on their own responsibility.

When the distant gardens need attention, it is the practice for the families to make camp near the place while they do the necessary work. The same thing is done at harvest time. In between times the gardens have to shift for themselves as other responsibilities require the owners' attention.

As for the flesh in their diet, there is plenty to be had. Wild fowls—ducks of many varieties, geese and swans—are plentiful at certain seasons and are easily obtained, but the bother of picking and dressing them makes them rather unpopular with the natives.

The hair seal is an important element in their diet. The seals are covered with a layer of fat or blubber an inch or two thick under the skin, which furnishes the seal oil of which the Indians are so fond. The flesh is black and, I understand, tastes like a mixture of fish and flesh, but it is valued as an article of food. In the early days the oil was tried out in the same way as the eulikon oil, by means of putrifaction and boiling with hot stones; now, however, the primitive methods have been discarded and stoves and cooking utensils are used.

The wild animals of many kinds—deer, bear, mountain goats and sheep, even the porcupines, contribute their share to the Indians living.

There is another greatly prized element in their diet, which, however, is available for but a very short time, and that is the eggs of sea fowl. Natives have told me of islands, of which Forest Island is one, where the gulls and other sea birds nest in untold numbers and at the proper season the Indians go and stock up and feast to their great satisfaction, each clan having their own special preserve. One day this spring I picked up some dark green eggshells, mottled and splotched with black, on the plank walk near the dock, and puzzled over how they could have come there, until it occurred to me that it was "bird-egg-time" and some of the natives had been to the "eggery."

When I see the vigor and vitality of the older generation of Thlingets, the keenness of their vision and the soundness of their teeth, I realize that nature, when depended upon, can furnish a far more valuable and suitable diet for the human being than he can provide for himself with all his artificial foods. I know a man here nearly 80 years old, who has a set of teeth that would be the despair of a dentist, so perfect and sound and beautiful are they; and there is not a gray thread in his thick thatch of black hair; nor a squint to his eyes, and he swings an axe with the vigor of a young man.

The situation is very different with the children, however. They have the child's sweet tooth and the wild honey they are able to get no longer satisfies them. Now they have the white man's sugar, and worse yet, his candy, and as a result it is hard to find a child in school with sound teeth. We try to fight the candy habit, but the indulgent parents are unable to deny the clamor for the nickles and dimes which are passed over the candy counter.

Of course the food of civilization has been adopted as well as many other things, and some of the natives make beautiful bread and cake, but others buy such things instead of making them themselves, and are very poor cooks from our point of view.

I musn't forget to tell about Andrew Wells, the "Ice cream king," because ice cream is to be had even in Alaska. Andrew builds boats in the winter time, but in the summer he makes and sells ice cream; and the interesting thing about that is that he has to ship in his ice from the ice plant in Ketchikan. How is that for Alaska? We get some ice here at Klawock, but ordinarily it does not form thick enough in the winter to be put in storage and keep long enough to be of any use. Neither does he have any cows to draw on so his milk is obtained with a can opener. On Sundays and on special occasions Andrew puts his freezer in a child's four-wheel cart and trundles it up and down the plank street, peddler-fashion. What he calls, and what it means, I have not the slightest idea, but he draws generous patronage. As for ourselves, for obvious reasons, we have never sampled his product.

We have been told that the natives have a dish of their own which they call "sopalally" or Indian ice cream, which is made by beating up with the hands crushed soap berries in warm water in a big bowl or dishpan. Sugar is added and the whole is beaten till a stiff froth forms. One beats, with sleeves rolled up, until weary; then another takes a turn until the proper stiffness has been secured. All then gather around the dish and eat it with spoons.

While the fondness for the native food persists, the natives now make free use of the prepared foods carried by the stores, and are very generous users of the fresh fruits which are shipped in from below. The life of a fisherman is a strenuous one at best and is especially so when the fish are running freely. The water in the butts on their boats gets warm and stale, and doubtless the salt air tends to aggravate their thirst, as well as the hard work, so the tartness of the carbonated drinks and the juicy fruits are exceedingly welcome and the quantity consumed is astonishing. There is also a heavy demand for fresh meats, especially during the fishing season. We were rather amused after Bob's return from below, to be told that he was having a half carcass of beef shipped up on every mail boat and was going to sell it at the straight price of twenty-five cents a pound, regardless. The meat was frozen solid, and not knowing how to cut up beef, he simply chopped off a chunk as was, until he reached the other end of the beef. There were spots where one fared well, but otherwise it was like buying one's meat from a grab-bag. Those who got meat might be satisfied, but those who paid the same price for little but bone, were otherwise. He decided shortly that there must be some better way to dispense meat, so he had it cut up before being shipped.

In spite of the readiness with which the Indians have taken to our foods, if a Thlinget is entirely separated from his own foods, he becomes a forlorn and homesick creature. I have had some tell me who have been outside, that they have actually been made sick by dreaming about and longing for their native delicacies, and had had to give up good jobs and return to their people from sheer homesickness; and the delighted letters that have been sent home from young people who have gone out to school at Chemawa, on the receipt of packages of fish-eggs, seaweed and other native favorites, rival those from our own children to whom we have sent candy and cake.

Chapter XX

MARRIAGE

When the missionaries came to work among the Thlinget Indians they found marriage customs which were entirely unfamiliar to them. Marriage was not a mating for love, but purely a matter of propagation and was arranged in accordance with native custom and totemic practice.

Just as the Thlinget babes are born larger than white children and show more rapid growth and development, so the girls mature early and at sixteen to eighteen are in full bloom. Marriage would naturally occur early, but native custom is apt to bring about marriage of mere children. Love or affection rarely entered into marriage in earlier times. There was no courtship. A girl rarely had any choice and the man not a great deal, for a union was generally effected through tribal council or through a request of one dying. As a result there were no old maids among the natives and few widows. Physical attraction entered very little into marriage considerations, but a girl's ability to do things was the great recommendation after caste.

Marriage must always take place with someone outside the clan and the only relationship considered to exist is that on the mother's side; the father and his connections are not considered relatives. The children are always of the same totem as the mother, therefore the members of that totem are considered to bear a closer relationship to the children than their own father. Under the rule of marrying into opposite clans, a boy could be married to his father's sisters, who were of a different clan than his mother; or to their daughters. That made possible the marrying of what we consider as "blood relations," and would not permit the marrying of those of the same totem, even though no blood relationship existed, as in the case of members of the same totem from distant unrelated villages. That totemic rule was so absolute that if a girl disregarded it and married one of her own totem, death was the penalty and she might expect to be strangled by her own father or brother in order that the stain on the clan might be removed.

To marry into a lower caste clan, for there was caste among clans as well as among individuals, was a disgrace. Custom and tradition required that both parties should be of relatively the same caste, although a girl member of a clan of a certain caste, if good-looking, was considered of higher caste than her clan and could marry a higher caste man; while a handsome high caste woman was considered very high caste.

When marriage was considered desirable for a boy or man, members of his family would go to see the mother of the girl whom they in council, had decided was of proper caste, properly gentle and modest and efficiently capable in those lines of work which devolved upon a wife. The agent, who would be the mother, a sister, or an uncle on the mother's side, would say to the girl's mother:

"I value the words 1 am going to speak at 40 blankets. If you are willing, accept them. Perhaps in two days I will speak to you."

That was to give the girl's family a chance to consider the proposal and decide whether the alliance was desirable and the gift offered valuable enough. If the decision was favorable, when the subject was brought up again the blankets, furs, or other price agreed upon, would be delivered. Such bestowal of property on members of a girl's family was called "putting gifts on their backs," and cannot properly be considered as a purchase price, but as a compensation to the girl's family for the loss of her services.

The girl's family of course desired a "good provider" for a husband, and if his hands were rough they would say they "looked like an eagle's," and considered him industrious; but hands "soft as a mat" belonged to one who was "no good."

In early days Ben Lindsey's "companionate marriage" was quite the approved thing, but "trial marriages" have been abandoned today under the teaching of the missionaries. The marriage tie was a very loose one. Marriage consisted simply of living together after the proper exchange of gifts and feasting. If the experimental marriage which was sometimes tried, looked promising, the bargain would be clinched and the marriage considered on a formal basis. The girl didn't go to the man, but the man went to live with the wife, generally in the communal house of the family, and had to work for his wife's family—so far as work was done; in other words, instead her becoming a member of his family, he became a member of hers, and if he should wish to escape from the situation he could only take his wife away by paying for the privilege in blankets or with some other consideration.

A woman was expected to bear many children, so one who remained childless was considered by her husband to have defrauded him and he could turn her back to her family and demand his money back. In the days of their communal life it was quite common for the men to loan out their wives for a consideration to their friends—a very natural consequence of such herding together; but that is not done today, although it is not surprising that the idea of chastity should be very loosely drawn and carelessly observed.

Theoretically the man was considered the head of the family, but as a matter of fact, the women were often the dominant element. Even today the men turn over all their earnings to their wives and consult them on all business matters—and the women are often the shrewder business men of the two. If the wife proved lazy and incompetent or sullen and intractable, the man could demand his payment back; and if she proved unfaithful, he not only could have it refunded, but would be entitled to compensation for the injury and disgrace brought to his clan. That price would have to be paid by the woman's clan, for the disgrace would be more than a personal matter—the whole clan would share in the injury and the other clan would be considered responsible.

Should he send her away or divorce her, for that is all that constituted divorce, without adequate cause, he would have to divide his possessions with her. If, however, she were to leave him and go home to her family, the father was under obligations to either return her to her husband, or repay half the number of blankets originally received for her. If she ran away with another man indemnity was due from her clan and her life might be forfeited, providing she could be caught.

Under the easy system of divorce and companionate marriage, there were few of the women of the older generation who had not had from several to many husbands. That is evidenced today in the variety of names to be found among the brothers and sisters of a family; but according to the nurse, there is just as great a variety of fathers to the children as there used to be.

When the missionaries first went among the Thlingets, plural marriage was a regular practice and was one of the first features of the native life attacked by the zealous workers.

Widows and widowers were an abhorence among the Indians and the plural marriage practice seems to have largely been the result of their effort to avoid that condition. It was quite a common practice among them for a married couple to adopt a boy and a girl to rear and take their places in the event of either of them dying—a sort of understudy as it were. If the husband died, the boy became the woman's husband; and the girl became the man's wife, should the woman die. If that provision had not been made, the members of the deceased one's family was supposed to furnish a successor. Under the totemic rule governing marriage, a man could marry the daughter of his wife by a previous marriage, his wife's sister, or his wife's sister's daughter; while under plural marriage, he could marry both the sister and her daughter. We know of several instances in the village where men are fathers of children by the wife; by the wife's sister; by the daughter or daughters of the wife by a previous marriage; and by the daughters of the wife's sisters, and I suspect that to be only a part of their parental history. Under our standards the children were born out of wedlock, but not under their old tribal practices; and while today they outwardly accept and conform to our ideas concerning marriage, it would be irrational to expect their old ideas to have been completely eliminated, or for them to feel towards the subject as we feel. That could not be done with one generation, nor probably with two.

One feature of their marriage practice which struck me most forcibly when I heard of it is the way their abhorrence of the unmarried state meets a condition which with us is met by life insurance. The only means known to them for the support of women and children was by marriage. The woman needed someone to fish and hunt for her and her offspring, and to build a house for her; while the man needed someone to mother his children, prepare his food, dress the skins he brought in, make the baskets, moccasins, etc. In the case of a widower, the younger children were taken over by members of the woman's clan, so that problem was met; but the other problems were usually met by mating him up with a woman in a similar situation. I refer to the dying request frequently made to some friend or relative, which carried with it an obligation that could not be escaped. When I asked blind Jumbo McFee if he was married, he answered, "No, not married," then he went on and told me that he had had a friend and the friend died, and before he died he said:

"'Jumbo, you have my money—you have everything I got— you take my wife.' So I did. No, I not married."

I don't know whether he meant that no marriage ceremony

had been performed, or that his wife was not of his choosing, but the fact remains that the fine old man is "taking care of the wife." She is "eyes" for him, and his broad back and stout muscles furnish the protection the dying man desired. When Jumbo starts his outboard motor, she does the steering. Jumbo rustles the wood and she splits it up; so two, who otherwise would be dependent, are independent.

It was quite the orthodox thing for a brother to marry his brother's widow, and if there was no brother, then the man's closest kin inherited the responsibility, or a friend, as in the case of Jumbo. In the polygamous days that simply increased the number of his wives, but after the natives were influenced to give up polygamy, if the party who inherited a friend's or a relative's wife were already married, he was forced to put away his wife in order to fulfill his duty to the friend—a strange practice that compelled a husband to abandon his own wife and children in order to assume responsibility for another's. But she was not neglected. Another husband was found for her in the same clan.

Should the man die and there be no "understudy," it was customary to find a young husband for the widow and he might even be a boy. This was generally the man's nephew, if he had one, or his nearest kin. In the same way, in case of the death of the wife, a sister, a niece, or some other close relative, became her successor, regardless of her age. Marriage being arranged on a commercial basis between two clans, it was up to the clans, if their members could not be kept alive, to make replacements; and because payment had been made once, there were no presents in case of replacement. The actual choice of the successor was generally left to the survivor and the choice was final, in so far as the choice was concerned. As compensation to youth for marrying age, if the older mate died, the survivor was allowed to select a young girl or boy, as the case might require, for the second mate.

These primitive people, being closer to nature than the higher refinement we are disposed to call civilization, are ruled more by physical impulse than by emotional stimulation, so they probably, like animals, follow the mating instinct without experiencing the spiritual tuning in called love that is supposed to accompany marriage among the whites; but as they pass farther from their aboriginal condition they develop mentally and take on the customs of civilization. Their spirit begins to quicken and there is a growing tendency to mate by the process of selection. It is evident that the younger generation is beginning to break away from the old tribal customs and is going to marry to suit itself. There are those here who can flirt as skillfully and ardently as any pale-faced lads and lasses.

We hear rumors through the nurse that certain marriages are being arranged, but they don't take place, so it looks to us as though some of those involved have other ideas and Custom finds obstructions in her path.

One day we were shocked to hear that Harriet Nickerson, a 14-year-old school girl in the seventh grade, had been married to John Dick, a forty-year-old, or more, widower. The primitive Thlinget marital law had been operating. I ascertained that there had been a real ceremony performed at Craig by the United States Commissioner, so there was nothing I could do without having more legal information than I possessed. However, I took steps to learn what protection was supposed to be furnished against the marrying of children, and found that the marriage was illegal; that the man was subject to court action for being a party to it; but I stopped to think: What chance had I, an alien among these people, a temporary appointee, even though representing the Government, to stem the current of age-old custom and check the operation of Thlinget psychology? It looked to me like a pretty good place to tend to what I *could* do and if I were to neglect anything, to neglect the impossible. Had we known in advance, we might have obstructed effectively.

One Sunday afternoon Harriet and her brother John came to the house and we had another experience—the revolt of youth, dusky youth—against ignorance and tradition.

John, who has been through the village school and out to the Indian school at Chemawa, took the initiative and told us that his sister did not want to be married to an old man like John Dick: that she wanted to go to school and get an education—that the United States Commissioner had been told what wasn't the truth, or he would not have married them; and they had come to talk with me and see what could be done about it.

When I questioned Harriet, she took up the story, telling it in the soft, low, unemotional voice of the Thlinget Indian.

"My mother sick long time—my father work. John Dick come sit in room, every day he come, night he come too. My mother say 'John Dick want to marry you.' I tell my mother I don't want to marry John Dick. I don't want to marry anyone; I

want to go to school and learn; but all time John Dick come and
sit in chair and say nothing, and all time my mother say she want
me to marry him before she die—she say he buy me things, but I
just little girl, I don't want to marry anybody. I want to go to
school. My father he say, 'You ought marry John Dick—he make
good husband for you,' but I say, no! My mother say, 'Come here
my daughter. You been good girl to your mother—your mother
going to die—she very unhappy cause she going away and leave
you. You marry John Dick and she be happy when she die.' My
father he say, 'You make your mother sorry you don't marry John
Dick—I want you marry John Dick too.' I want to make my mother
happy and my father, so I say I marry him. One day my father
say, 'I go over to Craig on boat—you go too,' so I do. When we
got to Craig there was John Dick, and my father say, 'John Dick
going to marry you today.' I say I don't want to marry old man
like him, but he take me where there was fat man. My father say,
'My girl want to marry John Dick.' Man say, how old she is? My
father forget to ask my mother how old I am, so he say I eighteen.
That wasn't so. I fourteen, but my father didn't know or he
wouldn't say I eighteen. Man he say to me, 'Are you eighteen?'
I didn't want to say I was, but if I say 'no' then he know my father
tell lie and maybe he put him in prison. I don't want my father
go to prison, so I say, 'yes,' but it ain't so. Then man marry me
to John Dick and we come home. All time he come to house—he
stay there all time, but he don't do anything. He eat, but he don't
say anything. He just sit in chair. I only little girl—I don't know
how to be wife—I don't know how to take care of man—I want to
go to school—I don't want old man for husband."

There it was—the operation of primitive custom and the
revolt of youth.

John Nickerson is an honest, conscientious, hard-working
man—none finer in the community—a boatbuilder—and I believe, as the girl did, that he did not lie about her age intentionally.
I know from our experience with the parents of these children in
connection with the annual census taking, that few of the fathers
do know the ages of their children. But she was right about her
age. I was able to verify it by going over the school records; and
there she was—a child of fourteen, though large for her age,
compared with white girls—married to a man over 40 years old
who had been married before. It seemed distressing to us, and
especially so to Alma, because Harriet had been so earnest and

faithful in her work and so eager to study, though not a brilliant scholar.

I was confident that the marriage was illegal and advised that she should not live with John, but go and stay with someone else while I looked up the law, and they went away.

That night Harriet moved in on the nurse. They do things that way; but the nurse is big-hearted, so she mothered her and made room for her, until she suddenly slipped out of the picture again.

The Commissioner admitted he should have insisted on some evidence of the girl's age and agreed to require in the future a statement as to the age of a young girl from the Government teacher, but it would require a court decree to annul the marriage, so the odds were against any release for Harriet. Furthermore, the pressure of native custom is something tremendous, so there would be small chance of a decree altering the situation.

In the course of time the nurse learned that John had been buying the girl dresses and that they were again together; and now she says Harriet is going to have a baby. So the round of birth and death has started.

A similar marriage antedated our arrival by a few months, only the girl was younger and the husband fully as old, though more pleasing. She, however, along with her old husband has a young lover more nearly her age, and she also is soon to become a mother.

So the old is in conflict with the new; and as a conspicuous evidence of the impending revolution, a young chap, David Smith, and his still younger wife, Blanche, a Hyda girl whose family lives in the village, go up and down the street hand-in-hand or arm-in-arm, as happy and as modern as two cooing doves—modern in more ways than that, for Blanche is very comely and is as sleekly and effectively boyish-bobbed as any snappy white sister. They will unquestionably sadly disturb the parents of more than one youthful Thlinget by their example. Several times the report has reached us of the impending marriage of two or three of the larger, marriageable school girls. They have dropped out of school for an interval, only to reappear; and when young chaps of the village have come to visit school and at recess time have slipped into the same seats with the girls, in the most approved white swain manner, we have concluded that the war between the tradition of Age and the will of Youth is on.

Chapter XXI

THE NURSE'S WORK

The Thlingets are a happy and industrious people in their way, but there is much tragedy in their lives, for disease is rampant with them. Their habits of life and their customs make the spread of tuberculosis easy and inevitable. Venereal diseases have been brought to them from the outside and have been passed along by contact and inheritance until whole families are afflicted, and few in the village are free from it.

Our nurse is a fine woman with a big Irish heart which keeps her up here in her mature years, where she can bring hope and relief to these people and she is doing a wonderful work.

The nurse truly belongs to the "restless sex," and the same spirit that won't permit her to sit in idleness while people are suffering, will not allow her to sit in silence while there are people to talk to, so she is a great accumulator of information and literally, comes in a dozen times a day with some bit of information, or the "low-down" as she calls it.

This is her first experience in Klawock, but she has had considerable contact with the Alaska natives at other points and at Juneau where she was for some time head nurse at the Government native hospital, so she well knows the problems with which she has to deal among the Thlingets. She assures us there is scarcely a home where the blood has not been corrupted by venereal disease, and the vitality lowered to a point where the *white plague*, tuberculosis, finds a fertile field for activity. The death rate is high throughout the native population of Alaska and the mortality among the babies is appalling.

The Thlingets, like all primitive people, had no sense of relation between cause and effect. They were well, or they weren't well. If only moderately sick, they bluffed it out, but if seriously ill, they had no other explanation than that evil spirits had taken possession of them and the shaman, or medicine man, was supposed to be the only protection against such an affliction. He had to be paid of course and, unlike the medicine men of the whites, he exacted his pay in advance and guaranteed a cure—no cure, no pay—so he had not only to refund in the event of failure, what had been collected, but was heavily penalized by the patient's family unless he found some loophole to crawl through, and he generally did. He worked on the principal that if the person with whom the spirits had taken lodgement were made undesirable as a host, they would move out; so his first efforts were directed toward throwing a scare into them. Nearly naked, face painted hideously, hair a frightful looking mass matted with eagles' down, the doctor arrived with a rush and leaped into the midst of those grouped around the sick man, with a rattle in each hand. He shrieked and yelled—made the most horrible grimaces, indulged in inconceivable contortions, jangled his rattles, abused and reviled the patient, and generally worked himself into a state of hysteria; while the watchers, of which there was always a plenty, droned wierd chanting, beat or pounded anything that was handy —each one doing his bit to help the shaman earn his pay. If it happened that the evil spirits were dogged and persisted in holding their ground; if it happened that the spirit of the Indian was also tenacious and withstood the onslaught which would have killed an ordinary white man, the shaman launched another attack, but from a different angle. From torture of the mind he went to torture of the body. If the evil spirits could not be frightened away, the body must be made untenable in other ways, so the patient was given a pillow of devil's club. I have known what devils club is ever since I took my first jaunt into the woods of Southeastern Alaska. It is a combination of everything prickly you have ever seen—and then some. It hasn't an occasional thorn, like the rose, but is comparable to the moss rose in appearance, only oftentimes large as a man's wrist, and every little hairlike needle pierces the skin and stays there, stinging like a swarm of bees. Conceive a bundle of such stuff being used for a pillow! It would stimulate even a dead man to activity. The Indians are very ingenious in their tortures—and very successful.

The shaman would have to rest and recuperate from his hysteria, and while the patient was allowed a day or two in which to gather strength, the medicine man accumulated energy for the next assault. He proceeded to work himself into a frenzy and would pretend to fall in spasms and then swoon, and while in that state would enter into consultation with his own special spirits. When he emerged with rolling eyes and frothing mouth, from the conference, he would attribute his failure to get results to the work of a witch who had taken possession of the victim. Sometimes he would charge one of the watchers with being a witch and if well established in his practice, would offer to name the evilly disposed one for an additional fee. A witch was what we would call a "devil's agent," and only the fear of suffering could discourage him from his activity.

The natives have no idea of nursing. The sick have been allowed to care for themselves in the past so the whole subject of medication, sanitation, disease, and attention to the sick is a development only of recent years and they haven't gone very far yet.

One evening not a great while after our arrival, Alma went the rounds with the nurse. They started at the clinic where the nurse lanced a tubercular swelling on the neck of a young girl six or seven years old, while Alma held the basin for her. She was astounded when the child manifested not the slightest trace of fear nor even winced when the lance cut in. The child had come alone and made not a sound throughout the experience. The nurse says the Indians make excellent patients because of their fortitude and self-control. Whatever they may think or feel they don't reveal.

From the clinic they went to see an old man who was supposed to be dying and who is the *big chief* in his influence in the village—the "blue-eyed Thlinget." A number of natives sat in a semi-circle about him, stolidly watching the flickering flame of life—but his time hadn't come for he had rallied and the nurse found him better. "T.B." the nurse said.

Then they called on a mother with a new baby—her eighth, and a buster—about 13 pounds when born the nurse says. She has told us that large babies are very common with these people and that they grow so rapidly a year old baby is larger and farther advanced in development than white babies at the same age. And so they went the rounds. Generally they were received stolidly—nowhere with manifested interest or enthusiasm. They were willing to be helped, but their age-old superstitions and practices still possess them and they often seem to resent the results obtained by the white man's methods. Never do they manifest gratitude, and they take what is done for them as an inalienable right. I suspect however, that their attitude toward one another is the same. Gratitude is one of the finer feelings that develops with the refinement of a race—possibly not the feeling, but its manifestation.

The nurse has regular hours for consultation and treatment

at the clinic, in addition to the hours given to home relief, but with nothing else to do all day, the Indians will come around in the night and rouse us all, to get cough cyrup or ointment or other remedies they could just as well have come for earlier. Charlie Chuck, than whom there is no one with less to do, will come around and pound her up and blurt "Want Vick's!" having reference to an ointment, which because of its aromatic, woodsy odor, appeals particularly to them. As for cough syrup, there is little they like better and an eight ounce bottle will last just as long as it takes them to drink it; therefore she has quit feeding it to them. Possibly one reason for their special fondness for it is that their medicine men make such nauseating messes for them to take that they feel anything which looks less attractive lacks power behind it, and the cough syrup looks bad enough to be promising. Their old time mixtures for disgusting and vile concoctions never could be surpassed. The idea was the same as that which impelled them to try and drive out the evil spirits afflicting the invalid by fear or by physical suffering. If neither of those methods was effective, they attempted to make the body abhorrent to the spirits causing the trouble, so naturally no mild or seemingly innocuous remedy of the white man was considered in any way effective. In the days when the missionaries were beginning their medical relief work they found it necessary to add coal tar, bitter aloes, or other substances with some offensive feature, to their remedies, before the Indians would take them. The blacker and bitterer the better, otherwise it was "halo skookum"—*not strong.*

As for following directions concerning the taking of medicine, there isn't any such thing; so the nurse no longer dispenses a box of pills, a bottle of cough syrup, Vick's, physics, or any other remedy. She administers her medicines on the spot. To them it was a saving of time and trouble to take the medicine given them, all at once. Besides, if a little of a thing was good for them, more would be much better and the action quicker. It often was, but the nurse is more for moderation in all things.

One of the girls in Alma's room when she was working with the beginners, was the oldest and largest child in the room. She wasn't stupid but she had such a lack of health as to be physically and mentally incapacitated for school work, therefore she has never attended regularly nor long at a time. "T.B.," the nurse said—"a hopeless case," but she decided to try the inocculation. The results were surprising. I never have seen such a rapid and remarkable change in a child. She told the nurse afterwards that never before in her memory had she gone to sleep without crying herself to exhaustion because of the aching and pain that possessed her, but she now goes to sleep almost instantly, and is eager to go to bed because it is such a pleasure to her. We saw her the other day running and playing with the other children— a thing people say she has never done before. It thrills us to see happiness and renewed life brought to these people when the world has seemed so dark and hopeless to them.

Very much to our regret, the family has just left town to go to Wrangell where the father plans to fish for halibut through the winter, although the treatment of the child has not been completed. The nurse fears the full benefit won't be secured.

Of course this work of hers is experimental, so the extent of the relief is problematical, but anything that will even temporarily lift the cloud from the lives of suffering people is worth while.

One of the scourges of the native Alaskans in the past has been small pox, and many a native village has been wiped out by it. If I remember correctly, Bob has told me that his mother and himself were all who escaped a raid of the disease in their native village—the rest of the clan dying from it. Well the nurse has taken no chance of an epidemic in her bailiwick, for she has vaccinated the entire school population—and it worked.

There is one point of similarity between the Mayor and the nurse: both like to make the wheels go round. There, however, the similarity ends, for the nurse dearly loves to tell the people what to do and the mayor just as dearly loves not to be told. He, however, is so eager for the advancement of his people and the modernizing of their life, that he can, with adroitness, be led into almost anything that seems to tend in that direction. Periodically the nurse has had a brain-storm over the unsanitary conditions surrounding the natives and the indifference they manifest towards many things that seem important to her. If she only had the absolute authority of the Medical Corps of the Army, how she would straighten out the kinks! But one day, while in a mellow and persuasive mood, she laid before the mayor the idea of outlining a daily program for the village folk. It looked impractical to me. I would as soon have thought of trying to designate when and where the dogs should gnaw their bones, as to attempt to regulate the daily lives of the natives; but the idea of a printed schedule of "do's" and "don'ts"—a Ruth

Ashmore guide to right living hung in the homes, she believed would have a strong moral influence. What if the people cannot read and write, and what if they do think they know how to run their own affairs? Of course I had to admit I might be wrong in my views; but she came exultantly one day with the news that the mayor was so pleased at the suggestion that he had promised to have the cards printed in Ketchikan at his own expense. It was a wonderful *Daily Regulator* she prepared. The people were told when to go to bed, when to get up in the morning, when to bathe, when to do their washing, what they should feed their children, how clean they should keep their houses, that they must pick up the tin cans on the beach and dispose of no more that way, how they should dispose of their garbage, etc. It made a fine showing when printed, and I spoke for a copy for our records, though unsuccessfully.

I wish I might have known the sentiments expressed throughout the village during the *klucking* that surely followed the promulgation of the ukase. These people are humorists and are exceedingly shrewd. I am sure I would have had entertainment. The nurse has a sense of humor too. She came in one day, shortly after the arrival of the cards, chuckling over some *low-down* she had accumulated. Yes, Bob had had the cards printed at his own expense, but she found he was collecting one dollar each for them from the citizens, he is a fine collector, and getting away with it. Again I wish I might have heard and understood the conversation resulting. Anyway, tin cans are in situ, and the dead dogs also, unless the tide has seen fit to move them, and the matter is now past history.

Another thing that has disturbed her mind is the danger of mal-nutrition on the part of the children, and to meet it she worked out a plan for a free noonday lunch for the school children. It was a good idea for some of the children lived at least a five minutes walk from the schoolhouse. Children never get too much to eat, and while we knew of no cases of insufficient feeding, it was certain there were many children who had no warm dinner, and some possibly, who had no lunch at all; so a bowl of warm soup would surely be acceptable and doubtless beneficial.

She took the matter up with the Alaska Native Sisterhood and found them in a receptive frame of mind. The Thlingets are always interested in eating—for that matter, who isn't?—but their enthusiasm cooled when they found they would be expected to furnish the materials for the lunch, and the labor connected with it.

That also became past history.

The Indians are very psychic. The nurse is also and some very interesting things have happened. She told us at supper time today that during the afternoon she felt an impulse to go to her medicine shelf and look for oil of wintergreen. She had no use for it and has not used it so far this year. She pulled out the cork, touched her tongue to the pungent solution, went back and sat down to the work she was doing—just as a boy came in and asked for oil of wintergreen.

But another recent experience is more interesting still. One of the larger boys who is very evidently rather short on mental endowment, is also in a disheartening physical condition and has been going down grade so rapidly that it has given us all the heartache to see the hopeless look in his eyes as he drags himself around. The nurse undertook to give him the venereal treatment, but after the first inocculation he failed to appear again, and one day she had been thinking about him and wondered if she should go out and round him up, or whether it would be more merciful not to disturb him for his course appears to be nearly run. While she was pondering about him in walked Jimmie. She told him she had been thinking about him.

"Yes," he answered, "I feel it." And he had come.

If one were to see the boy he would understand that it would be "feeling" he would experience, rather than thought.

Eagle Horse is very psychic and he has told us that he married his French wife because the spirits told him to.

This is an interesting atmosphere in which we find ourselves and we have all kinds of food for thought.

Chapter XXII

FISH-EGG-TIME

At last "fish-egg-time" has come! Last night the gulls billowed up and down the cove like a snowstorm and the water bubbled and boiled as the herring crowded the surface and the gulls plunged down among them. Today there are no gulls and a native who saw me gazing over the water, volunteered, "fish-egg-time—herring gone to Fish-Egg-Island—gulls go too." That is the way they go to spawn—here, then not here—and not only have the gulls gone, but the crows and ravens, the fish ducks and "whiskey bottles," the soaring eagles, and everything above and below the surface of the water that preys upon the little fish.

After the turmoil of the past three months, the screaming roar that has filled the air and the ceaseless drifting back and forth over the water, the silence and emptiness of the air seems almost deathlike. For weeks each day has been ushered in by the clamor of the birds and the rushing of their wings and only the settling shades of night have quieted the uproar.

This is the time my rotund and sunny-faced friend, Tecumseh Collins, has talked about to me with drooling mouth. Tecumseh likes to eat. The fruits of the earth and the sea look good to him. Away back last November he began to talk to me about the coming of the herring and fish-egg-time. I have been told remarkable tales about the herring that crowd into the bay, so my interest, if not my appetite, has been keenly whetted from the first. It was the latter part of November when I first heard the herring were coming. Whales had been seen in Big Harbor out nearer the open sea.

"Herring come—whale come—sea lion—seal—king salmon —everything eat herring, come—big time!" I was told.

Early in December one dark afternoon I saw the school children in a flutter over something and excitedly looking at the water of the inlet below the schoolhouse, so I looked too. Suddenly I saw a long snake-like head and neck shoot up from the water, only to disappear again, followed by a glistening, rounding back that curved gracefully and faded into the water. "Those must be sea lions," I thought, "that means the herring are here." They were, for while I watched, the surface of the water broke into a rippling, splashing disturbance and flashing fish struggled to get away from terror that pursued them from beneath. I have come to recognize that splashing and boiling of the surface of the water as indicating the presence of the herring horde and that their enemies are raiding them from below.

That day there were a number of sea lions in the inlet and how gracefully they bobbed up and curved back into the water, and how long it would be before they came to the surface again, and how far away! I wish I might have had a better opportunity to observe them, but the sea lions are not popular with the natives because of their pursuit of the herring and men across the bay began to shoot at them. They quickly became wary and kept beneath the surface when in the bay. Big brutes as they are, the Indians say they are as hard to hit as a hell-diver, for they are always alert and a puff of smoke will cause them to dive before a bullet can reach them. If mortally wounded they sink in the water and are lost to the hunter, so the only chance to get them is to kill them with a shot in the head.

With the sea lions came still more gulls and various other water fowl which were unfamiliar to me; but while the herring had come, they were only the advance guard of the great host and it was not until well along in December that one morning, while again ringing the school bell, I noticed the water below us, which had been smooth as glass and reflecting like a mirror the tall trees on the ridge beyond, suddenly began to simmer and then to boil as tiny silver flashes leaped from the water. With a rushing, screaming roar the gulls swept overhead and plunged like plummets, hitting the surface with a great splash. Each rose with a rapidly disappearing fish in its beak. Small dusky lads standing nearby noticed my interest:

"Herring," they told me, "lot herrings—gulls eat herrings—natives eat herrings—good!" and they smacked their lips.

But it was only for a short time that the fish were at the surface—the onslaught from the air was as frightful to them as that from below, and they riccocheted back to the depths.

It is claimed that while the herring are running for the two or three months prior to spawning, they do not feed. That seems probable, for while they are running they move in solidly packed streams of fish that flow ceaselessly, much of the time five to ten feet below the surface, and it would seem impossible for such a horde, so closely packed, to find food enough for the multitude. It was impressive to stand on the dock and see the living current flow beneath me—every fish headed in the same direction, packed as closely as sardines in a can, and with their mossy green backs looking like a muddy current flowing through the clear water of the inlet. I felt awed by such a manifestation of the curious ways of nature.

As the winter advanced, the population of both the water and the air swelled markedly, but the natives did not wait for that. The first day of their appearance everything that could float was out on the bay and the fish that were raked aboard within the next few hours made many a stuffed Thlinget that night. Canoes and rowboats were out with some one to row or paddle, and another someone at the forward end with a dip net, or more often, with a long pole in the lower end of which wire nails had been driven so that the sharpened points projected an inch, an inch and a half, or two inches. The boat would be worked over the moving stream of fish and the brailer would plunge the pole down and with a sweeping motion, bring it up through the mass and shake off in the boat the fish impaled on the nails. It may sound like slow work, but there would be from four to a dozen fish at a sweep, so the boats filled rapidly and would come in loaded deep in the water.

Our first meal or two of fresh herring were greatly relished, but they are so rich in oil that our taste for them quickly palled. The natives however, never tire of them. They eat them fresh— they dress them and string them on long sticks to dry in the sunshine or beside smoking fires—they shovel them into tubs, or even into holes in the ground to ripen, and cook the oil out for future use. They soak themselves in the fishy atmosphere of their cabins and saturate themselves with oil and gorge with the dried fish until their very bodies exude herring savor, so that after Tecumseh Collins has paid me a visit I want to open the doors.

As the weeks passed, those steadily moving, mossy-green currents widened and deepened and increased in number until they took on the proportions of a river of life flowing up and down the inlet, but ceaselessly in motion. It fascinated me to look upon them from above and see the way the streams would eddy and flow around the piling, while every now and then there would suddenly develop a whirlpool of frenzied flashes that would boil to the surface, as a king salmon or some other raider of the deep would surge up in their midst. And always in the air above, the gulls drifted like a blinding snowstorm, back and forth, ever winging and ever screaming. When the enemies below drove the fish to the surface, the gulls from above met them there and the water would fairly seethe with their plunging drives while their screams would swell into a continuous roar. The counter attack would drive the fish down and the gulls would settle on the water like a fall of snow, only to rise en masse like a fleecy cloud, in a few moments, with a rushing sound like a coming wind storm.

Often fortune favored the herring—temporarily—but more often the gull would strike successfully and after going out of sight in the water, would flash out with its prey in its beak. The fish is always swallowed head first, possibly so it can't come back, but more likely because of the spiney back fins; and the adroitness with which the bird would manage to invert the poor fish, sometimes so long one would expect to see it stick out at both ends, and swallow it while on the wing, was a thing to marvel at; but that skill would often be foiled by their own kind. Gulls are lazy and aggressive, as well as greedy, and many a gull which had captured its game would be attacked by another so fiercely before the herring could be put away, that the fish would be dropped, only to be caught in midair and be gulped down—possibly not by the original aggressor. One day I stood on the school grounds when the bay was almost solid with herring and the water so covered with gulls it looked like a snowbank, when someone across the inlet fired a gun. With the swish and roar of a hurricane the whole white river seemed to rise into the air and I heard a "plunk, plunk, plunk!" and a splash that sounded as though someone were throwing stones into the water. A keen-eyed, observant youngster standing near volunteered, "Gulls eat too much herring." They are terrible gourmands—I know nothing their equal—and they must have a digestive apparatus like a sausage mill for I have watched a single gull swallow herring after herring, when each seemed as big as their whole insides. But they really do have a limit, and the splashing was caused by the disgorged fish which had been spasmodically ejected, either through fright, or from the exertion of flying with too much ballast.

As the living tide continued to flow into the inlet big gas boats came in and cast their seines, and it was staggering to see what they carried away. The human beings are as greedy as the gulls. A boat which I was told was from Prince Rupert and not supposed to be in American waters, loaded and overloaded till its deck was almost awash before pulling out. A little later one of the natives told me that the boat had not reached its destination and it was thought it may have foundered in a storm that developed soon after it departed, but we learned still later that it eventually reached port, but a large part of its cargo had either been washed overboard or jettisoned.

Another day the "Confidence" came in from Ketchikan and from one haul of her purse seine loaded 300 barrels of herring and in three hours time after her entrance, had left the inlet after dumping the surplus haul of her seine which she could not brail out for lack of capacity, to float out on the tide, dead.

The herring is a delicate fish and quickly succumbs to the crowding and rough handling in the seines, so when they are dumped the mass will float, white bellies up, on the surface of the water and then begin to sink until the bottom twenty or thirty feet down will gleam white with the dead fish—tons of them. I stood on the dock one day watching them settle to the bottom, when a native beside me said, "Bimeby all come up—float on top water — make smell — make bad smell — make much bad smell."

The natives say the run of fish is small compared with other years and it troubles them greatly to have the power boats from Ketchikan and elsewhere, come into their dooryard and raid the herring flood to the extent of thousands of barrels; and in their greed and recklessness, leave other thousands dead behind them because they hauled more in their nets than they could possibly carry away. Herring are the "staff of life" for them and the spawn is another source of sustenance. What affects one, affects the other.

The seined herring are taken to Ketchikan where they are frozen in the cold storage plants for bait for the halibut and salmon fishing later in the season. The Indians realize the importance of having bait, but the needless and terrible waste of the seiners, whose only consideration is that of loading as quickly as possible and returning for more, alarms them for the safety of their source of food supply, and they became much wrought up over it. The whites, knowing they were ruthless, were cowardly in their greed and complained to the United States Marshal that they were threatened with violence by the Indians, and asked for protection. The marshal came over to see for himself, which gratified the Indians, because it gave him a chance to see what was going on. He came to me and I told him the situation, which fitted in with his own judgment. I advised the men to present their complaint both to the United States Bureau of Fisheries, and to the Territorial Legislature, then in session, through their capable representative William Paul, an educated Thlinget; and prepared letters for them which were signed by the village officials. To further clinch the matter, I took photographs of the Pirate and the Radio, two large gas boats from Ketchikan which were working close to the Commercial Company dock. The evidence was conclusive. It was too late to stay the waste for this season, but Klawock inlet, inside the red light at the mouth of the bay, has been barred to seines in the future.

The raid of the Pirate and Radio, working together, surpassed any other of the season. The Pirate drew the seine so full that the water was boiling with fish even before the seine was closed, and when the Radio drew in on the other side of the pond, as the closed purse-seine is called, to brail out the herring, the net was opened to let out a portion of the excess of the haul and the dead fish poured forth in such numbers between the bows of the two boats, that the water was solid with their white bellies. I was in a row boat with my camera and a solid white current flowed by me on either side like drifting snow and ice, until the dead fish began to settle to the bottom, which they did almost immediately.

The seiners felt uneasy under the surveillance, for other boats were making observations for future use, so their boats were allowed to drift down the bay with the tide, with the seine between them. I had snapped my pictures at 11:40, when they began to brail, and by twelve o'clock the boats were loaded to the limit of their capacity, had dumped their nets and were drifting out of the inlet, leaving the water white with the wasted fish and the air filled with a myriad screaming gulls who saw themselves utterly unable to take advantage of the feast spread before them.

As the herring flood swelled during the weeks of December and January, the sea lions increased in numbers. The shooting kept them wary of the inlet in daylight, but when darkness fell they came in where the fish were many and the chances for escape poor; and often before going to bed, regardless of the time of night, I have stepped outside the door or even gone down to the dock to listen to the pounding of the water and the splashing of the great brutes as they played and fed. One night as I stood listening to the boistrous splashing, the air was rent with a bellowing roar that was new to my ears. I was thunderstruck for it sounded like the roaring of lions; suddenly I understood why the sea lion was given its name. The resemblance was striking. The main disturbance seemed to be on the other, or channel side, of the long wooded peninsula which separates the inlet from the outside channel, and must have come from a large number of the creatures. The noise they made with their floundering made me wish I could watch them at their sport.

One Sunday, near "fish-egg-time," Joe Demmert went to Craig and told me afterwards that his boat had passed a small rocky island that showed above the water at low tide and there were at least a hundred of the big fellows basking in the sun on the rocks.

The people here insist the sea lions like music and they furnish evidence, which in their judgment, proves it. Bill Gardner told me the story first, but I have heard various versions of it since then. Several years ago the band was practicing in what is now the Salvation Army Hall which stands on piles alongside the plank street; and many sea lions were disporting in the moonlight in the bay. After the band had been practicing for some time they stopped to catch their breaths and heard a great thumping outside on the walk. Someone stepped outside to investigate. He jumped back, slammed the door behind him and stood there trembling. Others cautiously investigated the occasion for his fright and saw a mammoth uncouth form floundering around in the street. They were terrified almost to the point of panic, when someone discovered their visitors were sea lions. That relieved the tension somewhat, but the musicians were perfectly willing to remain inside and as there was nothing else for them to do, they went on with their band practice; and Bill maintains that the sea lions lined up outside and were most attentive and appreciative listeners. It sounds a little like a reversal of the Greek myth of the sirens. Anyway, it would seem that once drawn from their element, the animals made the most of the experience and made a thorough inspection of the village. One climbed up and sat down on Bill Gunyah's porch with its back to the door, like a big watch dog. Another investigated Bob's chicken house, while others ambled up and down the street to the surprise and terror of late pedestrians. Whether Bill was accurate in all details, I cannot say. The varying evidence depends upon the point of view. As for Bill, he said he was wending his way home to roll up in his blanket, when he felt the walk shake on its piling under his feet and suddenly what looked like a mountain loomed up right in front of him and, unlike a mountain, it had a head. He said there didn't appear to be room for them both in the street so he hastily turned back—he is instinctively polite—so his observations were not very detailed. However, regardless of inconsequential details, the fact remains (that is well attested) that the sea lions did come up out of their briny deep, whether to listen to the music of humans, or otherwise, and flopped up and down the city streets of Klawock. It is probably safe to believe also, that some of the superstitious natives were scared almost into spasms and Bill says he stayed sober for two weeks.

Other followers of the herring horde are the hair seals. The fur seals do not frequent these waters, but the hair seal does and is hunted by the natives for its flesh and blubber, which furnishes oil they prize for use with their food; and the hides, from which they make moccasins tanned with the hair on—bags and various other useful articles. The skins are interesting and some are very attractive, for there is a great variation in their color, some being very light with dark spots, and some very dark with light spots. They are apt however, to smell very fishy.

In earlier days the natives held various superstitious beliefs in connection with the seal and it was common for a hunter before starting on a hunt, to take a piece of bone from a seal's shoulder blade and talk to it: "Will you tell me what I am going to kill?" he would ask. Then he would spit on it and throw it in the air. If it fell in a certain position he knew he would kill something; if it didn't, then there was no need of his going for he would get nothing.

Because sea lions are so much larger than the seals, the Indians name for them means "biggest animal sitting on the edge on an island."

The natives maintain that the herring are diminishing in numbers rapidly and that is why they become alarmed when the boats come into the inlet to seine for bait. It is like having passersby come in and shake the apples off the tree in your dooryard.

Whether the stories which have been told me often since we have been here, of the herring massing in the inlet in such untold numbers that a boat could hardly be rowed through them, and that when the tide went out it would leave the fish piled several feet deep on the beach, are literally true or not, I cannot say, although their tales do not seem so impossible to me as they did when I first heard them; but it is certain that the run is very much less this season than usual and the Klawock inlet seems to be the only place in Southeastern Alaska this year where herring can be found at all, which explains in a measure, the raiding that has taken place. The scarcity alarms the salmon canners, for the absence of herring, the main diet of the salmon, means the absence of salmon.

I have been told that two or three years ago a ship came in and converted herring into fertilizer and oil; that seems to have been headed off here, at least. In those seasons when dead herring have been left heaped on the beach by the tide (we have a twelve foot tide here), the natives have covered their gardens with them for fertilizer. I doubt if anyone but the natives could have stood the stench that must have followed. I have been satisfied amply with the smell of the herring that have risen to the top a few days after the bait seiners' raids. At such times the village would hardly impress a chance visitor as a health resort.

The ceaseless activity of the great schools is interesting and fascinating to watch, and as they flow along in what seems to be a blind and utterly aimless way, one does not think of the moving mass as having any more intelligence than a similar stream of water; but Bob has a "pond," an area inclosed between the two docks with the wire chicken fencing used in making the salmon traps, and his men have several times cast their seines and shunted the haul through a gap into the pond, to hold as live bait for the halibut fishing. For possibly two or three days the dark mass would mill around and around in the trap and then would come up missing. Blindly and aimlessly as they swam, they still were quick to find a chance hole or opening and they would leak through it into the open, where they could drift as instinct willed.

"Fish-egg-time" has come — that for which the natives — grown-ups and children—have talked for weeks with watering mouths. The spawn must be a great delicacy—at least to them. The town is well nigh depopulated and I have been adroitly informed that last year school was closed and even the teachers went to Fish-egg Island near Craig, which is the spawning ground for this locality. There might be temptation to do the same this year were the weather not so bad. The school attendance is so depleted that so far as work is concerned, all might as well have gone.

The town is draped in fish eggs. I have eaten them, uncooked, for the natives eat them that way, like candy, but in my judgment "they aint much." They are translucent, about the size of pearl barley, and have no taste except a slight saltiness, yet they are a choice tidbit to the Indians.

Fish Egg Island has sandy, sheltered beaches where the spawning fish swarm, depositing their eggs in the water in immeasurable quantities, which cling to seaweed, gravel and everything with which they come in contact. At spawning time the Indians move to the island from all the country about. Some have permanent camps and others live in tents or improvised shelter, but each group always has its own section to work in, which is a private preserve.

The natives make use of various kinds of seaweed for food and these, with their burden of spawn, are gathered and dried together; but to facilitate the harvest, they cut hemlock boughs and immerse them in the water, anchoring their stems in the sand, and they accumulate spawn in astonishing masses. When loaded the boughs are removed from the water and the eggs are dried in the sun, if there is sunshine, or by fires or under shelter.

The village is literally hung in fish eggs. The big branches are split up into smaller ones, and on the porches of some of the houses clothes lines have been strung and the branches hang from them, swinging in the wind. In other cases spawn-laden kelp is suspended from lines in the dooryards. At another place a different variety of seaweed, laden with eggs, fills all available space; while the fish-net fence at another, is hung with hemlock boughs. They tell me that the spawning ground is no place for sensitive noses, but here, unless the eggs dry so slowly that they spoil, there is nothing unpleasant about the harvest. After the eggs are thoroughly dried they are scraped from the hemlock boughs, first being dipped into warm water to soften them, and then are compacted into cakes and are packed in containers for preservation. Those deposited on seaweed are treated the same way, except that they are dried and packed together and later, covered with herring or seal oil, they are cooked and are greatly relished.

Aside from its being the culmination of their anticipations and the occasion for their laying up stores for future use, *fish-egg-*

time is welcomed by all the natives as indication of the passing of winter and of the approach of spring. There is further confirmation of the coming change in the flocks of migrating robins which have been feeding on the school grounds for several days. It takes more than one flock of robins to make a spring, however.

A few days ago we had a fierce *southeaster*—the king of them all. Judd, a white man who works for Bob during the fishing season and who lives on his gasboat the year round, told me afterwards that the barometer on his boat dropped to 28.5, which in the east would indicate a cyclone. It was the lowest he had ever seen the barometer go. At 6 AM he said the wind was so fierce he got up and got out another headline to the float where he was tied up, for he knew something unusual was coming and he feared he might be torn loose and swept into trouble.

The wind and driving rain were so terrific I could hardly keep my feet to ring the school bell, and I couldn't face the storm —had to hump up my back to it like an old horse in a blizzard and cling to my slicker to keep it from being stripped off my back. The storm abated somewhat in the afternoon, but rain, hail and snow alternated much of the day. About the middle of the afternoon, during a lull, I witnessed the most remarkable snowstorm I have ever seen. The flakes kept getting bigger until they were floating down the size of the palm of my hand—so large that as they fell the resistance of the air curved the edges upward until they were deeply saucer-shaped, and when they fell on the board walk they left wet spots as much as five inches in diameter. I went down to the dock to try and get a picture of the unusual sight, and a native who saw me confided that something was going to happen. "No see it like that before," he explained. Superstition is always at work with them.

Later it started to snow again and kept coming with marked enthusiasm. The longer it snowed the more in earnest it got. There would be intermissions and relapses, but the next morning we found everything plastered with about eight inches on the level —dry on top and soggy beneath. The wire clothes lines was a white cable an inch in diameter, while every branch and twig was vastly enlarged by a white casing. The spruce and hemlocks were dressed in white—trunks and branches—and the limbs hung drooping towards the ground in graceful lines under their burden. When the sun rose its light first struck the snowy mountain tops north of us and colored them a beautiful rose coral, and as the sunlight settled down the mountainside the color faded into a pink which lasted until all our white landscape was tinted with it for a short time; but the water of the inlet was cold and black, and the black line of the beaches fringed the white banks as the tide went out. White gulls floated over black water, like big snowflakes, and long-drawn-out flocks of scoters streamed up and down the inlet against the white background of the snow-laden hemlocks on the other side, for the herring were still in the bay. Patches of blue sky, snow-white billowy clouds reflecting the sunshine, and black masses of storm clouds made the sky as interesting as the earth, but the snow passed quickly and was followed by rain.

Yesterday was typical of the weather which has prevailed of late—sunshine, rain, snow, hail, sunshine again and the same thing over and over again; blue sky with fleecy, billowy, beautifully white clouds floating about. Suddenly through Canoe Pass at the south end of the wooded peninsula which makes an island of it at high tide, would come a smudge and another of mist or snow, or a downpour of rain that hid everything behind it, flurried or beat about us, and moved on to hide the landscape on the other side of us—raw and biting one moment, then warm and balmy —but when the water wasn't pouring from the roofs in the form of rain, it drizzled from them as melted snow. From a landscape of bare ground, green trees and black water, everything in a few moments became snowy white, except for the black water— always the black water. That is "fish-egg-weather" the Indians tell me. It is what they always expect and get at fish-egg-time.

This morning the world is wonderful in another way. The temperature is not much higher, but there is a quality to the light and atmosphere that makes everyone and everything happy. *Fish-egg-weather* is storm and sunshine, but today there is a quickening which the Alaskan world feels; yet I imagine it will be weeks before we see real spring weather. The sea is a mighty body of water and changes temperature slowly.

Before the advent of the white man the natives had no calendar, but checked off the passing time by association with certain events. *Fish-egg-time* with them was the culmination of winter and the inauguration of something else.

Chapter XXIII

DOGS

"The dogs of an Indian village!" I understand the significance of that expression: It has a meaning for me it never had before.

It is moonlight and the "baying of the hounds at the moon" would be music compared to what is going on. The village swarms with the scrubbiest lot of scrubby mongrels—mostly a mixture of Spitz and something else which has passed through several generations of uuoluuunuss—which are noisy, yapping pests, absolutely of no use whatever, unless their prowling and fighting over the offal on the beach can be considered a use.

There is supposed to be a dog tax which contributes to the village coffers, but the mayor, who has something in semblance of a real dog, says he is the only one who pays the tax. If he pays it, he is doubtless correct, for I cannot conceive anyone paying a dollar to keep any of the swarming curs alive which are making life miserable for us.

In a way, though unwillingly, I suppose I have a measure of responsibility. There is a really beautiful dog—about the size of a small collie, with the long, black, silky hair of a cocker spaniel, and with a very intelligent head and adoring eyes. I don't know where she came from—she simply moved in on us soon after our arrival and seemed to center her admiration and affection on me. I sought to discourage her attentions by gentle rebuffs, but she forgave and persisted. More pronounced snubs were accepted with the same sweet spirit, but oh, the sorrow revealed by the worshipful eyes! I felt as I imagine a screen hero must feel in the presence of his lady fans—but maybe he doesn't feel as I felt. To me it was quite embarrassing to be the subject of so much admiration, for she dogged my steps wherever I went. But who is proof against adoration? I finally succumbed and we began to feed her. It wouldn't do to have even a dog dying on our doorstep. That settled, she began to take an interest in life—and what was worse still, all the dogs of the village began to take an interest in her and to parade up and down the school yard, strutting their stuff, except such times as they were engaged in a battle-royal, sometimes ten or a dozen deep.

It troubled us to be the center of so much attention, so I strove to learn who might be her master; but *Queenie* seemed to be a dog of mystery. Different ones were reputed to be her owners, but all disclaimed the honor; yet there seemed to be something in the background which I could not fathom. Skan Johnson seemed to be the one most involved and on my earnest representation that I did not wish to be a party to the alienation of even a dog's affections, he came and led her away at the end of a piece of rope. At the same time the mayor, whose sleep was also disturbed, delegated one of the six village marshals as dog executioner and the crack of a rifle was heard at intervals one morning and six canine carcasses floated out on the next ebb tide. That was six barkers less, but they were never missed.

Queenie stayed away as long as a rope might be expected to hold a dog with something on her mind, and she and the moon continued to inspire a nightly chorus and a daily stiff-legged parade of the canine beaus. It was treachery of the basest sort I'll admit, but I not only disclaimed any interest in her existence to the mayor, but dropped the suggestion that we would take no offense if she went out some morning with the tide; but the mystery behind her prevailed and she survived, and as there is an end to all things, there came a time when the haunted, worried look left her hazel eyes and Queenie wearily slept away the hours upon the door mat. Once more she became the faithful, worshipful follower and her coat became glossy and beautiful.

But the barking dogs of the Indian village continued their eternal yapping. I don't know whether they barked at the sea lions in the bay, at possible creeping foxes or stealthy deer in the wooded jungles of the hillsides, or barked to see which could out-bark the others: the results were the same—sleepless nights for us humans, and once more I complained to Mayor Bob.

When Bob returned in December from his annual business trip to Seattle, he was full of the ways of civilization which he planned to inaugurate and he gave me quite a talk on the undesirability of a promiscuous canine population. It was his idea to eliminate all of the barking, snarling, scavenging pests on which no one was willing to pay the license fee; but in Seattle things seemed wholly desirable and entirely feasible, which somehow did not seem so possible when he got home; so the barking of the dogs continued. I understood. Each yapping cur was somebody's dog, and in the primitive days dogs were cherished property; and besides, Bob was in politics, which makes a difference to an Indian as well as to a white man. So the raid in the fall had

eliminated only strays; but the limit of endurance was reached
a while ago and once more the popping of a rifle was followed
by a dog-laden ebb tide, and this time, it was after the municipal
election and Bob had been re-elected, the marshal was less dis-
criminating in what he shot at and the results were more satisfactory. But again Queenie did not take the ocean trip. The mystery seemed to persist and an unknown something protected her.
All right. But it puzzled me—were they avoiding the possibility
of displeasing me, or was there some element in the situation that
made a difference?

One morning I noticed some of the bright-eyed little "bugs"
from the primary room, deep in a thicket of brambles and salmon-
berry bushes in a corner of the schoolyard near us and much
interested in a big fire-hollowed stump. I stopped to investigate
and saw a pair of brown legs projecting from a hole which extended down into the cavity left by a big decayed root. The legs
wriggled out and a boy followed, dragging a little brown puppy.
A repetition of the squirm and crawl resulted in a litter of pups
of assorted styles and colors. The pups weren't much, but the
reversion to the habits of the wild on the part of the mongrel
bitch was interesting to me.

In the course of time Queenie waxed fat and sleek and then
she disappeared. I was not disturbed by it for her continued presence at my heels was more of an embarrassment than a pleasure.
I hadn't the slightest use for a dog. I didn't need a pet, and a good
deal of the time we really had nothing to feed her that properly
belonged in a dog's dietary. Canned wieners were acceptable to
her, but not an economical diet, while if she was left to forage
for herself, her presence afterwards, even at a distance, was not
always harmonious after a night spent with carrion. But one
morning Queenie showed up with a broad smile on her face, and
with much wagging of tail and squirming of body, made us know
how glad she was to be with us again. We could not help being
appreciative ourselves and half a loaf of stale bread was drenched
with condensed milk and placed before her. She attacked it as
though she had a rabbit to chase when she got through, and
faded as suddenly as the bread had done. I diagnosed her case,
for her nose was brown from rotten wood for several days before
she disappeared, and started a hunt. She was too big for the root
cavity of the stump in the schoolyard. She wasn't under the house.
I found a place where she had started to dig a burrow like a coyote,
in the mass of decayed wood and vegetation of a bank close to

the house, but she wasn't there. Finally, in a bramble jungle behind the teacherage, in a hole dug in the rotten wood of a big hollow stump, I found the litter of pups. She was a terribly proud dog, but she needn't have been for they were just as mongrel a lot as the school children had found—black, brown, black and brown, and "what have you."

It seemed unaccountable that a dog, which already had a home and a perfectly good master when we joined the village, should uninvited and discouraged by us, persist in attaching herself to us, even though we did not feed her, and virtually force us by her love and devotion, to accept her as one of the family.

Well, I have learned the secret, a matter of dog and Indian psychology: I had made the acquaintance of a man named Bill Peterson—antecedents unknown—not a native of the village— whose complexion proclaims him a Thlinget, but who seems to have more of the white man's slant on life than is common with them, so he doubtless has white blood in his veins. Bill saw the dog following me today:

"I wondered what had become of her," he remarked to me.

"Do you know her?" I asked.

"Yes, she is a good dog," he said. "She belonged to the foreman of a lumber camp on one of the islands, but he abandoned her when he went out. The cook took pity on her and fed her, but when the camp pulled out she was left behind. One day I was passing in my gas boat and saw her on the beach, so I took pity on her myself and went ashore and got her. She lived on the boat with me for some time and seemed perfectly contented, but last fall when I was over here, she went ashore and took up with Skan Johnson—left me cold—but Skan told me later that she left him too, and though he tied her up and tried to keep her at his place, she always got loose."

That was the explanation. Queenie was a white man's dog and wanted to continue so .We feel a new sympathy for her. She will be lonesome again when we go.

Chapter XXIV

PETER LAWRENCE AND
GEORGE SAUNDERS

Peter Lawrence, the "nephew of a chief," came to see us today and we enjoyed the visit. He was in good spirits. He had recently, on invitation, attended a fish bake or whatever the Indian equivalent of that would be, at Hydaburg. He is in much demand because of his boundless store of Indian lore, songs and dances, and he was the guest of honor—at least that was the impression left with me.

Besides being an historian, a raconteur, and the nephew of a chief, Peter is a good deal of a humorist. He is the Chauncey DePew of Thlinget after dinner speakers, and takes the same pleasure in talking that DePew did.

Peter was called upon to speak at the picnic and the story he told them, with its moral, as accurately as I could get it, was this:

"A man was created named Crow.

"Crow had no fish hook, so he catch no fish. He hunt round and round and find piece of stone—stone blue—he tie rag around stone, put feather on top so it look like man.

"Crow made ridges of sand in shallow water like fish trap; then he tease salmon to make him mad—call him 'black mouth, long tooth, big head, big bone,' not nice names—like that. He say 'come here see this man.' Salmon make dash for man—get in trap.

"When Crow see king salmon in trap he make excuse—go into wood and get club—hit king salmon with club—kill him. Crow send all his men to find something to cook king salmon in so to keep sand off. Men go look—bring back big skunk cabbage leaves. Crow say, 'No good! My wife's body burned where those leaves grow—go over the mountain and get leaves.'

"When men all gone away, Crow roll king salmon in skunk cabbage leaves, put him in ground and make fire on top—roast him and eat all fish himself.

"When men come back they ask, 'Where king salmon?'

"Crow say, 'King salmon gone away. See that stump? That stump fall on top him—go away, don't bother me.'

"Blue jay one of Crow's men—he very sorry king salmon all gone—he sit by fire—burn his breast.

"Crow call brown squirrel, 'You go away, go far off—go up in tree and never come down!' Brown squirrel scared—he run up in tree lot excited.

"Chick-a-dee, nother one Crow's men—he feel very bad— he cry and cry, rub his eyes with his hands like small boy, make black streak over each eye.

"Wren, he sassy and scold at Crow—Crow say, 'Get out of my sight—don't like to see you—go under stumps and bushes.' Wren go, but jerk his tail in air—show he don't care.

"To woodpecker Crow say—'Don't like way you look—go way off and don't come back. Pound on tree so I know where you are.'

"He tell swallow he little bird—go way up in sky and stay. Swallow go, but when he fly he keep pretending he going to come back, then change his mind round and don't.

"Crow tell everyone his men go way. He lie to them cause he eat all king salmon himself, so he don't like to have them look at him—make his back ache.

"You, my brothers, not like Crow—you don't catch king salmon and roast him in skunk cabbage leaves. You don't eat him all yourself and lie to your friends—You catch king salmon and cook him and then say to your brother, 'Come eat king salmon, and Peter Lawrence come too.'

"I come and see you and eat with you, and I not sad like Blue Jay, and brown squirrel—I don't burn my breast like robin; I don't cry and make dirty face like chick-a-dee. I don't have to crawl under bushes and I don't pound on wood so you know I way off. I come up close and talk to you—I happy to be here and eat king salmon with my brothers. Goona cheesh, ach ho nay! (Thank you, my friends.)"

He is a born story-teller and thoroughly enjoys the part.

It is interesting to see how much these people enjoy talking, and they enjoy listening just as much. With us, the two things rarely go together.

George is a close second to Peter as an interesting character and he is a humorist too, but they all do enjoy fun and a joke on someone else is a delight to everyone that knows about it.

George also came to see us soon after our arrival. He is a handsome boy of 76 summers—erect, vigorous, keen of eye and bright of smile; every tooth is in his head, sound and beautiful;

and every hair appears to be on his head—I can see no room for more—black and glossy. It seems inconceivable that he should be the age he gave us, but people tell us that it is so. I regret that there was so much of what he talked to us that day which we could not understand. His English was of a different brand than ours, but we did understand that he is a devout believer in the "Good Ke-an-kow," the white man's God, and is a seer of visions— a dreamer of dreams—which he considers are inspirations.

It is evident that the villagers hold him somewhat in the same awe as they did their medicine men of the olden times, and Charlie Chuck asserts with all confidence, that George understands the talk of the ravens; while his weather prognostications are given much weight. In that connection however, I know of one time when he fell down. Some friends of ours, the C. W. Kelloggs, wanderers on the water, who come occasionally to Klawock for the fine trout fishing up the creek and in the lake, invited us one day to take a trip with them in their gas boat, the Gypsy III. On our return we approached the burial island in front of Canoe Pass and because it was later than we had planned, Charlie questioned whether it would be possible to get through the pass with the Gypsy. I had been through it at high tide on Joe Demmert's boat: true, the hull had scraped, but we made it—and I thought it was a larger boat than the Gypsy, so with encouragement from me, Kellogg decided to try it and I undertook to direct him how to get around the island. Right there I got beyond my depth and a sudden scraping of the Gypsy's keel showed the reverse was true of her. We had missed the winding channel through the sandbars and were grounded, with an ebbing tide. Charlie knew what we were up against and I speedily found out, for in less time than it takes to tell it, the boat began to list and our efforts to get supports under her lee rail to keep her from lying down on her side, hardly kept pace with the falling water. It was astounding how rapidly the sandy bottom rose to the surface and soon both of us leaped overboard into the shallow water and were able to work to better advantage; but by the time we had succeeded in our efforts, the ladies were able to drop down upon relatively dry ground. Instead of hastening our return home, we were high and dry on a sand bar, with the next tide due about 2 AM. My nautical ignorance was responsible, so with Kellogg's help, we dragged his skiff through the shallow water and over the dry channel of the pass and slid it into the water of Klawock Inlet and I rowed the little bobtailed whirligig, for being very short and very small, it spun around on the water like a piece of bark—down the inlet to the village, got our own boat and returned with the two of them to the pass and dragged the skiff back again to the Gypsy. We ate on the boat—a tired and chagrined party—and there was where George Saunders came into the picture. He was trolling for salmon when he saw us and came over to console us.

"No go through pass that boat," he assured us, and we knew he was right. "Boat too high, water too little." Again we agreed that he was right. He chuckled to himself—George is a great chuckler—he finds himself excellent company—and pointed to the channel. "Go wrong way," he volunteered." "Thlinget know right way—teacher he know wrong way—boat no go on land." I felt the truth of his remarks, but my chagrin was turned to concern when he looked about him—at the sky—at the setting sun and the mountain tops, and added,

"Bad weather maybe—morning wind blow—big waves—lot rough."

I asked him how he knew.

"Thlinget know by mountains," and he pointed to a mountain on an island in the glowing west, where fleecy clouds, like a lady's veil, both hid and revealed its top. I accepted his prophecy at face value and though Kellogg vetoed the idea, I resolved to be with him at high tide. Who could know? Those props might fail to meet their responsibility and let the Gypsy down on her side, to fill with water before there was enough to float her. I rowed Alma back to the village through the golden water, leaving them companionably smoking in the twilight on the deck of the boat.

True to the promise I had made myself, I was rowing up the inlet in the starlight on the rising tide, some hours later when I heard the "put-put" of a gas boat coming around the red light, and the shadowy Gypsy chugged by me to an anchorage. The tide had outstripped my reckoning and had safely floated the boat. But our Indian for once had missed his guess about the weather. There was no wind, no rough sea, nothing but a starlit sky.

But George had his inning and put one over on me and I am still wondering about it. I wonder whether it was a carefully worked out practical joke to which a number were party; whether I was the accidental fish caught when the bait was floating upon the water; or whether Indian slyness skilfully side-tracked a white man's curiosity about something which did not concern him.

It started one bright sunshiny morning when Johnnie Skan told me he overheard George Saunders, who is cutting wood on the ridge behind the North Pacific Packing Company's cannery across the inlet, telling Bob the night before about finding a box in a hole in a tree—very old, not made with nails, but fastened together by roots passed through holes in the corners. He thought there was something in it—"wanted honest man to come and look at it—wanted everybodys see it." I pricked up my ears, for I had heard how the medicine men would hide their charms which gave them their supposed power, in holes of trees and other out-of-the-way places when they were about to die, and it seemed possible that I might see something of ethnological interest. I had no superstition—I was perfectly willing to open the box.

I promptly went over to Bob's store and questioned him about it. Bob said, "Yes. George he say he find box when cutting down tree—very old—box different from way make box today. He say he want everyones come see it." I decided I would be one to see it so I borrowed a boat and went over, taking my camera with me . . . The experience was worth the effort anyway for when I returned I had discovered what that ridge which we have looked at so often, was really like. Hemlock, fir and cedar stand on it in a beautiful dense green growth. A fringe of fishermen's huts and the cannery buildings line the beach or stand on piles, casting effective reflections in the water as we see it from our side of the inlet. Beneath the forest trees appeared to lie the forest floor, covered with a jungle of undergrowth; but when I climbed the steep bank above the cannery that morning, I found a hog-back of granite covered with a sodden blanket of decaying wood, so spongy and loose that I could only keep from sliding back as I climbed, by clinging to the shrubs and overhanging undergrowth. Once on top of the bank, the situation was worse still. What, from the village, had looked like solid ground beneath the trees on which George and Peter worked, was no ground at all. Trees had fallen criss-crossed in years passed. The trunks had been held off the ground by the branches and the space beneath had filled up to a semi-solid mass of undergrowth, bracken, moss, decayed wood, and pine needles—all soaked with the constant rain like a sponge, so that if one stepped off into it he would plunge down as into mire. The men were only able to keep on top by means of planks laid across the mass, or by walking the trunks of the fallen trees.

George was working still higher up and I called to him and told him I wanted to take a picture of the box he had found.

"Me no want picture!" he exclaimed, with sober face.

I concluded he must have some superstitious belief concerning it, so I said, "All right. I'll leave the camera here, but I would like to see it."

Then he began to chuckle to himself.

"I make mistake—I burn it in fire," and then he told me it belonged to some old medicine man and he was afraid of it, but added, "You want take picture, you come," so I climbed over the spongy mass of roots and rotten logs. He joined me and we worked our way several rods back where he pointed out a tree he had sawed down—a perfectly sound tree but of a very peculiar growth; three trunks growing from the base of a big stump. He showed me where the tree had fallen and where the box had been, although he had cut it out and sawed the log into blocks. According to my understanding, the box must have been fifteen or twenty feet from the ground. He said it was about the size of my camera case—about a foot long, and seven inches deep and wide. He was afraid of it, he said. Long, long time ago the natives had all been afraid of it. He had been baptized—it couldn't hurt him— and he went off into an incomprehensible story, but in the end I understood that if a white man touched it, it would make him sick so he would die. A white man had handled one once and "long time afterwards—two years maybe, man couldn't eat food—got big and hard in belly, he die. Medicine man put something in box make man die. Me fraid—make big mistake—make fire, burn it—lie there week. No want people see it—last night got it out, carry it in sack, pile brush on it. This morning forget—make big mistake—make fire burn—all gone—big mistake—schoolmaster take picture—big mistake."

Was he spoofing me? He showed the embers of the fire, but I suspect he feared I would scratch around among the ashes, which I felt inclined to do, because he began picking up roots and hemlock branches to throw on the embers. So I left him and had to content myself with photographing the village across the water, and its background of beautiful snow-capped mountains.

I concluded Bob had intended to say that George *didn't want anyone* to see it, instead of that he wanted everyone to see it. I have noticed that the natives in interpreting Thlinget talk for us, often say they "have to turn things around," but I have not understood just what they meant by the statement; though in disciplining the school children I have found that they give assent when they mean "no." Maybe I shall get the reason for it some day.

But that was all I found out about the box.

Some time afterwards I asked Peter Lawrence about it— Peter was working on the wood job with George but didn't happen to be there that morning. Peter threw back his head and how he laughed and how his eyes twinkled!

"He make joke," he said. "George like make joke on boys. He tell Bob, to make joke on Bob. You go over—want make picture of George's joke—George feel funny—he don't know what to say—he tell you he burn it up—George laugh inside—he feel funny cause make joke on schoolmaster."

Peter was wrong. I was the one who felt funny. Now, however, after prolonged and earnest rumination, I don't know that "George make joke." One cannot tell about these primitives. The instinct for concealment is as ever present as with other wild life. George has been baptized, but that may not prevent him from playing safe and concealing from the white man that he still fears and holds in awe the discredited medicine man and his belongings. Our own children know that there is no such thing as goblins and ghosts, but just the same, their eyes grow big when they look into the shadows at night.

Chapter XXV

NATIVE ENTERTAINMENT

It is a brilliant moonlight night with snow on the ground. As I look through the window the dark hemlock and fir on the ridge beyond the playground loom blacker than ever in the white light; while the "whoo-who-whoo" of the big owl drifts across to me. His mate answers and they talk back and forth. I wonder what the Thlingets who hear them are thinking. They hold the owl very much in awe. Peter Lawrence told me one day: "Owl bad spirits, all same witches—lot bad—natives fraid owl—owl can't talk Melican, just Indian. Thlingets know what they say— they understand. Owl know everything, but he big coward. He fraid big Thlinget—not fraid little ones. Little boy, little woman go out by self, big owl come along say, 'whoo-who-whoo,' turn little Thlinget heart upside down. Owl talk bad to everybodys— don't know good words. He big tief too. One time Thlinget in house, big owl stand in dark tree and talk bad at Indian. Indian come out to scare owl away. Owl say somebody going dead. Thlinget no like owl say that—make Indian feel bad—owl no good."

A Thlinget legend, which, however, the older generation and possibly the younger also, consider to be a fact not a legend, is that once upon a time an old blind woman lived where Sitka now stands, with her son and his wife and a time came when there was no food. The son was a fisherman and every day he hunted and fished but without success, so he and his mother lived on the roots and berries he was able to find. Each day they grew poorer and weaker, but his young wife kept fat and sleek, though no one could understand why that was so. They grew so hungry the old woman would wake up and ask, "What have you to eat?"

"Nothing," the daughter would say, "I have nothing."

"But I smell fish and I hear oil dripping on the fire," the mother insisted.

"No, you are so hungry you think you smell fish, but there is nothing here." And the poor woman would fall asleep.

"What are you eating?" she would ask again, because her hunger would not allow her to sleep long. "You have fish. I hear you eating."

"I have no fish. I am chewing the gum of the spruce because I am hungry too," answered the daughter.

Now the young man's wife was a witch and when midnight came she would go to the rocks at the edge of the sea and wave two branches before her and young herring would leap from the water and fall at her feet. She would fill a basket with them and take them back to her home where she strung them on a stick stuck in the ground before the fire and roasted and ate them all. And every time the old blind mother would smell the fish and hear the oil sputtering in the fire. Then she would ask the daughter what she was eating, until one day the girl grew angry at her questions and grabbing a roasting fish from before the fire, she told the mother to hold out her hand and she should have some. The old woman did as she was bid and the girl tore the insides from the hot fish and dropped them in the outstretched hand and burned her badly.

When the son came home he asked his mother why she cried. She said nothing, and the wife told him she didn't know but he knew his mother wouldn't cry for nothing, so he resolved to find out the reason. He told his wife to go to the woods and get some bark lining to fasten the heads on his arrows because he was going hunting. While she was gone his mother told him what had happened. On the wife's return, he took his bow and arrows and went away in his canoe, but when he got around a point of land and out of sight he landed and hid in the bushes till night; when he went back towards the village until he could see the beach and waited. At midnight he saw his wife approach the beach, wave the branches and pick up the herring that leaped from the water. He followed her back and saw her cook and eat the fish and refuse to give his mother any. He went back to his canoe and the next day was so fortunate as to kill a hair seal which he took home and he made his wife eat so much of the fat that she fell into a deep sleep—so deep that she did not wake up at midnight; so he went to the beach and did as he had seen her do and filled his canoe with the fish that fell on the ground at his feet. Then he wakened his wife and told her to go get the fish in his canoe. She went and when she saw the canoe full of fish, she called to him to bring baskets, but he wouldn't and commanded her to fetch them. That she wouldn't do, and stubbornly sat on the beach all day. When night came and the moon rose she started up a gulch intending to follow it to the top of the mountain, but she came to a big white stone and sat down on it and turned into an owl.

"That is the reason," Peter says, "why owls fly around and hunt at night and talk when the moon shines."

Charlie Chuck says he knows the story is true about the woman because the stone is in front of the Sheldon Jackson School at Sitka: "You can see it if you go there."

Last night there was a fall of two or three inches of snow which covered the ground with a blanket of whiteness. Later the shining moon flooded the earth with chilly white light, while stars winked and flashed their colors in the sky. It was one of those winter nights that are described as *radiant*. I had worked late at the everlasting Government reports and Alma had lent moral support by keeping me company; while the nurse held a soiree upstairs with the three young men, Aaron Isaacs, Charlie Chuck and Willie Brown. All their conversation, the sound of which carried through this thin shell of a building, had been interspersed with the singing of the boys to Willie's guitar. The boys all have good voices—Charlie's is an uncommonly rich baritone—and while their repertoir was very limited, they made real music and furnished us a rather pleasing background while we worked.

I imagine that the nurse reached a point where she was ready to rest from her fancy work, for the boys clumped down the stairs sometime after midnight and out into the moonlit night, and we supposed they were headed for their blankets; but not so! We heard the strumming of the guitar and the boys' voices lifted up to the tune of "A red-hot mama" and the drinking song, "Show me the way to go home," repeated over and over again. Finally we looked out and saw them on the playground, dancing in the snow and silvery moonlight, and it was one of the most interesting and unusual sights I have seen as they posed and postured, with waving arms and swaying bodies—pranced and danced and wove figures in the snow, keeping time with their singing and the strumming of the guitar. It was sharp outside— keenly cold for Klawock, but they continued their dancing for nearly an hour, just for the enjoyment of it—because so far as they knew, they had no audience. It brought home to us how destitute the people are for somewhere to go and something to do and we felt that while it was impossible for us to have them coming in on us, with all the night work I had to do, it was a blessing to them that the nurse should have the time and the willingness to have them around. Doubtless it filled lonesome hours for her, as well as for them.

Another night back in November made an impression on us all. It was in the days when the big town hall was still a "disappointed hope," with the few rafters rearing into the air like the bones of a skeleton, and the uncovered floor joists bearing their piles of lumber.

Along about nine o'clock one wet night, while I was working at the kitchen table as usual, with Alma on the other side, we heard voices singing, which struck us as unusual, as it is almost as quiet here after dark as in the forest. The singing continued until curiosity prompted me to investigate, and I found it came from the big rain-soaked hall. I slipped over in the wet and peeked through the yawning doorway, and back in a far corner, sitting on a pile of lumber, with no light but that of an electric torch, sat half a dozen young fellows, including the three dancers of last night, entertaining themselves in the cold and dampness, but with shelter from the wind. They had attended the Christian Endeavor meeting at the church and when that came to an end, still wakeful and tuneful, with no place to go, they had sought out that poor shelter, and there they sang for two hours. It touched our hearts: that need of youth for some use of their time—for some place to go—for something to do, and the expression of that need in song.

We talked the matter over, the nurse, Alma and I, at the supper table the following night, and the nurse volunteered to act as chaperon if I could arrange to heat an unused room adjacent to her clinic so the boys could use it for a club room. We thought that if they had some comfortable place where they could gather, they would enjoy reading such papers and magazines as we could round up between us—could sing, play games and pass the time under shelter. We tried it, but the young fellows had no more interest in work than their slave-holding ancestors. No one cared to do the chores connected with such an enterprise—to build the fire, get the wood in, empty ashes, sweep, or otherwise assume any responsibility for their entertainment.

In the same way the nurse's attempt to organize a sewing club among the young matrons, through which she hoped to indirectly inform them concerning maternity, the proper care of babies, and many other things useful for them to know, tapered off into nothingness. She had a creditable attendance the first night—fewer the second, and none the third. No explanation was offered for the lack of interest. There may have been some sub-surface influence—possibly the opposition of the native midwives—headed her off; but it takes patience and perseverance to put a thing over, and a close study of the psychology of those to be helped. Novelty always interests. Repetition isn't novelty, and when novelty wears off it is very difficult to hold the interest of primitives and children—and some others.

The nurse belongs to the "restless sex" and likes to have something doing, and she gets a special "kick" out of making the wheels go round, so she conceived the idea, when things seemed to be in a condition of stagnation, of holding a birthday party. Whose birthday party? That was a minor detail. She was expecting to have a birthday in the near future herself, if anyone was going to be fussy about it, but the idea was to stir things up socially. Winter is always the social season in New York and Seattle, so why not in Klawock? Calmer consideration however, suggested that as a birthday is apt to be associated with some definite age, it seemed better to avoid personalities and call it a community affair. But as it was engineered by the nurse, it most naturally was called "the nurse's birthday party." Of course one thing leads to another, so the nurse, exercising her woman's prerogative, changed her mind once again and the ultimate consequence was to be a carnival held in the town hall and the proceeds were to be utilized in paying off the debt which Bob had incurred for the new planking for the village street, and for the lumber that made it possible to complete the hall. Bob was still holding the sack, so when the proposal took on that aspect, he became deeply interested and quite enthusiastic.

The nurse enlisted the services of Eagle Horse as producer, and some of the young blades of the village as participants, so the carnival was a great success. Incidentally, over $300 were taken in for the evening—some returns from an Indian village of 400 souls.

Peter Lawrence, as *nephew to a chief*, is very high caste, he also is probably the best informed on Thlinget history, legend, and lore of anyone in Alaska—and 76 year old George Saunders is a close second. Peter had been very busy for several days in preparation for his share of the entertaining, and had paid me several visits in the effort to find just the particular shade of red that he needed for his make-up. Neither the red ink I had, nor the mercurachrome from the clinic, quite satisfied him, for it seems that the ceremonial red had to be just so red and no redder; but eventually he had to be content with the mercurachrome. When I saw him at the carnival I understood why he had been so busy, for his was a fearful and wonderful make-up. In the old days when the native dancing played a large part in the lighter side of their lives, regular regalia were among the most valued possessions of the chief and other "big men." Each tribe had its ceremonial hat—a high, conical affair, often woven from the fibrous lining of cedar bark, or from spruce rootlets, or was made of wood—which bore the crest of the clan. It was a certain identification of the wearer with his clan, as in the case of the *raven hat*, the *whale hat, king salmon hat,* etc. and if anyone not a member of the clan were to wear it, trouble immediately followed.

Tribal masks also were worn at dances and feasts, but were not so important a feature as the hat. In addition, each clan had its ceremonial blanket on which the totem of his clan was painted, or as in the case of some we have seen, outlined by pearl buttons sewed on to make the pattern. There was also characteristic painting of the face.

In addition to the identifying features of the costume, each dancer sought to make himself appear as fantastic and terrible as possible; and would tog himself out in furs, feathers, seals' whiskers and anything else that would make him appear awesome. Further, they painted their faces in black, red, yellow, etc. in diagonal, horizontal or vertical stripes and carried drums made of deerskin stretched over a hoop; or rattles, whistles or anything with which they could make a noise. Oftentimes they attempted to represent some creature by their costume and acting, as when one would paint one half his face white and the other black, to represent a halibut; while another would represent a grampus, or killer-whale, by swathing himself in his blanket, with a cedar stick protruding from his back to represent the big dorsal fin; and still another would act the part of a frog.

Peter had explained to me that their dancing told stories concerning their totems, or enacted legends, much in the nature of charades or theatricals.

Well the regalia of Peter and George was somewhere else, if any of it had survived the onslaught of the missionaries, so they had to improvise to the best of their ability.

With the two men danced a Thlinget woman from Craig, who

put all the verve and native spirit into it that characterizes some of our modern jazz-hounds; but Peter looked the wildest of the three, as behooved his rank, draped in a bearskin and blanket, with a bone skewer thrust through his nose, a fierce mustache of seal's whiskers, a band of eagles' feathers around his head, and eagles' down matted into his hair which he shook out with spasmodic jerks of his head. His face was painted, of course, and he had a feather duster fastened to his nether region, like a turkey's tail.

The carnival stirred dormant memories in the breasts of the natives, and three nights later the old-timers put on a real Indian dance in the town hall. One might think their dancing was merely an aimless hopping around, but it is far from that. Every odd and eccentric motion has a meaning all its own. The dancers may be imitating the characteristics of some totemic animal such as the bear, whale, raven, etc.; or it may be a story of prowess, a legend, or an incident which they are portraying; or in earlier days, dances were of war, peace, for the dead, or the marrying. In the good old days the dancing was done in the communal houses by the light of cans of burning fish or seal oil, and everything considered, one can imagine a little something of the atmospheric condition that would develop. That night, however, we actually had electric lights, for Bob had had wires run into the hall and donated the illumination. Probably under the old setting of dim light, foul air, and hideous figures, the experience would have been much more weird.

At one end of the big hall, Peter, duly caparisoned, leaped through the doorway chanting weirdly to the pounding of a young chap on the Salvation Army drum and opened the ball. Others sifted in, one or two at a time, men, women, and girls, until there were twenty or more dancing, surrounded by spectators who crowded so closely as to leave scant room for the dancers to perform.

Peter wailed and roared, twisted and postured, gestured and acted out his narrative in a spectacular way, and all to the rhythmic beat of the drum and his own droning chant. Every part of his body was spasmodically tense and seemed to play its own game independently of the rest. He would crouch and creep, straighten, twist and turn, dramatizing his story, I suppose or imitating some animal. As for the others—the ballet, or chorus, as it were, they surrounded him and chanted unceasingly their

The casket, about to be taken to the boat, is covered with a ceremonial blanket. The wreaths are of artificial flowers. The mourners would have liked to hold up the American flag behind the coffin, but it would have hidden the people.

Four boats lashed together and about ready to start for the burial island for the Jackson potlatch at the erection of the grave stone over Mr. Jackson's grave.

Burial island outside of Canoe Pass, with its "dead houses." At the right may be seen the gravestones of Chief Tom Takite and Jennie Bell.

A grave covered with a tent and a ceremonial blanket hanging by it with the pearl buttons outlining the pattern of the whale killers, shelling off because of the rotting thread.

A new grave with the enclosing concrete still in the form, and with food and cooking utensils—a graniteware teakettle containing water and an aluminum kettle containing food and fruit and a bottle of pop.

Thlinget grave houses at Sitka.
Photo B. C. Towne—Oregon Historical Society

Grave stone of Chief Tom Takite on the burial island outside Canoe Pass. It is of white marble and is weathered and heavily pitted by the salt air.

Grave stone of Jennie Bell.

Indian grave houses at Ketchikan.
Photo F. H. Nowell—Bancroft Library

Mortuary totem poles at Ketchikan.
(Note: The photos of the oldsters from here on through page 196 are through the courtesy of "INDIAN PRIMITIVE" by Ralph W. Andrews, Superior Publishing Company.)

Indian graveyard, Hawkan.
Photo F. H. Nowell—Bancroft Library

Mortuary totems at Sitka.
Courtesy Provincial Archives, Victoria, B. C.

Indian doctor, healing? Dyea, Alaska.
Courtesy California State Library

Shaman healing sick woman.

Thlingets in Potlatch dancing costumes, Sitka.
Case & Draper Photo—Bancroft Library

Ravens in Potlatch dancing costume.
Case & Draper Photo—Bancroft Library

Thlinget dancers.
Case & Draper Photo—Bancroft Library

Skak-ish-stin—108 years old.
Bancroft Library

Chief Cow-dik-ney in Potlatch dancing costume 1906.
Case & Draper Photo—Bancroft Library

Dah-clet-jah 1905.
Bancroft Library

Thlinget houses.
Courtesy University of Washington

Drying seal skins, Wrangel.
Courtesy Provincial Archives, Victoria, B.C.

monotonous "he-he, yo-yo, he-he, yo-yo!" to the jangling of their rattles and the drum beat, and kept time with funny spasmodic twistings of their bodies and the stiff, jerky motions of their arms and legs, that suggested the eccentric motions of an automation or robot.

In the front rank was Annie Collins, Tecumseh's granddaughter, and it would have been hard to tell whose heart was more thoroughly in the game—little Annie's, or wrinkled old Kitty Collins—she of many children and husbands and "Kewpie's" erstwhile dying wife. They were both there, not only with both feet stamping to the tom tom, but with every muscle in their bodies actively at work. It was a performance impossible to effectively describe, and very spectacular. As the dance progressed and the blood of the dancers warmed up, they lost themselves in an ecstacy of motion and sound. The raconteur, or soloist, Peter, waved his club, darted forward as though to brain his enemy—fell back as though in self-defense, crouched, lunged, leaped into the air and spun around, bent backward with his face up-turned to the sky, bowed to the ground, twisted and turned in all manner of grotesque and seemingly impossible attitudes—shaking his head till the eagles' down flew in a fluffy cloud, and chanting throughout, the tale he was enacting. Possibly he was killing a bear or fighting a killer-whale, or he may have been in mortal combat with his enemies. I was on the outside and could only guess, but the natives were living again the days of yore. One could see the flow of blood in their veins quicken—the veneer of civilization slough off and the primitive man emerge at the beat of the tom tom, for no sooner had they begun to warm up, than out of the past appeared the old native drum—deerskin stretched on a wide wooden hoop—with old fire-eating Peter Anniskett as drummer.

Suddenly my eyes fell on "Kewpie" Collins sitting flat on the floor with his legs sticking straight out in front of him, like a sitting doll, bouncing himself up and down like a rubber ball, and pounding his heels on the floor in his glee; while happiness radiated from his round face like the sun's rays from a burnished copper kettle, and I'll wager herring exuded from every pore.

The white man's world was forgotten—they were in the days of long ago. I withdrew with a feeling that to stay would be a serious breach of etiquette.

I understand now why the preacher thinks the Indians should not dance.

Chapter XXVI

TOTEM POLES

The totem pole has been a characteristic feature of Thlinget life in the past, as it was with the Haidas and the Tsimpsians; but when the Henya Thlingets abandoned their old village of Tuxikan for Klawock, they left their poles behind them. There are only three poles in this immediate neighborhood; one, on the left bank of Klawock Creek, and two on the right bank—all about a mile from the village.

One cannot say that the totem pole originated in Alaska for it has been found among primitive people in many of the unfamiliar spots of the world, but the idea behind it seems to be much the same wherever found—the recording of ideas. Among the Thlinget Indians the totem pole served four different purposes. One was the genealogical pole, which gave information to those who could read it, of the ancestry of the particular individual, usually a chief, who erected it.

The historical pole recorded in the same way, the high spots in the history of the clan.

Other poles recorded legendary history, and still others were mortuary poles and were erected in commemoration of some individual whose ashes would be inclosed in a cavity of the pole. Such poles lacked the extensive carving of the other poles and generally were topped by the totem of the dead man. There is one such near here—the one I passed on my hunting trip and which I have since photographed.

It is a difficult matter to get two stories of any pole, that resemble one another closely. That is not surprising because the Thlingets have no picture language and have merely attempted to fix in memory some ideas, much as we tie a string around a finger to remind ourselves that there is something we want to remember. Those *ideas* were executed in whatever way occurred to the artist who carved the pole and their meaning was preserved by word of mouth. Of course the details varied in the course of time with the telling—some embellishing the tale, and others forgetting parts.

A totem pole, as found in the older Indian villages along the coast of Southeastern Alaska, is generally a yellow cedar log, ten to seventy-five feet long, set on end; on which are carved grotesque figures that resemble animals or birds, often with marked human characteristics. These poles usually stand close to the homes of the owners or are fastened against the front of the buildings. The figures are usually weird, but the carving, which is done with a small adz-like tool, is very symetrically and skilfully done. Occasionally the poles are painted or stained with dyes, but commonly they are weathered to a silver-grey.

The simplest totem pole consists of a straight, smooth pole twelve to eighteen inches through and ten to twenty feet high, with the carved figure of some animal or bird on top— the totem of the clan. More often however, the poles have a series of figures carved one above another. Such poles may be historical and tell the story of intermarriage with different clans; or they may commemorate important events in the clan history, or in the life of the chieftain, as in the case of a small pole which has the figure of a beaver at the base, a halibut next above the beaver, and a man at the top, which indicates that the man caught halibut and trapped beaver. Another pole carries a figure of a raven with a frog in its beak, which is supposed to show that the raven and the frog clans had conflict and the raven was victorious.

In the summer of 1898 a party of Seattle businessmen made an excursion to Alaska, sponsored by one of the daily papers, and one of the sights visited was the old Indian village with its totem poles, on Tongas Island. The village was deserted and the poles abandoned, so they looked like available souvenirs. One of the party told me in Seattle, that the boat anchored for the night and late, when all was quiet on the ship, a small party landed with a crosscut saw and laid low one of the poles and cut it into several sections so they could handle it; then towed it out to the ship. The next morning the party beheld the pole which the day before had stood on the island, lying prone on the deck of the ship, and on their return to Seattle it was presented to the city.

Although the poles had been left behind by the Indians when they abandoned the old village, they were not forgotten and the owners of this particular pole were much aggrieved at the vandalism committed by the white men. It represented more than a sentimental value to them, for its carving had cost $250 a figure, or a total of $1750. When the situation was understood the clan was reimbursed by the city.

There are several quite different versions of the Seattle

totem pole, but here is one written by a Tongass youth of the clan that owned the pole. There are seven figures carved on the pole, which is sixty feet high. The topmost figure is that of a raven who told the man below him that he knew of a woman who wanted to marry a good looking man. It was all right with the man, so they were married. She belonged to the frog clan, which is shown by the figure of the frog.

The flood came, which is a universal tradition among the natives of Alaska, and sea food, of which the raven is very fond, became very scarce, so he married the lady mink, who had the reputation of being an exceptionally good provider.

The flood receded and food became plentiful and the raven waxed fat and forgot his wife, the mink; but after a time he grew lonesome, which is shown by the lugubrious figure of a raven below the mink, so he married the killer-whale, which is indicated by the figure next below.

The last figure, at the bottom of the pole, is that of an eagle, the father of the raven.

At that point the story takes a turn and recounts that the world was in darkness for a long, long time and old Eagle, Raven's father, was the only one who could make it light because he kept the sun and moon shut up in a box which he alone could open.

One day while young Raven was very small, he asked his father to let him play with the sun and moon, and when his father refused he began to cry and cried so loudly and so long that he made himself sick. That frightened his father, who feared the child would die, so he let him have the moon to play with, but admonished him not to let it get out of doors. He played with the moon many days, but one day he was bouncing it on the floor and it bounded up through the smoke-hole and soared away into the sky, where it hung and gave light. After a time, when his father had forgotten about the moon, Raven asked Eagle to let him play with the sun, and when Eagle refused, he again began to cry, and his father gave in and let him have the sun, but told him he mustn't let it get away from him. One day, in spite of his father's caution, he took the sun outdoors to play with and it escaped and went up in the sky as the moon had done, and ever since the sun and the moon have made the world light for human beings.

A radically different version of the story supposed to be told by the Seattle pole is that Raven, whom the Thlingets called "Yalth," was the greatest of all men and wanted to make the world a better place to live in, but he was opposed by another (the raven shown in the middle of the pole), who controlled the sun, moon and stars. Yalth had a friend, represented by the frog, who was an enemy of the King of Light previously mentioned. He told Yalth that the King of Light had a daughter of whom the king was very fond, who, because she was a virgin, could only drink from a certain spring, and was always attended by her woman companion. Yalth was interested and had his servants, the mink, help him to change to a spirit which went to dwell in the spring. When the daughter of the King of Light came to the spring she drank and conceived a child who was Yalth, which greatly delighted the grandfather. As Yalth grew older he always kept in mind his desire to improve the world for human beings and he thought it would be a fine thing if the world could have light, so he plotted to secure the sun, moon and stars from his grandfather and turn them loose. He began by pretending he was sick and cried a great deal. To quiet him his grandfather gave him first one thing and then another, so when the child cried for light one day and would take nothing else, his grandfather had a servant get a small box which contained light from a large chest in the house and gave it to Yalth to play with. The grandchild got under the smoke-hole of the house and opened and shut the box, making it first light, then dark, until all the light had been used up, thus making daylight and darkness. When Yalth found all the light had gone away he began to cry loudly again, so the King of Light had a servant bring another box which contained the stars, because he did not want to see his grandchild die. When he gave Yalth the stars to play with he cautioned him not to toss them into the air, so the boy rolled them around on the floor until he had a chance to toss them through the smoke-hole; but even then there was not enough light in the sky, so once more he cried and cried until his grandfather let him have the sun. He allowed the sun to get away, as he had the stars, but when night came he found the stars gave only a little light—not nearly so much as the sun gave in the daytime, so he tried his old trick again of crying and was given the moon to quiet him (grandfathers are apt to be just that indulgent and trusting), but that time the King of Lights sat under the smoke-hole so the moon couldn't get out and Yalth had to be satisfied with rolling the moon around on the floor until it rolled near the door, when he quickly opened the door and pushed the moon outside; then he changed himself into a raven, seized the moon in his beak and flew up in the sky with it, where he left it to light the night along with the stars, while the sun lighted the day.

After that he started to fly to a far land where he heard they needed help, for his reputation had gone all over the world, but after flying many days over the ocean he grew very hungry because he couldn't catch fish from the sea, like the gulls, so when he saw a whale come to the surface to blow, he dived into the whale's mouth and fed on the fish in the whale's belly. He rode in the belly of the whale four days and nights and feasted on fish till he was happy, but at last the whale reached his destination and Raven hopped out and landed on the beach where he has lived ever since.

Still another and more elaborate version is most interesting, because the legend and the related history illustrate various phases of Thlinget psychology. According to native history, the wife of a Tongas chief nearly one hundred years ago, was a high caste woman named Shawat. It would have been proper to have called her an Indian princess, although they did not. In English her maiden name would have been "Shining-face-of-copper." After her marriage she was known as "Great Whale." Because among the Thlingets names changed with unusual experiences, she was known as "Chief-over-all-chief-women," after the birth of her first child; which was equivalent to calling her *Queen*. The name of the father was "Everybody-looks-up-to-him," a fitting name for a big chief.

After many years tidings came that her sister was very ill at her home on a far distant river and while attempting to cross a river to get to her, Chief-of-all-chief-women was drowned, so her brothers and her children had this pole carved and erected at great expense to honor her and to record a native legend of a chief and his wife who lived happily together for many years. A time came however, when the wife was unfaithful to her husband, and to escape consequences, she pretended to die. The deceit was discovered and her lover was slain. The woman had a son who decided to take a journey into the sky to marry the daughter of a chief. To do that, he and a friend clad themselves in the skins of woodpeckers, one red and the other black—for they had heard that the girl's father killed all suitors. At that time the world was always dark, but the woodpeckers found a hole in the sky where fire puffed up and down through it. They flew through the hole, but were singed by the fire, so they cast off their woodpecker skins and became sandpipers which were caught by the chief's daughter and carried home. The chief was very angry at the trick that had been played and at first was going to roast them both alive, but the girl talked him out of it and he decided to accept them as sons-in-law. In the course of time there were children and one day a son of one of them dropped through the hole in the sky and fell near the home of old Everybody-looks-up-to-him and was found and taken in. That child became head chief of the Raven clan and is represented by the figure at the top of the pole; but he was a terrible gourmand and was "taken for a ride in the country" and left to die, however a soft-hearted old woman took pity on him and fed him crabapples to keep him from starvation. He changed to a raven and made the acquaintance of four other young men in the guise of a squirrel, a crow, a robin and a blue jay. Later they were joined by a mink—shown on the pole—and all decided to travel and see the world. At that point the killer-whale arrived (he is the fifth figure on the pole), and he proposed to go with them and took them all in his mouth; but they grew hungry because they had brought no food with them, so the raven made a fire inside the whale and undertook to cut some fat off the whale's heart. He cut so deep that he killed the whale, whose carcass drifted around on the sea for a long time, but at last they felt it bumping on a beach. People living on the land saw the whale drift ashore and cut a hole in its side to get the blubber, when the raven and the mink came forth all shining with oil. The mink rolled in rotten wood to dry himself and has been brown and glistening ever since. This is believed to have happened at the Haida village of Yakwan (the Thlinget legends all have definite locations which is considered proof of their truth), where it was always dark.

Raven knew that the old chief kept the sun in a box, so he decided to find some way to get it, and as the first step in the right direction, he married the chief's daughter who bore a son. When the child was partly grown he teased so hard for the box that held the sun that the chief had his slaves give it to him. He took the sun out and played with it till he tired, then he told it to go up in the sky, which it did and there has been light ever since. The boy then changed to a raven and flew out of the house (he is the bird on top of the pole), and eloped with the pretty daughter of the chief of the village. She was named Go-dah. Her father was frantic over the loss of his daughter, but four years later he saw a frog coming into the house late one evening. He called to it: "Whose child are you?" and when the frog answered," "Go-dah, Go-dah," the chief knew it was his grandson and told him to go and bring his father and mother because he wanted to see his daughter again. The frog went behind the house and jumped in a pond, but the next morning the chief's daughter came into the house carrying a frog in her arms, and behind her came a large frog. The chief felt very much ashamed and had the bull-frog and the young frog killed, but spared the daughter, who continued to live with her father. She is the second figure from the top.

That seems to be the end of this story. My own opinion is that the Thlingets could easily qualify as fiction writers, but they insist by all that is sacred that everything they tell is true. They can show the raven, the crow, the robin and the jay, the mink and the frog, and also the rotten wood. What further proof could anyone want?

Chapter XXVII

THE SALVATION ARMY

Last night Alma attended the Salvation Army meeting at the invitation of Captain Benson. I would have gone also had I not had mail to get ready for the mail boat which would be in before morning.

A white man, Mr. Caruthers, from Wrangell, major in the Salvation Army, is here helping with revival meetings. He preached a sermon using as a text, "I am the Vine, ye are the branches," and Captain Benson stood beside him and interpreted paragraph by paragraph, because of course, the sermon was in English. The listeners paid the closest attention and showed keen interest and appreciation. The sermon was followed by singing, accompanied by the band instruments. As they sang and talked they waxed stronger and stronger in spirit, until it seemed as though half the congregation were on their feet, swinging their arms and stepping to the music of the horns, drums and voices. Whenever they paused someone would give a testimony. Captain Benson came down beside Alma and interpreted the testimonies for her, but almost needed an interpreter himself. He said to her, "You can give testimony if you want." So in a few minutes she rose and told them she was glad to be shown the beautiful lesson of the tree and its branches—that Christ is the tree and we are the branches—for God is Life and what we express to our fellow men is the fruit. Jesus said, "By their fruit ye shall know them," which means that the world can tell a Christian by the life he lives. Good words and good deeds are spiritual fruit and show to the world that we are followers of Christ. We are the branches of the living Vine and so bear good fruit. The Captain jumped to his feet and translated her testimony to the interested listeners. Their black eyes shown and they watched her and listened intently, apparently sensing her sympathy and understanding, with the Indian intuition, though they did not understand her words. They smiled and nodded and "amenned" on every side, then went into an ecstacy of singing.

The first meeting we attended was not a great while after our arrival. We understood they were to have a special meeting, so when we heard singing and the playing of the band down on the street one evening, we went over to their hall, which stands on piles over the water and apparently was once a little church. There was a goodly gathering for a small village; the women assembled on the benches on one side, the men on the other side, while two or three benches in the rear were occupied by younger men and boys.

Captain Benson, Envoy Collins and Sergeant-Major Anniskett occupied the platform, and a woman, Mrs. John Darrow, in some capacity; while those who played the band instruments sat in front near them. Captain Benson talked, of course in the native speech, but while we could not understand what was said, we did understand the spirit and were deeply interested in seeing the earnestness with which all participated and the genuineness of their worship. Different ones prayed and anyone and everyone was willing to talk when the time came for the experience meeting. It wasn't a man's meeting, for women talked as freely as the men and prayed as long and as earnestly; while Mrs. Darrow, who can use some English, with the utmost courtesy, struggled to express her ideas in our tongue so that we might understand, and she carried more meaning to us than one might suppose.

These people take their religion so seriously that when they are opening their hearts before their associates, they open them wide and tell the most intimate experiences of their lives with all the frankness of the confessional, and they are eager to do it. Where, in a similar gathering of whites, there would be long periods of silence and of embarrassing waiting for someone to talk; here there was nothing of the kind. Men and women talked eagerly and fluently and if anyone thought another had talked long enough, or if he could no longer control his pent-up emotions, he would leap to his feet and start in with his own story. The interrupted one showed no resentment, but accepted the situation in the right spirit and joined in the listening. Soon someone would burst forth in song—the speaker would sit down, as was, and the band and voices would peal out a favorite hymn.

Children sat quietly through it all and the nearest approach to restlessness we saw manifested, was a little tad quietly chewing the buttons off an older sister's coat; and in that we saw demonstrated a perfect illustration of brotherly, or possibly more accurately speaking—sisterly love, for the girl, instead of interfering, would considerately find a new button for the child when the last one had been chewed up and spit out. The buttons lasted through the service—both came to an end at the same time rather to my regret, for I would have liked to know what would happen next.

Throughout the service Captain Benson considerately explained to us the substance of what had been said, and it was surprising how much he could tell in a few words. When I rose and expressed the interest and sympathy we felt in their work, he very carefully translated my thoughts into the native tongue.

We came away so conscious of the earnestness and spiritual understanding of God on the part of those present, that we felt we had attended a stimulating religious service.

At another time we found the little hall full and the meeting in full swing when we entered. William Stuart, a big Tsimpsian, was the speaker. He gave a talk which Josie Snook, an attractive young widow, interpreted. They stood side-by-side in the pulpit, each holding a Bible in hand. He read from the Bible, then talked about each passage and she translated, paragraph by paragraph, into Thlinget, for the leader spoke in English, not being a Thlinget himself.

He read from Christ's Sermon on the Mount,

"Ye have heard that it hath been said, An eye for an eye, and a tooth for a tooth: But I say unto you, That ye resist not evil: but whosoever shall smite thee on thy right cheek, turn to him the other also."

"My brothers," he went on, "if I never hear those words our Saviour spoke, I would be a murderer. When I young man I work on dock in Ketchikan. I Indian. White man try to make me fool— laugh at me cause I Indian—call me bad names—say I coward— try push me down fish chute. I not so big as now, but I strong— strong like grampus. My fingers jerk—I feel hot in my body— my mind fierce like wounded bear—I want hit that man. I kill him if I hit him—oh, I want to kill him hard—I double my fist—I make step at him, then I think, 'No I Clistian.' I remember those words I read. I didn't turn my cheek to man, I turn my back. That made him fierce mad, but other mans turn white man round— make him go way—say to him, 'You drunk—you fool to make Indian fight. He Clistian Indian—Bill good man—if he hit you once you be dead man—go way.' Man go way and I glad I keep my hands from choking him. I been baptized—I want to be good Soldier of the Cross."

A fine specimen of a young man named Robert Armour, with a rich, deep base voice sang a solo, with a quartette singing the chorus. But to describe what followed would be difficult. The drumming, the beating of tamborines, the playing of the Army musicians, singing, the waving of arms, clapping of hands, embracing of one another, choosing leaders—all seemed to follow some definite program, but the cue was not evident to us. We were confident however, that they would depart feeling, in the trite words of the country newspaper, that "A good time was had by all."

One interesting feature of the meeting was the confession made by two young men of their sin in attending the big party at the town hall the night before where they had danced. They were blessed and duly forgiven by the older members, but we heard the next day that they afterwards laughed and joked about their confession. Quite likely. It is possible that their profession of repentance was purely a prank, but I am inclined to believe that for the moment they felt the contagion of the crowd and acted on a genuine impulse which the jollying of their mates later caused them to repudiate. Human nature is very prevalent, even among the Thlinget Indians of Alaska.

On our way back to our quarters we saw what we have never seen before—a rainbow encircling the moon. A long thin cloud floated across the face of the moon like a veil, and the moon shone through it in a ring of prismatic colors.

It seems to us that the Salvation Army offers the most natural and appropriate channel for religious expression for the natives. As a church it fits their needs splendidly. Their minds, their thoughts and their experiences have been very simple. They are entirely unhampered by the whims and individualistic ideas which have been responsible for the endless number of religious sects the world has known. In their primitive days they recognized a power greater than their own, but did not go so far as to worship it; but when the white man came and told them things about that power, and gave them a name for it, "God," it seemed to explain everything for them. It seems easy for them to understand that God, being the power or principal that rules the world, must always exercise that power for right and justice. They realize that there is no room for two Ke-an-Kows (Great-Ones-Over-All), one good and the other evil; neither is it possible for a "Good Ke-An-Kow" to be both good and evil, therefore the unreality of evil is easily accepted by them. They see and hold the one idea of a good and loving God. That is enough for them. It would be enough

for us, wouldn't it, if we could only see it and give up our incon-
sistent whims and fancies. To think of God makes them happy;
to think of their own failings makes them sad; but the assurance
that their loving God is always with them, gives them new courage
and enthusiasm and, like children, they manifest their joy with
song and praise and musical instruments. Children, when happy,
jump up and down. These people are children in their experience
with our world and are not yet hampered by the inhibitions that
bind us. The Salvation Army, because it is doing its work all over
the world among those who are children in understanding, adapts
its methods to the child's psychology. Religion is a very simple
thing with the Salvation Army, which makes it the natural church
for such people.

What does the doctrine of *original sin* mean to a Thlinget
Indian?—No more than it means to me. They take what they
can understand and ignore the rest; therefore they have the
simplest of beliefs—that of a loving, Almighty God. It is vain to
expect much more with them, and why should we?

During the winter months, which is a dormant period with
the fishermen, there is a great activity in the Presbyterian Church
and in the Salvation Army. They charge their religious batteries
for the rest of the year by visiting neighboring groups, or in being
visited by them. Two days before the end of the year the village
heard the playing of a band, and a gas boat rounded the red light
and chugged up the inlet with its deck crowded with singing
natives. It was a visiting Salvation Army delegation from Hydaburg. Their coming was unexpected, but they were joyfully welcomed and were billeted around the village. A series of enthusiastic
meetings followed which gave a fine opportunity to indulge their
fondness for prolonged prayers and extended speaking. They all
love to talk in public, and never show the slightest embarrassment.

When the boat again chugged around the red light, everyone was tired, but happy. We felt the effect of it in school, for
everyone attended everything—adults, children and babies. Bob
gently voiced the regret to me that their coming at that particular
time had spoiled their plans for dedicating the town hall.

The natives of Klawock are religiously alert—according to
their lights—and I can confidently assert that they slip and slide
no more than we do ourselves.

Chapter XXVIII

DEATH

There was another funeral today—this time, a young man who very evidently was doomed when we came to the village. The father and the clan had already spent much money in seeking medical relief. He had been taken to accessible towns where doctors could be reached and some had taken their money and made promises of recovery which were wholly unjustified, for the nurse assured me venereal contamination and tuberculosis left the poor chap not a chance in the world. Her pronouncement was justified, because today they have taken him to the island cemetery.

Only a few days ago I stopped to speak to him, as he sat in the sunshine on Bob's dock, and my heart ached for him. I wondered what was in his mind, for surely he knew his fate, but he smiled wanly at me and cheerfully expressed his enjoyment of the warm sunshine.

I think nothing has interested us more in connection with these people than their attitude towards death. Probably we are far from comprehending their actual psychology, but there seems to be two phases of the subject; one, their attitude before the advent of the white man; and their present attitude. I wonder why the primitive man faces death fearlessly, while to the more intelligent races it is fraught with terror. I suspect that it is because their ideas are simpler and are more fully accepted, while our minds are full of questions and uncertainty. Death has no terror for the Thlingets. It is never absent long from their midst and no home escapes its visitation. They are fatalists, in a way, for if resistance is to be made, it is made for them by others, not by themselves. In the old days it was the clan that invoked the medicine man, not the individual; and when one comes to understand what a patient experienced at his hands, it is easy to believe that he would rather die in peace than be cured by the shaman.

The primitive Thlingets believed that there were spirits, good or bad, in everything, which naturally took the form of animal, bird, fish, or even inanimate things, but which could take the form of human beings at will. There was nothing consistent, logical or plausible about their beliefs. They just believed them, that was all, and no crazy inconsistency evident to us, could be so crazy as to trouble them.

Like most primitive people, they accepted the immortality of the spirit without question. Spirits were indestructable, therefore they always survived whatever they might go through, but the natives' ideas of what ultimately became of their spirits depended largely upon those things which most influenced their lives. The red men of the States had their "Happy Hunting Ground," because hunting was the great feature of their lives. The Thlingets, however, instead of thinking of a happy hunting ground as the abode of those spirits whose bodies had been left behind, thought of the "other world" as "The beautiful island" surrounded by green water so great in its expanse that no spirit could find its way across alone. And to the beginning of that water, the way was so long across the land, and the hazards so great, that careful and extensive preparations were necessary for the trip. When death seemed certain, all effort was directed toward insuring a comfortable journey. Food must be provided, clothing and blankets for warmth, and the other necessities of travel; and the body must be properly cared for because the bond of sympathy between the spirit and the body was supposed to be so close that the spirit would suffer if the body was neglected; consequently it was considered most reverential to help the dead in the other world. The living could be neglected—they could care for themselves—but not the dead; and it was that loyalty to the departed that justified the lavish expenditure of money and property at the time of death. A great feast in honor of a departed spirit helped to establish its social status in the "spirit house" on the "beautiful island." It was not an unusual occurrence in the olden days for the remains of someone long departed to be exhumed in order to pay honor to the spirit by ceremonial feasting, because those responsible for such an event were the ones who actually profited by it. It was a case of being honored by honoring, and it is told that two relatives who conceived the idea at the same time, of thus honoring posthumously a departed spirit, quarreled over which should take the bones from the old dead-house and rebury them. The difference of opinion became so acute that they grew angry and one spitefully threw the bones broadcast into the surrounding bushes. It consequently became necessary for the other to hire members of the opposite clan to reassemble the remains, and they were reburied in a new dead-house with great pomp and much feasting. The heavy expense connected with the affair, instead of being begrudged, was most cheerfully welcomed, because by offering opportunity for a lavish outlay, just that much more credit was earned by those involved and the angry one was put to mortal shame by being unable to make such display himself.

The death of a shaman called for an especially large and expensive series of functions. The community house would be packed with Indians sitting on the floor in family groups, each with as big a dish as could be obtained in their midst, which would be filled with a stew or goolosh, consisting of boiled meats, fish and what have you. Each individual would proceed to help himself with spoon and fingers. Fruit, dried fish and many others of their relishes would be dumped in heaps in each group, while seaweed, fish eggs, eulikon, seal and herring oils would be supplied in tightly woven baskets or wooden bowls. If the supply of food surpassed the individual and collective capacities, the surplus could be carried away, but that was a limit not easily reached; therefore it became as much a matter of family pride to surpass the point of saturation, as it used to be to the convivial hosts of the Middle Ages to drink their guests under the table.

Because the road was so long to the green water—over two mountains with a great valley in between—there were many traveling the trail at the same time, and on the shore at the end a great host waited to be carried across. Wearied with long watching, the waiting spirit would drop into deep sleep, when canoes would come to take the good spirits across. Bad spirits never did get across, but waited in vain on the shore of the great sea.

Unlike many among the so-called, civilized races, who believe that the spirits of the sinful burn in everlasting fire, the Thlingets' idea of future misery was suffering from cold, which was the explanation of their burning their dead.

When a Thlinget felt he was about to die, he was apt to say, "This house is beginning to fill with spirits. They are waiting for me." Maybe that was so. The natives are very psychic, as psychic as wild animals or children, with none of our inhibitions. With us there are many who have seen faces brighten with the delight of recognition of loved ones who have gone ahead, as the spirit separated itself from its mortal shell and winged its way—where? If we, who are skeptical as a whole, see that happen, why should not these *little children,* to whom nothing is impossible, be conscious of those waiting to greet them.

There was a great unwillingness to touch the dead, so the sick were often dressed two or three days before the end came, and when coffins came into their experience along with the white man, they would often be placed in the coffin to die. The dead were dressed like the living in preparation for the end, and when the last breath had been drawn, the body would be lifted from the house by ropes through a hole in the roof or in the side of the building. The dead were never carried through a door, and a dog was always taken out along with the body in order that any evil spirit might enter the dog and on that account be unable to return to the house and injure other members of the family. If the dog were not taken, some one else in the family would surely die. After the removal of the body, the opening would be closed speedily to prevent any possible return of the dead one's spirit, for once separated from its accustomed abode, there was no telling just what the spirit might do.

The dead were never taken to the funeral pyre or the grave, from the house where death occurred, but were removed to a house of the opposite clan, which took responsibility for all service rendered in connection with the burial. From the passing of the spirit, to the final disposal of the body, some one was always present with it, and the wife sat on the floor with her back to the body until its removal, while lights were burned all night to prevent any possible return of the spirit. The first time we heard Bob's Diesel engine throb all night, we wondered what could be the explanation, but learned the next day that there had been a death and the lights had been kept burning on that account; which shows that the old ideas persist.

All service in case of death had to be paid for extravagantly, no matter how trivial the service might be—the higher the caste, the more extravagant the outlay, and it was a common practice to hire mourners from the opposite clan to add to the effect. It showed that there was no counting of the cost. The obligation to honor the dead was so absolute that no one thought of slighting it in any degree. To have done so, would have brought disgrace upon the dead and no crime could be greater than that.

When the white man came to Alaska, the disposal of the dead among the natives was always by cremation, except in the case of slaves who, being unworthy, were simply cast into the sea; and the medicine man, who was accorded special treatment.

The burning of the dead generally took place at a spot not too close to the village, because the spirits of those burned were supposed to hover about the burning ground. Here in Klawock a point of land which lay between the Demmert and the Peratovich sections of the village was originally used for that purpose, and long after cremation had been abandoned, it was looked at askance by the natives and given a fairly wide berth. Eventually the feeling was largely overcome, the village crowded around the spot, and a house was built upon it which was torn down a year or more ago. One of the natives has told me that he intends to build a house upon it again. I wonder if he will.

The theory of cremation was that the man whose body was burned passed his future life in bodily comfort; while those not burned were forever cold and seeking to get warm. For that reason Thlingets have had a greater dread of death by drowning, than of death in any other form. The spirit of the drowned was supposed to be caught and dragged into a hole in the bottom of the sea by a land otter, where it became a goosh-ta-kah (hobgoblin), which was never warm.

The missionaries made strenuous opposition to the native practice of cremation, which seemed to me to be a narrow-minded and prejudiced attitude, because cremation is increasing steadily among us, until I learned that so many practices accompanied the burning as to give it the nature of an orgy, and the custom, if continued, would have seriously interfered with lifting the people out of their paganism. Evidently the missionaries won out and the practice is entirely one of the past; but those who first obeyed the insistence of the missionaries had to meet the full force of native prejudice and the most active opposition of the medicine men, who were quick to turn any misfortune which might visit the families of those who buried their dead, to advantage, and place the blame on the misery and unhappiness of the spirits imprisoned in the cold ground. As a result, in the early days of burying, the bones were not infrequently dug up and burned so that the spirits might dwell in the spirit land in warmth and comfort; and a big feast was held to propitiate the unseen powers.

The shamans or medicine men, were an exception to the practice of burning. Their bodies were embalmed and deposited in a dead-house, tree, or in some secret place in the forest, or in a cave beside the sea.

Because the Indians believed that the spirit of the dead one hovered about before starting on its long journey, they threw food into the fire. A little food burned, meant a large amount received by the spirits. Clothing and blankets were cast into the fire that the spirit of the departed might not suffer from cold; the dead man's weapons, special belongings, and even his canoe, were put on the pyre in order that he might in no way suffer for lack of anything needed; while in the case of a chief or "big man" of the village, slaves would be killed as his spirit fled, in order that their spirits might continue to serve their master, and their bodies were burned with his. Sometimes the wife threw herself upon the fire so that her spirit might accompany that of her husband.

The bones and ashes of such a great one would be gathered and deposited in the cavity of a totem pole or in a dead-house constructed for the purpose.

It was believed by the natives that once upon a time a soul came back from the "beautiful island" to tell the people how departed spirits should be treated. It said that:

"Weapons should be burned with the bodies so that the spirits might have spirit weapons with which to defend themselves.

"That there should be coverings for their hands and moccasins for their feet, to protect against devil's club.

"That water should be thrown into the fire so that the spirits might quench their thirst.

"Food to nourish the spirits, because when the fire crackled it was a sign the spirits were hungry and must be fed.

"Songs should be sung in order that the spirits might have the encouragement and moral support of the living."

On the night following the cremation, unless conditions were unfavorable, the mourning feast was held. It was managed by the opposite totem group (if the husband died—the wife's clan; if the wife or a child, the husband's) and because it must be in every way a creditable affair, contributions were received from the clan of the deceased, and they were always cheerfully and liberally given.

The feast was to honor the memory of the dead; to further supply the spirit with food for its long journey; and to compensate all who had in any way assisted, no matter though it might be so trivial as putting moccasins on the feet of the dead for the burning. At the feast, food was again thrown into the fire and the name of the dead one called, for they believed the spirit of the dead to be still present, and that it feasted (of course on spiritual food), and rejoiced with the living and basked in the honor that was bestowed upon it. There was singing and dancing in which the spirit also participated, for the songs and dances dramatized the native life and ideas, and interested the spirit as well as the mortal Thlinget.

Last of all, as great a store of blankets, cotton cloth, furs and other evidence of wealth, as could be assembled, were piled before one who acted as master of ceremonies, who proceeded to divide them by tearing or cutting into suitable sized pieces which were distributed among those present of the opposite clan, according to their rank and the service they had rendered. As a rule the pieces would be too small to be of use by themselves, but they were valued, nevertheless, and when combined often produced garments that would rival Joseph's coat for effect.

At the end, the heir of the deceased became husband or wife of the relict and on him devolved responsibility for erecting the mortuary pole or other repository of the ashes. That called for another feast, with the accompanying gift-giving to all who had taken part, it being an invitation affair. Thus, often, a large part of the inheritance would be expended upon the original owner, but it was never begrudged, for honor and respect shown the dead redounded greatly to one's credit among the living, and was a great help in improving one's social status or caste. I suppose the idea was that in exalting one's progenitors, he exalted himself.

Such were the conditions the missionaries found, and while they have wrought remarkable changes, I suspect they are not all as complete as one might suppose, and among those of the older generation, are probably very superficial. It is true they no longer burn their dead, and they no longer have slaves; but while the old time mortuary feast and the potlatch have become ancient history, the idea persists with them, though the observance is of a symbolical nature. From those old customs there has been a gradual change along various lines. Burial in a coffin is now the accepted practice and is often keenly anticipated by those who know they are drawing towards the close of life; and in order that the enjoyment may be theirs while they can still take pleasure in it, the coffin is sometimes bought in advance of the need and kept in the same room with the ultimate tenant, where the eyes can feast upon it and the pleasure be shared with friends. The same is true of the clothing to be worn on the final occasion. That pleasure is clearly not due so much to appreciation of the beautiful color, the silver handles and the satin lining, as to the honor which is being bestowed by such lavish outlay.

Recently an old native woman died, Mrs. Cook-Jack. She was a very influential old lady among the members of her tribe— what the reporters of the city papers would play up as an *Indian princess*, although there is no such thing. She was the proud possessor of a big 12 by 20 foot American flag. Equally precious to her—possibly more so—was her ceremonial blanket with two big figures of a grampus, the totem of her family. She had once promised to sell the blanket to the nurse, who is an accumulator of souvenirs, for $20. The nurse paid the money and the blanket was to be delivered after the demise of the owner, which was supposed to be imminent. Well it wasn't and fuller consideration convinced the old lady that she should not separate herself from her ceremonial robe, a decision easily reached since the money was already in her possession, so the deal was off, and when the end finally came the blanket went to the grave draped over the casket. One of the sons later reimbursed the nurse in a measure by reproducing the Chilkat blanket pattern on a dressed deer skin.

Mrs. Cook-Jack had three sons, three married daughters, and some property, probably mostly in money, in which her husband hadn't even a community interest, for the husband doesn't count among the Thlingets; so she called her daughters together and told she wanted Fred to have her property, because the other sons would simply waste it and drink it up. The decision was accepted by all and was as absolute as a probated will with us, but think of such a procedure "getting by" without a contest in our civilized society!

So Fred, who told me about it, bought her a beautiful casket and had it taken into the room where she lay, so she could enjoy looking at it; and after her death he asked me to take a photograph of it so they would have something to remind them of its grandeur. I photographed it in the house where they had hung the big American flag and the ceremonial robe on the wall behind it; and again outdoors, in the rain that was starting, with the daughters, two sons, and a grandson, and the treasured blanket spread over the casket. They again wanted the American flag in the picture, but it would have concealed the people, so it had to be omitted.

She was taken over to the island cemetery a mile distant, where today we can see the immense flag rippling finely in the breeze above her grave from a pole prepared in advance for the occasion.

Of course the dead are no longer taken out through a hole in the side of the house, and dogs no longer play any part in the passing of a spirit—so far as we know—but burials still do not take place from the house in which the end came. Possibly that is because the opposite clan still takes charge of everything that has to be done . . . They know . . . I don't. And I saw another ancient practice evident. When I went in to take the picture, one of the daughters sat on the floor with her back to the coffin and another sat in a chair nearby, while before the coffin a dish stood on the floor with money in it, of which a twenty-dollar gold certificate was the most conspicuous element, although there was currency also. There was a low interchange of their guttural speech between the women and the dish was put out of sight; which I did not interpret as casting any reflection upon myself, though I was curious to know the particular impelling motive.

I would like to attend one of their funerals some time, but I have never been invited to do so and I have the notion that a white man's presence would be more of an embarrassment than a courtesy. So many relics of their pre-civilization days linger around, which haven't yet been bred out of them, but which they feel a little sensitive about, that they do not crave curious observation. I have no doubt they have their feast following the funeral, for the funeral obligation must be settled, but the old mortuary feast has been much modified. I had an illustration not a great while after our arrival at Klawock of the persistence of old customs. A high caste woman who claims to be the master midwife of the village, though not without dispute, came to me hugging her arms, and asked me to pay her for taking care of the boy's wife. I thought it a good joke at the time, though I concealed my amusement and tried to make it clear that I had no responsibility whatever for anything of the kind; but later I again saw the gaunt figure haunting the school ground and was greeted on my appearance with the same request.

"Him no good. He no pay—You pay," she insisted.

If persistence were always rewarded, I would surely have paid her.

It was not until we knew a great deal more about the Thlingets and their customs than we did at that time, that I realized that according to their practice, I *was* personally liable for the debt. Of course it was the nurse who attended the population party, but the Thlinget code of etiquette permitted anyone to participate, whether invited or no, and any service rendered, no matter how trivial, must be liberally paid for. There was where the debt came in: My responsibility was due to being the representative of the Government. If it hadn't been for the Government, the nurse would not have been there. Had it not been for the nurse, the woman would have taken care of the baby, and if she had taken care of the baby she would have been paid without question; but since she had not been paid, the nurse had wronged her, and I, being the "Big Man," should pay the nurse's debt. Their responsibility towards their native obligations, I have noticed, are taken much more seriously than those to the Whites. But who can blame them for that? If I didn't pay a just debt owed by my clan, the United States, to the defrauded midwife, why should they pay their debts to other members of my clan? It had been an age old rule that a clan was responsible for anything done by one of the tribe, and war was certain to follow any repudiation of responsibility. The rule still looks good to them, but today, under the influence of civilization, they make war in other ways. Such is progress.

Chapter XXIX

BURIAL

Our curiosity was early aroused by the marble gravestones which we saw standing in several parts of the village. They were clearly gravestones, though seemingly out of place. Two of them were of a style found in every cemetery in the States, but others were radically different. Of these, one, standing in the midst of a fair-sized strawberry bed and between the street and a really modern looking cottage, was a white marble shaft about five feet high, on a base, and capped by an eagle's nest with a mother eagle brooding over her young.

Then, beside the walk which leads from the school playground to the street, we daily pass two stones; one, quite ordinary in type, is made extraordinary by its inscription, "Mary Ha-Clan, Age 112 years." It was some time before we learned that the little, shriveled, bent, hardly human form whom we occasionally saw moving about, was Mary Ha-Clan—still living—but whether 112 yet, or still, we don't know. Probably no one does, but she is entitled to the benefit of the doubt.

But beside Mary Ha-Clan's memorial stands another affair. Sitting on a block of white marble is a chubby figure of a bear, designed according to Thlinget ideas of realism. On the bear's head rests one of the tall, conical dancing hats of the early days; and on top of that, balances the virile figure of a grampus, the killer-whale. On the base is inscribed "Jackson Takite," whether living or dead; and what the marble totem pole tells, are other things we haven't found out. In American schools we teach our children, "If you don't know, ask questions," but in Thlingetdom— ask questions, and you still don't know. The information given may be valuable; the only trouble with it will be that it isn't so. One gains information here by accident—not by seeking it. I haven't forgotten my experience with George Saunders and his mysterious box.

We alleged to one another that these were gravestones, but in the absence of graves, and due to the presence of the living, we denied the allegation. Then what?—The accident happened. One day, as I stood ringing the school bell for the afternoon session—the bell is on a frame in front of the building, where I can enjoy the outlook as I ring—I noticed an activity down at the dock which I did not understand. A fog hung over the water so one could see but dimly, but my curiosity was aroused (a chronic state here), so after I had given the bell a final clang, I seized a camera and went down to see what was going on.

There at the float, were four of the larger gas boats lashed together abreast. Flags were flying from their masts, people crowded their decks, and on one of the boats I saw one of the alleged gravestones which we had passed down near the water front daily, with its white marble limb reclining in white marble clover. Men were loading boxes of apples, cases of pilot bread, barrels of pop and cases of canned goods and candy. There was much clucking in the native tongue—lines were cast off—and the four boats, moving as one, swung out, circled around and headed down the inlet, with the band playing on the deckhouse of one of the boats. As I turned to go I met Eagle Horse and asked him what it was all about.

"Well," he answered, "in the old days that would have been a potlatch," and he went on to explain that the Jackson tribe was going to erect the stone which I saw on the deck of the boat, at the grave of the husband of Mrs. Jackson, near whose doorstep the stone had been standing ever since our arrival. Only the two clans, his and hers, were represented and he said all were high caste. Eagle Horse was not of either clan, so he, like myself, was a stay-at-home spectator. He said that on such occasions in former days, instead of a grave stone, a totem pole would have been erected, with all the accompaniments of a potlatch. The potlatch and the totem pole are now passe with the Thlingets and have been succeeded by the grave stone and the "light lunch" of fruit, pop, candy and other prepared edibles, but the natives still enjoy the anticipatory honor that will be theirs when the *day* comes for them, so they sometimes buy the gravestone in advance, as they do their coffins, thus assuring themselves that they will have one, and at the same time, suiting their particular tastes. They erect the stones close to their homes till such time as they shall be needed and in the meantime they can daily look out and dream of what is coming to them.

When not provided in advance, it is the practice to order the stone as soon after death as may be practicable, and when it comes, to erect it temporarily in the village at some convenient and conspicuous place until the fishing season is over and the natives have returned from their various fields of work.

I have no doubt that is also the explanation of an incident that happened during one of Tecumseh Collins' frequent visits. The particular thing he had in mind for me to do for him that morning, was to write a letter for his wife, the devoted Kitty, to a Chinaman, Sing Li, who lived elsewhere in Alaska, and who, in her fondness for children, had been raised from childhood by her as her own. (Yes, possibly—well, never mind.) Anyway, he had been raised by Kitty like the rest of the collection and gave and received the affection of a son.

In short, Kitty had said, via Tecumseh and myself:

"I forget not, dear son Sing Li, that you have promised to get a gravestone for me when I die. I talk to Tecumseh all time about it. I pray for you before I sleep that your business may grow and prosper. I kiss you my son.

Your mother, Kitty Collins."

Of course I recognize that the whole sentiment may have originated in the poetic mind of Tecumseh, who is thrifty and willing to share domestic responsibility. It is also possible that he still carries within his heart thought of the young wife he is to have when Kitty tires of this earth and he is cast adrift, and wished to have all details carefully worked out. Probably he was simply seeking to gratify his wife's natural longings. The point is, that the gravestone, like the coffin, enters actively into plans for the future.

In connection with the Jackson affair, a little sidelight on the native psychology has recently come to us via the nurse. Jackson died early in the year, leaving a widow whose home is between our quarters and the plank street along the waterfront. About the same time Jackson Coombs became a widower through the death of his wife, and not long after our arrival we heard through the *daily paper*, that Jackson Coombs and Mrs. Jackson were married. That looked plausible for they were living together; and sensible, because it costs less to maintain one home than two; and it struck us as quite romantic. We enthused over two hearts picking up again the thread of life and plodding along the road to the hereafter hand-in-hand. Well, no harm was done, but we live and learn.

Two or three months later a white major in the Salvation Army visited Klawock and he told us one of his errands was to marry Jackson Coombs and Mary Jackson, and he did it in the approved white man's way, although neither of the parties could talk the white man's language. Because of his delayed trip, they had met the emergency by marrying the Thlinget way. And why not? They are respectable people and earnest Salvation Army workers. Besides, who gave the white man the right to decide for the world what shall constitute marriage? Anyway, the skeleton has been taken from the closet and the grave stone removed from the dooryard—Jackson has been honored and his spirit can hover contentedly about the gatherings of the clan and will not be deprived of its spiritual food, even though no more food is thrown into the fire to be spiritualized—but is that so? What does a white man know about what goes into the fire?

But to return to the interesting subject of burying! We puzzled for sometime after our arrival, over the odd little structures we saw on the shore of a small island in front of the Demmert end of the village, before I found the time one day to slip on rubber boots and wade through the slime of the intervening channel at low tide, for a "looksee" at the little affairs. They might have been children's playhouses, they were so small. Two or three were in the jungle which had grown around them, making it impossible to get to them; but one stood closer to the edge of the rocky bank. It was inclosed and roofed over, with windows in the front which revealed a grave within; while in front of the little house stood a broken shaft of gray marble, with the figure of a "kit whale," or killer-whale lying in the grass at the base.

The odd affairs were "dead-houses" in which the natives buried their dead when the missionaries had weaned them from cremation. They were evidently very old and their nearness to the village indicated they were among the first made.

Later, when we rowed through the channel from the inlet to the bay into which Klawock creek flows, we saw a picket fence standing on the steep rocky slope of the shore with two kit whales carved in wood on each of the front corner posts. Within was a concrete slab in which the body of a little two year old child had been buried; and close by lay the decayed remains of an old mattress. What else there may have been originally, was concealed by the rank growth of brambles.

At another time, on a trip to Craig, we passed a small rocky knob sticking out of the water in front of Canoe Pass. On it were several of the dead houses and when Alma and I rowed around to it later and landed, we found beside the dead houses two weathered marble totem stones—one, erected to *Jennie Bell* who, the stone said, died in 1850; and the other, to *Chief Tom Takite*.

It was an odd stone, designed like a block of marble with the after end of a whale rising from it, tail in the air; while from the side of that block oozed out what might have been taken for a bear, except that the fore feet were those of a lamb. I suspect it was a dramatized Thlinget idea, flavored from the white man's country, because a lamb is not a Thlinget institution.

Only one of the dead houses bore indication of its contents, but about that were piled what was left of an iron bedstead, a bed spring, and a mattress. I understood that, because when the natives became Christianized, gave up cremation, and took to burying their dead, they could no longer spiritualize the food, clothing, weapons and personal effects of the deceased by burning them, so they adopted the only other possibility—that of piling all such things, even to sewing machines and phonographs, about the grave where they would be accessible if needed by the spirit, and free from molestation, for who would rob a spirit by stealing from its grave?

One day John Dick came in to consult me on some matter and told me that when his brother died he left everything to him— his gas boat, a new rifle, a fine big phonograph, etc.

"But," he explained, "I no had use for phonograph, so I put him on grave."

It sounded strange and weird to me at the time, but later, when we came to understand more about what has gone before with these people, we could see the breaking down of old customs going on. There was the instinctive impulse to pile the belongings of the dead man on his grave, but it had been modernized by self-interest to a point where only those things not desired by the living were so dedicated.

John possibly is not musical, which would be unusual for a Thlinget, or he may already have possessed a phonograph of his own, which is most likely. He had use for the rifle and the gas boat, but the phonograph he could spare.

Self-interest is displacing the rule of custom with the Thlingets.

Often during the months we have been here, have we heard the band playing a dirge and when we have looked down upon the plank street, have seen the procession of natives, maybe carrying the flag-draped casket down to the dock, or possibly trundling it along on the baggage truck. Behind would walk with solemn mien the members of the interested clans. It used to be that mourners would be hired for the occasion, and pall bearers, in order to make a pretentious showing and properly honor the hovering spirit of the departed. Whether that is still done I do not know, but I am under the impression that the native funeral is strictly a clanal affair. A funeral cortege is never a cheerful sight, but somehow these stolid, unemotional followings of mortal remains down to the water's edge—the drifting of the gas boats with their burdens down the inlet and across to the *beautiful green island,* with band playing and the stars and stripes waving, stirs a feeling in the breast akin to awe, and we have felt a strong interest in what might lie at the far end of that boat trip. The other day we put on our rubber boots and rowed over to the cemetery. It is in sight of the village on the near end of an island a mile or more distant—one of those rocky Alaska islands which is covered with a jungle of forest growth—a tangle of everything imaginable —windfalls, big stumps, standing trees, salmonberry bushes, the ubiquitous devil's club, immense brakes and much else. There is no soil. The rock is covered by a spongy mass of rotten wood, partly decayed vegetation and roots reeking with water, and offers no firm footing for the trees, so they have toppled over from their own weight or have fallen before the wind and lie criss-crossed in an impenetrable snarl, while the rapidly growing brush and brakes and the fast accumulating moss choke the interstices. Think of trying to make a cemetery out of such a location, but it has to be done if there is to be burying.

Of course real burial is impossible under such conditions, so the natives clear the jungle in a little patch big enough for a grave, dig a shallow hole to contain a box made of rough lumber, and when the casket has been placed in the box, the whole is buried in a big slab of concrete, possibly six by twelve feet. This is oftentimes largely on top of the ground, sometimes as much as two feet above the surrounding surface. Then they may build a little pavilion over it, which may be simply a shingled roof supported on four posts; others may be completely inclosed, some with windows on one side, others without any; and in those shelters they will place the cherished belongings of the dead. In one little dead house open on one side, there was a shelf running around the other three sides, on which a little child's playthings were carefully arranged—dolls, toys, a doll's carriage, even the little white hair brush which is found among most babies' belongings. It was a heart-touching sight.

Artificial flower wreaths, crosses, etc. are freely used in decoration and the American flag, while the older generation generally displays the ceremonial robe or blanket, which is a valuable and greatly cherished article.

Of course the graves show great variation in appearance due to the amount of money spent upon them. In the older buryings concrete was not used, and simple frame houses, sometimes floored, were erected. In one corner of the jungle a small tent had been set up over the grave and the brambles and weeds grew as rank within it as in a hothouse. In other places, simply a low fence surrounded the grave, while in some cases the graves have already become so encompassed by the fiercely growing jungle as to be completely inaccessible.

On some of the graves a teakettle sat on the concrete slab, containing water; and on one, besides the teakettle, there was a new aluminum kettle with a lid, containing oranges, bananas and other food, and a bottle of pop; while on others were plates on which food had doubtless been placed at one time which the ravens and other creatures of the wild had diverted to their own uses.

Near the tent-covered grave hung a heavy Hudson Bay blanket on which totem figures of the grampus, like the one on Mrs. Cook-Jack's, had been outlined in pearl buttons. When I touched the blanket many of the buttons rattled off upon the ground and the rest will soon follow, because the thread was so decayed as to have lost all its strength.

We were at a loss to explain the frequent appearance of the teakettle on the graves, but our information bureau told us that the natives are great hands to drink from the teakettle. They pour the water down their throats from the spout . . . The teakettles were there so that the thirsty spirits might drink.

Besides the funeral, with its accompanying obligations, there are numerous other occasions which call for feasting and ceremony, such as the building of the rough box, the coffins are usually bought today and are carried in stock by Bob, digging the grave, doing the concrete work, making the grave fence, building the dead house, setting up the grave stone, and so on. All such labor must be paid for generously, but expense is coveted and pride and satisfaction follow—never regret, with the Thlingets.

Chapter XXX

INHERITANCE

My first lesson in connection with inheritance among the Thlinget Indians came through an early interview with John Dick, a native fisherman. John came in one Sunday afternoon: I didn't know why he should come, and I didn't know why he had come, after he had gone. As I have thought about the matter since in the light of some of the things I have learned, I think I understand.

In November, 1926, Charlie Brown died. He was a Klawock resident, and quite contrary to the usual custom among the natives, he left a will, drawn by the school principal, in which he devised his gas boat and other property to his three children, of which a son, Edmond, was the oldest. This will was probated before the United States Commissioner at Craig, and so far as I could see, everything was O.K. and settled, and there was nothing more to be said or done about it. But it seems there was. The matter was far from settled as it stood, because the whole proceeding bumped up hard against native custom.

Charlie Brown had a brother, Charlie Jackson, living in Klawock; another brother, Charlie Johnson, living in Kake, a Thlinget village on Baranoff Island; and a sister, Maggie Jackson. When I asked John Dick about the assortment of names, he explained that Charlie Brown's father was called just "Charlie" by the white men, so all the boys were called Charlie, with other names attached. As a matter of logic, the sons should have been called *Brown Charlie, Jackson Charlie, Johnson Charlie,* and the girl, *Maggie Charlie,* but they weren't.

John Dick was a cousin, which I suppose means, on the mother's side. He explained that the brother, Charlie Jackson, married Charlie Brown's wife. I understand now that that was quite the orthodox Thlinget practice, and that because he did so, he should have been heir to Charlie Brown's gas boat and other property, as well as to his wife and children—a case of inheriting an undivided estate of which the wife and children were a part; but knowing nothing of the native psychology, it looked to me like rank injustice to deprive, what appeared to be the natural heirs of the deceased, the wife and children, of their inheritance as decreed to them by the court; yet I could see that John, evidently acting as spokesman for the clan, was hoping that

I would see things from their point of view and overturn the Commissioner's decision. Evidently they preferred to do things in accordance with the white man's law, if it didn't interfere too much with their own ideas of justice. I am afraid I disappointed him, but maybe he didn't understand me any better than I did him, and failed to comprehend my views on the matter.

In the course of time I learned that the question was settled in conformance with Thlinget custom, regardless of the probated will and of the moral support I had given it, and Charlie Jackson was the recognized owner of the boat. And now I know it was right to be so. Charlie Jackson has married the widow, Kitty Brown, not from love, but because she had to be supported and the children raised, and he was the one elected by native custom and the clan to take over the responsibilities. It is very easy to make mistakes when one does not understand what he is doing, and mine was the usual white man's conception of inheritance.

It would be quite unfortunate that the Thlingets should be entirely subject to the white man's law and courts, which the natives cannot comprehend at all, were it not that where law is administered with a desire for justice, the white man's court makes its decree and turns its attention to something else, while the natives quietly adjust things to suit themselves.

Not very long ago, Sam Thomas, a very intelligent native of the village, came to see me one evening and asked me to go and make a will for James Skinna, who was dying, so I went with him to the Skan Johnson house where Skinna lived. It is a large house, somewhat on the order of a modern community house, and several families lived in it. His old mother was at the bedside and Skan Johnson and his sons, J. S. Johnson and Sam Thomas, who is Skan's son-in-law, were also in the room. Sam acted as interpreter. The man himself, was scarcely conscious, but the people talked among themselves and with Mrs. Skinna, and Sam told me the results. Everything was to go to the mother, including his gas boat, the "High Wind," his row boat, the stock he owned in the Klawock Commercial Company, etc.; and after considerable talk among themselves, Sam explained that several years before, after a prosperous fishing season, Jimmie Skinna had turned $500 over to Jim Johnson (they trust one another in that way) and Jim, in accordance with the native practice, had turned it over to his wife Bessie, to take care of—quite the orthodox thing for him to do. Bessie, however, proved to be rather in advance of her race and stepped "high, wide and handsome," but no one suspected where the money for the stepping came from until she deserted her old husband and, to make the chasm of separation complete, told him that it was Jimmie Skinna's money she had spent, which was a violation of trust according to the native code, that cut deeply. Jim had repaid part of the money and proposed to repay the rest as rapidly as possible, but the mother insisted that it must be Bessie who repaid it. It was finally decided that Bessie must repay $100 of the amount and the husband could repay the rest and the will so stated. It touched me to see how keenly all present felt the shame of Bessie's conduct. She is married again and it would seem doubtful to me that she would ever repay it, but it is evident that the clanal influence is a powerful one and it may prevail.

About two weeks later Old Mrs. Skinna came to me, with Annie Brown to act as interpreter, and wanted to know about the will. She was so distraught that night that she could not remember what was done. Before leaving Annie told me that Bessie was in town again and information as to her use of Jimmie's money had been communicated to her totemic group and caused great excitement. A meeting of the tribe had been held to consider the matter and the shame that had been cast upon them all. Unless the old customs have broken down more than I think, they will see that the disgrace is satisfactorily wiped out.

Inheritance among the Thlingets passes not, as with us, from father to son and other children, but from the father to the father's brothers or to the sisters' sons. When I first learned that I became considerably *steamed up* over the injustice there, for so far as the children are concerned, the father doesn't count. He is purely an accident in their lives, which may in a way, explain why there are so often several "accidents" in the same family.

At the same time the mother's property goes, not to her husband, but to the members of her own family, even though her husband is turned out of doors thereby, as in the case of old Cook-Jack. When his wife died he had to leave the house to someone else and step out and find a hole of his own to crawl into.

In earlier days a chief's property—holdings, power and influence would descend to a sister's son, and that inheritance involved taking over the widow as wife by the heir, even though he be a mere child and she an old woman. If he already had a wife, he married the second one—in the primitive days—but later, when the missionaries had driven out polygamy, he had to leave the first wife for the second, and the clan in turn, saw that the abandoned wife was properly provided with another husband in the same clan.

A house in the event of death, did not go to the heir, but to the one who helped most in its construction, unless it happened that the owner definitely named the one to inherit it. Such a wish was always respected.

A man's widow may dispose of her husband's effects—canoe, gun, traps, etc. as she sees fit, unless he himself has indicated who should be the future owners.

The nurse shocked us greatly when she told us how Cook-Jack had had to leave his home and how the members of the clan had stripped the place clean, but it was not nearly so bad as it looked, for each one coming into possession of any of the dead one's possessions would have to amply compensate the family with generous gifts at the ceremonies and feasts which would follow.

Chapter XXXI

WITCHCRAFT AND
THE MEDICINE MAN

One morning after school had called, John Darrow and one of the village marshals came to the schoolhouse and wanted to see a girl in one of the rooms. She was allowed to go out to them and after much talk in "native," the men tapped on the door and said they would like to talk to the children.

It seems the little girl in question, in her association with the other children, had referred to Mrs. Darrow as a "witch." The idea of course, did not originate with the child, and it did not stop with her, for it evidently had been repeated and was going the rounds of the village, or more accurately speaking—had gone the rounds.

The days of the "Salem Witchcraft" are so far in the background and the whole episode seems so ridiculous to us today, that it is not easy to believe that people ever took the idea of witches seriously. To suddenly have it erupt directly under our noses and be of so serious a nature as it appeared to be, was decidedly startling.

The incident had passed before it came to my attention, but the teachers pursued the proper course—let the natives handle it themselves—and John and the marshal did that. Of course the teachers could not know what was said to the children in Thlinget, but the big eyes and sober faces showed there had been some plain and emphatic talk. After talking very earnestly to the children, John turned to the teacher and explained in his halting speech that the little girl had been telling that Mrs. Darrow was a witch. He said the people in Klawock are Christians now. They have been baptized and know there is no such thing as witches, but it is a terrible thing to accuse anyone of being a witch and it must not be done. The marshal then took a hand and told the children that he would arrest any child and put her in jail who talked about anyone being a witch. The children's faces showed they took him seriously, for they were a very subdued lot.

It was evident that something very disturbing to the community had happened, but we could not understand why it should be so disturbing at the time. Through the nurse and other channels we have gathered information that makes the incident a little more intelligible.

Charlie Chuck one day, during one of his voluble spells, confided to the nurse that his aunt, that would be one of his mother's sisters, became blind. To the Thlingets there could be but one cause for such a misfortune—someone had bewitched her—so, according to Charlie's tale, two of the young men had decided that a certain man in the village was the guilty party. They took him out in the wilderness and tied him nude to a stake, where they left him for two days, without food or water, unable to sit or lie down and at the mercy of insects and the weather. On their return they beat him with devil's club, then took him in a boat where the water was 100 fathoms deep, and threw him overboard. When he came to the surface and tried to struggle into the boat, they beat him off with their paddles. Charlie said he sank deep down into the sea and when he came up he had a skull with something in it. They pulled him out and threw him in again on the other side of the boat. Once more he sank and was gone a long time. When he came to the surface he had something else and they spared his life. As a result of the treatment of the witch, Charlie's aunt was cured and has been able to see ever since.

That isn't a yarn, but the account of what Charlie emphatically knows to be true. There is his aunt. Anyone can tell that she isn't blind now.

As for the chap who was bullied into calling off the evil spirits, I don't know what he thinks about it, but it is plain that he either is thoroughly broken in body and spirit by what he has been through, or that he was an incompetent in the first place—an abnormal—and possibly was picked on that account; either because it could be done with safety, or because they explained his abnormality as due to his association with evil spirits.

These incidents are of modern times when religion and education are supposed to have freed the natives from their benighted ideas. Imagine the situation then, in their premissionary days, when belief in evil spirits and witches was universal and the shaman, or medicine man, was their sole means of protection. The more insight we gain into the Thlinget psychology and superstitions, the more we realize that their belief in witches was unquestionably one of the strongest influences in their lives, and the story of witchcraft must perforce, be the story of the shaman

—a Russian term applied to the native medicine man, or "Iht."

They believed that spirits were everywhere and in everything, and that those spirits were largely evil or ill-disposed. Consequently the great effort of their lives was to keep on the right side of the spirits and to placate those that had taken offense for any reason—and they were easily offended. For instance, the birth of twins was considered so offensive to the spirits that in their primitive days members of the clan hastened to pacify the offended spirits by stuffing moss into the mouths of the infants so they couldn't cry, and abandoning them in the jungle to die from exposure or wild animals.

If the northern heavens indulged in an unusual display of the aurora borealis, that was taken as an evil omen, for it indicated that some one was to be killed to go up in the sky: not very unlike our childish belief that every time a star fell, some one died.

Most sickness was attributed to the action of evil spirits, especially in the case of a wasting disease, or one that had weird manifestations such as delirium, epilepsy, insanity and other mental troubles—just as the Bible tells of those "possessed of the devil." Witches were supposed to be responsible for the activity of the evil spirits, and it was the business of the witch doctor to identify the one who was exercising the malign influence. If the medicine man, by his incantations and exorcisms was unable to drive out the demons and the patient died, the shaman placed the responsibility on a witch and undertook to identify him. Individuals sometimes made accusations, but the doctor was considered the official witch-finder and he was very jealous of his prerogatives. There were only one or two Ihts in a community—competition may be the life of trade from the white man's view point, but the shaman did not crave it. Some communities had none and were forced to. patronize their neighbor's.

Medicine men were supposed to be born, not made. Occasionally the office was passed on by heredity, but more commonly not. As a rule any peculiar differentiation of a child at birth, such as red hair, cross eyes, or other peculiar marks, resulted in the infant being consecrated to the profession, and from that moment he was held in special awe and no water, comb, or shears was allowed to touch his head. Like Samson, of the Bible, his power was supposed to lie in his hair; the more matted and frightful became its appearance, the more power lay behind it.

To put a shaman out of business—again the resemblance to Samson—it was only necessary to shear his tangled mop.

As the child grew to manhood and entered upon the duties of his profession, he affected mannerisms that might add to the general effect and indulged in weird eccentricities, and practices in eating and otherwise, of the most disgusting nature. He would fast for long periods, then would feast on the bark of devil's club and even eat parts of dead bodies. The more revolting his habits and ways, the more evident it was to the Indians that the Iht was not as other men, but was especially marked; and indeed he became so, for he took on a peculiarly frightful expression. His eyes became deepset, with protruding pupils—fiercely keen— but concealed by a furtive manner. It must have given the superstitious native the "creeps" just to look upon a shaman.

The power wielded by the medicine man seems astounding to us, and often it became a vicious influence in a community, especially if the medicine man and the chief leagued together for the purpose of extortion, as sometimes happened.

The customary fee for the services of the medicine man used to be ten blankets, or so many skins of a certain kind, or "what have you?"—this, regardless of whether the patient came to his office or the doctor had to make a call; and was on the scale of the best city prices for medical services today. The "doctor" of those days however, had more confidence than the medical men of our day, for he guaranteed results—"cure or money back"—in the event of failure, the charge was not only refunded, but the medicine man was heavily penalized by the patient's clan for malpractice. That issue however, was usually avoided with the help of a smoke screen, by placing the blame for the innocuousness of his efforts on someone among their number who was a witch—just who that party might be, however, could only be revealed on the payment of another generous fee, for it was a delicate matter and a heavy drain on the vitality of the Iht.

Quite wisely the witch doctor generally discovered the guilty party to be a slave or someone of little importance in the community—an odd character, one who was already looked at askance, or someone against whom the Iht had a grudge; but there were times when influential and prominent individuals were accused by the shaman, and so absolute was the confidence of the natives in their medicine man, that such a charge would be accepted without question. Even the accused party not only never thought of denying the accusation, but would even admit it and would accept the consequences without opposition.

When the witch was definitely identified by the shaman, who would throw himself into a convulsion followed by a trance, during which the guilty party was revealed by his special spirits, the witch was promptly seized and, with a near relative of his clan acting as master of ceremonies, he was put through a course of torture that was limited only by the imagination of those presiding. The victim was beaten with devil's club, stoned, slashed with knives, pierced with splinters thrust into the flesh, or tied to stakes at low tide so that he slowly drowned from the splashing waves. Frequently he would be rigidly bound with the knees against the chin and thrown into holes beneath the houses where he was allowed to starve and his naked body suffer from the cold; or he might be thrown bound, on a bed of thorns or devil's club; or left lying on the beach under the heat of the sun and the chill of night, and subject to the attacks of insects and hungry dogs.

No one dared furnish relief to an accused witch or even approach him, for the terror of witches was so great, and no accused person escaped when his guilt was once established. Should one survive through any miracle of endurance, he remained an outcast for all time and was subject to mental torture as great as the physical. Whether those accused were thrown into a condition of hysteria through fright, which caused them to admit they were guilty, or whether everyone believed so implicitly in the shaman that no one thought of doubting his assertions, is hard to say. Probably both things were true.

I seem to catch a glimpse of what these people have been going through. It is not surprising that in the few short years that have passed, they have not emerged entirely from the shadow of the woods.

That the shaman should reach his position of power is not surprising. He was a psychologist and a fraud; but it is also possible that he was self-hypnotized and that he actually accepted as true all the power attributed to him by the natives. We can see just such power exercised today among supposedly intelligent people, although the manifestations do not take quite the Thlinget form.

The idea that the Thlinget medicine man was more than human, was firmly established. In the event of death, his spirit was supposed to enter another body, such as a red—or curly-haired child; while his body, which it was believed could not be burned, was held in terrible awe and was wrapped in the finest furs or blankets. The face was painted red and the hair was dusted with eagles' down. The body, bound in a sitting posture with the knees and chin together, and wrapped like a mummy, was placed in a dead house made of logs or boards supported on posts and located on some high point of land on an island, overlooking the sea, or hidden in a hollow tree, or placed in a box in the fork of a tree in the forest, or otherwise hidden. When the place of sequestration was known the locality was given a wide berth by the natives, but if compelled to pass near it, they made some sort of a peace offering to the spirit of the shaman to placate it.

Cherished belongings of the Iht were treated in somewhat the same way. They might consist of peculiar stones or pieces of wood, perforated shells, rags, bits of blankets, finger nail fragments, tufts of hair, the dried tongues of birds, frogs or mice, or anything weird and unusual to which he had attributed power as great as that of the "sacred relics" known to the white man.

It all sounds strange and impossible. Yet we have had the left-over influence of their primitive days break to the surface before our eyes, and I am not at all certain that there is no one in the village at the present time who is considered to have the power of a shaman. We are utterly ignorant of what has been going on about us among the natives, but it is evident that the tongues have been busily clucking, and terror has been stirred in the hearts of—who knows how many? Over what? . . . It would be interesting to know, but impossible to ascertain.

Again I am impressed, as I was during my work among the peasants of Central Europe and the primitives of Albania, with the tremendous effect upon the people of the traditions and customs and the influence of ancestors. Let such people be removed from their environment, as when they leave their native land to come to America from Europe or Alaska, and that influence is minimized, but let them remain in or return to their native heath, and the progress is smothered under the blanket of what has gone before.

Chapter XXXII

FISHING

This is a village of fishermen. Before the coming of the white man, the Thlinget had no occupation other than the struggle for existence which was not a very serious one—except when nature went off on a tangent, as sometimes happens—because she furnished food, clothing and shelter.

The sea furnished a wide variety and by far the greater share of their food, but the sea diet was supplemented by the game which filled the forests. Hunting the wild goat, bear, deer, seal and other fur-bearing animals, originally supplied them with attire, such as it was; and their houses consisted mostly of bark and pine bough shelters.

The early Russians brought ideas which modified the life of the natives somewhat and increased their needs. Blankets took the place of the skin and fur clothing, and crude houses replaced the cruder, frail shelters. They learned to carve and make a fiercely stimulating drink called "hooch-i-noo"; to use fire arms and some of the white man's tools; but fishing remained one of the main activities. They had carried it on along the fish streams with primitive spears tipped with sharpened pieces of bone, which they used very effectively when the salmon were running. They fished for the deep water halibut with exceedingly crude hooks fashioned from wood and bone, and lines made from the fine rootlets of the spruce which were so skilfully woven as to be almost imperishable.

When the white man came with better equipment the natives were quick to adopt it and fished to much better advantage.

Their first "ships" were the big cedar war canoes in which they traveled great distances—even so far as the Puget Sound country—in their hunt for adventure and slaves. It seems surprising that that should have been possible because they had no compasses or scientific knowledge; but their keenness of observation was highly developed because their very existence depended on noticing and interpreting little things. It was that struggle for self-preservation that has made them such close observers of the weather and the ways of the wind and the sea; and their eyes have searched the heavens also and found stars by which they have been able to guide their boats. The Big Dipper is their old

238

standby, but the Little Dipper, or Pleiades, is an old friend which they call by the Thlinget name for the sculpin, which is one of the fish of the sea. They have noticed the three stars of the constellation Orion, which they call "the three men in a line," while Venus, when a morning star, they call "morning round thing."

Undoubtedly they have their legends for all these figures of the sky, as they have for Pleiades. That one in particular, enters into the training of their youth and is used to inculcate modesty and discourage boastfulness. They say that Yalth, the raven, the mythical figure of many of their tales, saw a sculpin on the beach one day and hid in order to see what the sculpin might do. The latter, after a time, swam out into the ocean and went down out of sight. Yalth followed at a distance and opening the door of the ocean, went down into the house of the sculpin, which was hidden under a great rock, and called, "My younger brother, is this you?"

The sculpin denied that he was Yalth's brother, but Yalth insisted it must be so.

"But how can I be your younger brother," insisted the sculpin, "when I am a very old man?"

Yalth wasn't to be discouraged and insisted, "My home is in the sky and I want you there with me. There will be many sculpins, but you shall be chief of all," so he caught sculpin by the tail and with a mighty heave, threw him up in the sky where he stuck.

"That is so," the Thlingets insist, "because if you look up on a starlit night, you will see him sticking there. White man call sculpin Nippen Dippen," Little Dipper, they say.

The natives are quick to see and apply a lesson, so when one of their number assumes to know more than the others, someone tells the story of sculpin and ends with, "If sculpin could not make Raven believe he was old and wise, you can't make us believe you are old and know more than we do." The story teller wins.

Probably the natives fished from their canoes when the salmon were running strong, though they did much of their spearing from the overhanging banks of streams, or improvised ways of getting the fish into shallow water where they could toss them out on the bank. The canoes were necessary however, for the halibut fishing and when the herring and eulikon were running. Later, sailing craft supplanted the canoes, for they could range over greater distances, but now the gas boat is in universal use.

The halibut is a flat fish which hugs the bottom of the sea in deep water and sometimes reaches enormous size—even five or six hundred pounds. I have seen them hoist fish from the holds of the native boats at Bob's dock by means of a winch, that tipped the scales at 120 pounds and were as long as the height of the men handling them. Bob says they are often much larger.

The halibut belongs to the flounder family and is both a very peculiar fish and a great delicacy on the table. They tell me that when the halibut is young it appears to be a normal fish and acts that way, but gradually it takes to lying on the bottom of the sea and waiting for its food to drift around to it, instead of pursuing it like an active, self-respecting fish. As that habit grows on it a peculiar thing happens: one of its eyes gradually travels over on top of the head until both are on the same side, and the fish lies on its side with the two eyes staring upward. But that isn't the only peculiar thing about it, for I am assured that in the northern hemisphere the halibut lies with its left side to the bottom and the left eye does the traveling; but south of the equator it lies on its right side and the right eye travels around to keep company with the other. Now why, I ask, should that be?

Not satisfied with all this freak conduct, the halibut proceeds to deck itself out in white on the underside and a slate color or brown, on the upper side, but the Bureau of Fisheries man who told me all this, says it is not a matter of darkening on the "sunny" side, because no light whatever penetrates the sea to where the halibut lives its lazy life. Evidently it is simply one of nature's provisions for concealing the halibut from its enemies, or more likely, from that which it preys upon, just as the plumage of birds that live on the ground, and the skins of snakes, blend in with their surroundings.

The boats that specialize in halibut fishing are easily recognized by the nature of the gear piled on their decks and by the goose-neck-like affair at the stern over which the lines are hauled in.

Halibut fishing is done by means of set lines fastened to long heavier lines which are kept on the surface by means of floats marked with red flags on a floating pole. The set lines are baited with herring and dropped down to the bottom. In the days when the Thlingets fished with wooden fishhooks, they used to carve the clumsy affairs in the shape of animals, and hooks representing the raven and the land otter were thought to be the most successful because Raven was believed to have made the world, and the land otter was supposed to take people away from the world and make hobgoblins of them, and to run things under the sea. To see themselves portrayed on the hooks was supposed to develop an amiable feeling on their part towards the fisherman so they would encourage the fish to bite. Flattery was known even in those days.

While baiting the hooks on his halibut line, the Thlinget used to talk to them and to the floats, calling them "brother-of-my-wife," "father-of-my-wife," and other intimate names, because they believed if great respect were not shown to them spirits were supposed to occupy everything, and among the Thlingets the *in-laws* on the mother's side, were taken very seriously, the spirits would feel ashamed and mortified and would not let the fish bite. He would also spit on his hook and say to it, "Go right to the fireplace—hit the rich man's daughter." When that was done the hook would not be ashamed.

After the halibut line was set, if the fisherman felt a twitching at the corner of his mouth, he knew he had hooked a large fish, and if the twitching were on the right side, that he would have good luck and land his catch.

To what extent these beliefs and practices are still entertained, I cannot say, but I think it would surprise us if we did know. Bob has told me that when he was a boy and the salmon were running, he and his mates would go to shallow places upstream, and imitating the grown-ups, would make traps by pushing sticks down into the sand of the stream-bed to form a barrier across the current, then would arrange stones or small boulders below the stakes somewhat like a dam; then the boys would stand on the bank and talk to the fish in the stream—cajole them and taunt them by calling them insulting names with the idea that if they could please or anger the fish, they would leap the stone dam into their traps when the boys would wade in and toss the fish out on the bank.

The salmon were the great standby of the natives in the primitive days and they still are today, although salmon fishing with them is a very different thing than it used to be.

There are five different species of salmon in the North Pacific waters: the *chinook,* or king salmon—sometimes called the tyee, which means chief in the Chinook jargon; the *sockeye,* blueback, or red salmon; the coho, or silver salmon; the *hump-*

back, or pink; and the *chum,* or ketah—often called the dog
salmon. They differ in size and habits and make their runs at
different seasons.

Unlike those of the Atlantic, the salmon of these waters
spawn but once and within a few days die, after their mission in
life has been fulfilled. It seems a strange thing, but it is claimed
that the Pacific salmon always return to the stream to spawn
in which they themselves were spawned and that they do not
feed at all during their spawning migration.

The men have told me that years ago, before the tremendous
inroads had been made on the salmon population of the Pacific by
the canneries, that the run of salmon was a most remarkable
thing to see. It is still for one who is not accustomed to it; and to
watch the struggling horde push its way up a fish creek, regardless
of obstacles, fills one with awe.

Today, instead of the old spearing and primitive trapping,
the salmon are caught in great traps or are seined by the natives
for the canneries, although in securing their personal supply
for the winter, they revert more or less to their old methods and
spear them from the high banks along the narrow channels,
where the living tide of lunging fish surges upstream in an almost
solid mass.

Besides salmon and the herring, there is a fish called the
eulikon, or candle fish, about a foot long and on the herring
order, which is finely flavored and is considered a great delicacy
by the natives. I haven't seen it, but they talk about the eulikon
run as they do about fish-egg-time. These fish however, are found
only in certain localities like the Stikine river, which is quite a
bit to the north of us, and only for a period of two or three weeks.

Both the eulikon and the herring are brailed from the stream
either with a dip net or by means of the long poles I have described to you. When a generous supply of the eulikons had been
secured in the early days, they were dumped into holes in the
ground where they were allowed to putrify or ripen, which developed a special flavor much appreciated. When ripe the mass
was dipped into canoes and heated stones were dropped in to
cook it and try out the oil which rose to the top. When cool the
oil on the surface resembled butter or lard and was used in the
same way we use those substances.

The holes for ripening the eulikon were used year after
year and as one might suppose, the oil saturated ground took
on the odor which the whites would go a long way round to

escape. A slaughter house smell is said to be mild compared with it. There are people who eat limburger cheese and enjoy it, so why shouldn't it be possible for the natives to consider ripe eulikon a delicacy?

I have been told of another delicacy in the way of fish food which is prized by the Indians—that is the snout of the humpback salmon, which becomes much elongated at running time; and the raw head and tail of the silver salmon—that is, it is raw to our sense, but the natives do not consider it so because they say once upon a time a raven cooked those parts and they have remained cooked ever since.

But of all their delicacies, eulikon oil is chief, and after dipping off the oil that rises to the surface of the cooked mass, it is put into receptacles of any and every nature, even including the immense hollow stems of the kelp taken from the sea. Dried salmon, herring, venison and various other cured foods are dipped in it and eaten; while berries, salmon and herring roe, seaweed, and others of their winter stores are packed in it for winter use.

At their feasts the natives gorge themselves on the oil until they become saturated with it to a point where it pickles them, as it were, and makes them resistant to cold. When the oil is carefully skimmed it becomes almost as white as lard on cooling, can be spread like butter, and remains sweet a long time.

The eulikon was put to another use which gave it the name *candle fish*. Because of their remarkable richness in oil the natives were accustomed to dry them and run the pith of the cattail or rush, or strips of the inside of cedar bark through them like a candle wick. When stuck headfirst into the ground and light was applied to the wick at the tail, the melting grease would burn like tallow. Of course the light was hardly like that of our incandescent electric lamps but there was no reading to do, so all the light they needed was enough to see to get around.

Of course the contact with the whites has brought many changes into the lives of the Thlingets and things are not done as they were in the good old days, but their native foods are as dearly loved as of yore. The candle fish is no longer their source of light, but it still tastes as delectable to their palates; and while fishing does not play so vital a part in their lives as a means of sustenance, it plays a more vital part in furnishing them the money to purchase those things from the white man's world which have come to be necessities to them—as they are to us.

Chapter XXXIII

THE CLOSE OF SCHOOL

The school year closed April 29th and the closing was a big event. Alma and the other teachers planned an extensive and rather unique program and once under way, it had to be carried through to success.

What form our "doings" of the last day should take, was quite a problem. The program needed to be entertaining and impressive in order to stimulate the proper reaction in the village, but it was one thing to see what was necessary, and quite another to see how it should be accomplished. A school of over one hundred pupils offers plenty of material, but when the ages run from six to twenty-one, the material is not very uniform. It was desirable to have a joint program and eventually, after carefully canvassing the situation, we decided to take advantage of the dramatic instincts of the native children and prepare a program that, instead of being arranged on the old bromidic lines of the *last day of school* in the States, should present dramatically something of the life of America's aborigines. Each teacher, taking the material she had worked with in the classroom, sought to contribute an element to the general program, and of course a good deal of extraneous entertainment was furnished in addition.

The main features of the entertainment were a scenic reading from Hiawatha, and a tableau of Pocahontas and John Smith, by the older pupils; a drill, a "Frolic of the Frogs," by twenty of the younger boys; and numerous ornamental and pretty drills by the primary children; with much singing.

We had the big town hall at our disposal for our doings, but the stage lacked curtains and scenery, so we had to improvise our own equipment. We would have liked to stage the program out of doors, but the weather was too cool, and we always have to figure on rain. We used the floor of the hall for our stage and seated the audience along one side, while the school children sat on the other, which left the basketball floor in between. I had constructed two teepees. It may sound odd that I, a white man from the States, should be the one to make teepees in an Indian village, but this is not the country of the wigwam up here—too much rain, I imagine. Well I erected two teepees, one at each end of our stage, and had cut and dragged in good-sized young spruce and hemlock trees, which I grouped about the wigwams—standing them in nail kegs filled with stones. Old sails strewn with moss and leaves served for the ground, and mossy logs and shrubbery completed an effective setting. Because we couldn't shift scenery, we changed ends of the stage when we needed a change of scene.

The stage was set for scenes from Hiawatha. At one end
"Stood the wigwam of Nokomis . . .
Dark behind it rose the forest
Rose the black and gloomy pine trees."
At the other end stood the home of Hiawatha and
". . . . . . . the Ancient Arrow-Maker,
On the outskirts of the forest."

Indian blankets, baskets and other paraphernalia of primeval man gave realism to the wigwam.

Elsie Armour, the best reader in school, stood at one side and read from the poem the selections we had staged. The actors recited their parts.

Ella Gunyah, a frail, dark-skinned maiden, with marked Thlinget features, took the part of Nokomis. Hiawatha, the baby, a huge doll, lay in his 'linden cradle' (improvised), while his grandmother sang
"Ewa-yea! my little owlett"

Ella has psychic power—strong, even for an Indian—to visualize the unseen, and she carried her audiences with her as she taught to little Hiawatha spirit stories, legends and songs. When he grew out of babyhood into a little boy, Lawrence Demmert took the part. Lawrence is a sturdy, keen little youngster six years old. His black eyes flashed the spirit of the poem as he pointed his stubby little finger at the moon, conveniently hung up among the rafters of the hall, and hoarsely whispered, "What is that Nokomis?"

Harold Jones, a lithe, graceful lad of fourteen, represented the youth, Hiawatha, as
"Out of childhood, into manhood," he entered.

His wooing of Minnehaha stirred romance within our hearts. We had chosen Bessie Dalton, a very winsome and typical Thlinget girl, to take the part of the Indian girl of the poem, but she was so self-conscious that we were fearful she would spoil the play. At no time during rehearsal would she drop her shyness and act, but that night she actually became Minnehaha herself,
"the lovely Laughing Water." It was thrilling.

The part of the "ancient Arrow-Maker" had been assigned to Henry Johnson. He is one of the older boys of the school and one of those intensely earnest, serious plodders as a student, that delights the heart of the teacher. In addition, he has seemed to typify the finest of his race. He is tall, finely proportioned, dignified in bearing, and almost stately in his actions, and has been very earnest in all his work; but the nurse has pronounced his doom—has said that the dread enemy of the Alaskan natives—T.B.—is getting in its work. The pressure and excitement of the close of the year's work affected him and I am confident we have no understanding of the heroic self-mastery that carried him through the final days. We were conscious that all was not right with him, but were too deeply engrossed with the work we had to do to consider everything that came to our attention. Maybe it is just as well. He rose from his bed and with feverish eyes and his dusky face flushed, came to his work. But it was not alone a sense of duty towards his school that upheld him and carried him through; but his psychic nature placed him too, as was the case with Ella, in the character he portrayed, and he lived the part. I believe it was the supreme moment in Henry's life when he stood by the entrance of his wigwam and watched Hiawatha's departure,

"Leading with him Laughing Water."

It was a heart-stirring scene to us all as

"Hand in hand they went together,
Through the woodland and the meadow,
Left the old man standing lonely
At the doorway of his wigwam . . .
And the Ancient Arrow-Maker
Turned again unto his labor,
Sat down by his sunny doorway,
Murmuring to himself, and saying,
'Thus it is our daughters leave us,
Those we love, and those who love us!' "

The most spectacular number on the program was the tableau of the prevented execution of Captain John Smith. The tall pines, their pungent odor in the big room, the dim lights of the hall, and the shadowy forms of the stalwart Indian boys in native costume, moving noiseless with moccasined feet, as they brought in their captive, bound him and laid him with his head on a small log, sent shivers through our own hearts, though I caught a gleam in the eyes of some of the old-timers. It was as a living scene. My heart actually seemed in my throat when the executioner raised his axe. With a wild scream, Pocahontas, acted by pretty Pauline Jones, threw herself between him and the prisoner and shielded Smith with her own little body. Chief Powhaton, again Henry Johnson, strode forward with a commanding gesture. The executioner halted. Pocahontas sought mercy for her friend at her father's feet. He spoke, and Captain Smith was released.

We were not mistaken in my choice for the chief. It seemed to me that no one else could so well express the spirit of those magnificent old chieftans, as Henry. He seemed to embody their spirits. We forgot him and thought only of the patriarchs—we saw them—not the modern youth, and in his taut muscles and gleaming eyes, we sensed the authority and domination that his imperious gesture bespoke. To us it was a dream. To the gray heads of the audience, it was their life that had been, and the youth, steeped in the legend and lore of their race, were living the lives of their forebears. I doubt if any who witnessed the tableau of that historic event will forget it, though without doubt, some will make their own interpretations of it.

The funniest thing we had was the frog dance which I took from one of the educational journals. We intended it simply as a "filler," and it was good, but we were astonished at the way it was received by the audience. The appreciation seemed to be beyond any justification that we could see. During rehearsals the boys' frog antics convulsed us teachers, but the boys never cracked a smile. Being frogs was a serious business to them. We couldn't catch the psychology of the situation. One youngster in particular, Embert Collins, grandson to Tecumseh Collins, a special crony of mine, was almost uncanny in his portrayal of a frog. He squatted on the mossy log with the others, puffed out his cheeks, protruded his belly, stretched his long thin arms and legs, bending them grotesquely like a frog's at elbows and knees, and if ever a boy was a frog in spirit, Embert was one. At each rehearsal he was all over the place, just as a frog would have been, and he sorely taxed my patience. It wasn't that he was trying to appear cute in the eyes of the others. For the time being he actually seemed to be a frog and lived up to the part, but everyone but ourselves took him at face value. The night of the program the boys were dressed in "Twenty little coats of green" and were a scream. They fairly croaked their frogdom, and how they did delight that audience! These Thlingets! I wonder if a white man will ever understand them!

Another feature of the evening was one that might have been viewed with mixed feelings by a white audience. Annie Collins is sister to Embert Collins, the realistic frog, and she is just as interesting as her brother and her rotund grandfather.

We had seen Annie and some of her mates on the school ground one day, entering with much abandon into something which we at first supposed to be a game. They appeared to be acting something out and we assumed that it was simply an eruption of the native dramatic instinct, but the more attention we paid to them, the more interested and curious we became. Finally we asked the children to come in and show us what it was all about. Shy as the little things are, they came, and Annie told us they were dancing the bear dance and singing about what happened when the women saw the bears. It was a confused notion we got of the story, but it intrigued us to watch them and try to interpret their actions, for they put on a "by request" act for us there in the kitchen.

When we decided on the Indian program for the last day, we allowed Annie and her friends to act out their bear story; but we were somewhat astonished at the result.

It was worth seeing that group of a dozen or more dusky girls, ranging from ten to fourteen years, when they got under headway. They chanted a monotonous repetition of some kind, to which they kept time with swaying of the body, stamping of the feet, twitchings of the hands and arms, and jerks of the head; and their eyes shone like black beads as they entered into the spirit of the dance. It had been one thing on which there was no need of coaching—they didn't need coaching any more than a kitten that pretends it is playing with a mouse—and it was something we knew nothing about. We simply told Annie she and her friends could dance the bear dance. It started easily, but was not so easily stopped. We couldn't tell when the dance came to an end and apparently, neither could the children, nor did they care. We finally had to call time on them, much to the seeming regret of Annie, down whose face the perspiration was making shining streaks—and of the audience, many of whom looked as though they would like to get in the ring also.

When it was over we couldn't tell for the life of us, whether it had been a mistake or a successful feature of the program. We thought it was a folk dance, but was it? We sensed something in the air, but didn't know what, nor do we know anymore about it now.

There seemed no way in which we could use the little ones in connection with an Indian program, but it was necessary that they have a share in the day's doings. They certainly had it. Mrs. Millard, the Primary teacher, is an indefatigable worker and she had trained the little soft-eyed youngsters to do many things. They appeared in beautiful many-colored crepe paper costumes which she and Mrs. Range had laboriously devised for them; and represented fairies, butterflies and flowers. They sang and acted their little songs—spoke their parts and airily graced the occasion, delighting the enthusiastic parents. Of course the entire program was interspersed with the singing that so delights the natives, and waves of music rose to the rafters of the big barn of a hall. I think the harmony of the Indian children's voices was one of the inspiring features of the day. They do so love to sing, and they all can sing—every one of them. Even big, uncouth Jimmy Jacobs, rumbles along with the crowd, like the booming of a big bass viol.

That is the story of our last day, but it isn't quite all of the story. It is the story as we saw it at the end of the day, but we have been thinking and talking about it since—Alma and I—and we wonder if it tells it all. It is a strange experience we are having with these Thlingets. Somethings transpires and we behold it as we would an interesting event among our own kind: then, one day, unexpectedly an idea seeps into our minds—we find a question stirring around in our subconsciousness and eventually we become aware that we had unwittingly peeped in on the native psychology. We are coming to the belief that we had several peeps on that last day of school.

Alma had selected James Johnson for the leader of the frog dance. He is a younger brother of Henry and is a fine type of the native youth—beautifully made and with a joyous heart and a smile that won't come off.

In a composition class one day, Alma had told the pupils to write a little description of some teacher they had had and liked. The class got busy, but James sat with a puzzled look on his face. She asked why he wasn't writing and he naively answered, "I can't remember anyone but you." That was James all over. Well, he took great pleasure in the frog dance and seemed very appreciative of the preference that had been shown him, but when the dress rehearsal was staged for the forenoon of the eventful day, James did not appear and all the information forthcoming was that he had gone to Craig. In all the strenuous ordeal of preparation through which Alma had gone, nothing had upset and peeved her as James' defection at the critical moment. But when the frog dance was staged, James was there—the biggest bullfrog in the puddle. We learned later through the nurse, that he had gone to attend a trial that morning before the United States Commissioner, an essential witness for a friend who was in trouble. How he got back in time we haven't learned, but he got back and fulfilled his obligation. The whole proceeding was strictly Indian. What Indian has ever felt that an explanation for anything was due, either before or after? They no more think of offering an explanation for an act, than they think of apologizing for walking into your house without knocking. Their acts are as spontaneous as those of a wild animal. Also, nothing interferes, so far as they are able to control the situation, with their carrying out what they feel to be an obligation. Their idea and ours may not agree, however, concerning the obligation.

Then the frog dance! It was an entertaining fantasy to us, but I suspect it was more than that to the boys and to their audience. We are wondering if the frog isn't among the Collins totems, and if Embert may not really be a "frog" after all. We have been thinking about Annie's bear dance, and are wondering if the frog dance was not also something that had a significance to the natives which we never suspected. We are confident that they saw something more than the funny antics of a lot of boys— but what? Again we are on the outside, without even a knothole to peek through.

And the bear dance—what about that? We don't know, but we have a strong suspicion that under the delusion we were allowing the natural tendency to dramatize, to exercise itself in presenting a folk dance, we were staging an old time Indian dance, pure and simple—not to an audience that was mildly entertained, as would have been the case had the prevailing complexion of the audience been different, but to reminiscent and sympathetic spirits, to whom the thump of a tom tom would have been music, and the flow of whose blood was quickened by the droning chant of the dancers. There may have been reason for the gleam in the black eyes of the spectators and the physical restlessness that possessed them. Annie did not make it clear to us, but by putting things together, we have a notion the story they enacted was that of the chieftain's daughter who went berrying up in the mountains.

What a joke on the white teachers sent up to train the Thlingets in the ways of civilization, if they had instead, set the blood of the primitives surging through their veins and carried their spirits back to the good old aboriginal days! I have a suspicion that the dance to the Thlingets was like the jangling alarm to the city fire horse of days that have passed, or the clamor of battle to the war horses of old.

There is something else that has puzzled us. We know our program was a success. It would have called forth much enthusiasm had it been given in a white community, not alone because of the fine work that was done by the children, but because of its original nature. We know that the townspeople participated most heartily in the pleasure of the evening, but not a soul has said a word to us about it. Now what is the reason for that? Is it due to the Indian trait of non-expression of their emotions? Maybe so! Or is it because their old instincts were so revived and stimulated that their minds have been carried away from the present, back to the glorious past? That is possible. But there remains another possibility. By night of the following day, Klawock was deserted. Everyone who had been waiting for school to close, had slipped across the water to their camp at "The Hole in the Wall." They had no time for polite amenities.

Anyway, school closed with a bang, and it was a closing the children won't forget; while I'll wager the tongues of their elders have done some busy clucking in "native," and many a tale of old has been recounted.

Chapter XXXIV

TROLLING TIME

I went trolling one evening with one of the natives, Bill Gunyah. We started at 5 P.M. at high tide and rowed through Canoe Pass to the outer channel, where we trolled along the shore line for a mile or two towards Craig.

The big king salmon were leaping here and there in a way to tickle a fisherman's enthusiasm, but they did not seem much interested in biting.

Gunyah rowed, as the natives all row, facing the bow of the boat and pushing the oars, while I sat facing him and rowed in the usual way. It is interesting to watch the natives row for they do it so easily, but they do not get the speed of the other way and must have to change in heavy going, because there isn't the power back of it. One cannot push under such conditions as effectively as he can pull, but their method has the advantage of showing them all the time just where they are going. It is doubtless the result of their old paddling days when they always faced the bow of the canoe.

Bill had a heavy line—about a 72 strand line—with a No. 6 spoon—one half copper, the other half nickel or German silver, which he polished like a mirror, while he told me a joke on himself.

To get results the spoons must be kept as bright as possible and the fishermen use a prepared liquid polish and a piece of chamois skin and he says when the fisherman is rubbing up his spoon he says to himself, "Shine em up! Shine em up!" as he rubs. At one time Gunyah was down to Vancouver in some connection and as he walked along the street he heard some one say, "Shine em up! Shine em up!" He looked around but he couldn't see any fisherman polishing his spoon, so he went on. "Pretty quick," he said, "some one say gain, 'Shine em up! Shine em up!' I stop—I look all round—no water—no fishermans—no shining spoon. I go on. Gain man say, 'Shine em up! Shine em up!' and I begin get mad. I think he make laugh at me cause I fisherman. Just as I make my mind up to hit him, he say gain, 'Shine em up' to nother man and man he stop—he get up in high chair and shine man he make his boots black and he rub them bright till shine like my spoon. It make me feel funny—I laugh and I laugh. Next time man say to me, 'Shine em up!' I get up in high chair an man make my shoes shine like never before." He chuckled. "Shine em up! Shine em up!" he said to himself and continued his polishing. At last he was satisfied with his shine. He attached a one and a half pound lead weight and let out six fathoms of line and we started to row leisurely. He had a strike, but the fish didn't stay with it. Eventually however, he hooked and landed a 20 pound king salmon—a beautiful fish which put up a game fight and sent fisherman's thrills tingling up and down my spine. As for myself, I only got gnat bites, but I got so many of them that life was a torment to me for ten days. The pests got in my eyes—I breathed them in and sneezed them out—they bit at everything they could see and then crawled up my sleeves and trouser legs and down my neck until they met, biting as they went. They are called "no-see-ums" by the Indians, but they are "sure-feel-ems." I have read of the torment endured in Alaska from gnats and mosquitos. I now know some of the possibilities. I would almost as soon have fleas, and my European memories are well punctuated with that curse.

When I got our boat in the spring Alma and I anticipated the delightful evenings we would spend on the water in the summertime. We saw ourselves drifting on the surface of the gently heaving water while we langorously watched the changing tints of the gorgeously colored western sky, as it slowly faded from crimson and gold, to orange and yellow, then into the pale luminous tint through which the stars would prick and twinkle, and which at this season simply blends from sunset into sunrise with no actual darkness in between. We tried it once, but "never again." The drifting we had planned to enjoy took us into a mist of stinging insects and what we didn't drift into came to meet us. By the time we had realized our mistake our skins were burning as though we had rolled in a nettle patch and when we finally reached cover of the house, we were suffering the torments of the damned. And yet, in spite of that, I innocently went trolling with Bill Gunyah.

To see the king salmon flashing from the water in their great lunges—to feel the shock of their strike at the trolling herring, sets one's nerves to vibrating and quickens the heart action, but I am wondering which is going to exert the stronger influence next time—the stimulation of the anticipated sport, or the inhibition of the remembered torture.

As soon as school closes here the entire native population,

except the few who remain to help get the canneries in shape for the packing season, load up their gas boats with dried herring and other food supplies; with their camp outfits and few belongings, including the children and the dogs; and go to the outer fringe of the Alaskan islands some twenty miles distant, to a place called, "The hole in the wall," on San Esquibel Channel; where they establish camp for the salmon trolling season.

The Hole in the wall is a narrow channel, almost a canal, which cuts through Noyes Island on the edge of the open Pacific and it furnishes a wonderful natural shelter for the fishing fleet from the winds and rough water of the ocean. It is an interesting sight to see the hundreds of power fishing boats parked on both sides of the channel, like automobiles parked several deep on a crowded city street; while the shores of the rocky islands are populous with the tents and little frame shacks of the campers behind which the dense jungle of cedars and undergrowth rises.

This summer village is not confined to native Alaskans, though the Indians have their own locality, for there is a still larger population of white fishermen with their gas boats from Ketchikan, Seattle, and the Puget Sound country. Stores are maintained in shacks on the shore or on barges, which are towed to the island by the concerns who buy the fish for shipment to the fresh fish markets. A cannery on nearby Steamboat Bay consumes part of the trolling catch, but a generous part is sold fresh. The supply obtained by trolling is not great enough to supply the canneries.

When the fish are biting well excitement and enthusiasm runs high among the fishermen, especially among the natives.

The whites live on their boats and spend the summer fishing out in the open sea. The power boats have long poles, often twenty or thirty feet long, which are rigged to either side of the mast in such a way that they can be lowered at right angles to the keel of the boat, so that the lines which trail in the water from them are kept clear of the boat's propellor. Frozen herring are used for bait and are fastened on the spoon hooks with curved sticks thrust through the length of the herring in such a way as to make the dead fish flash and dart about in the water as though alive.

The natives who go over to the camp from Klawock stay until the Fourth of July, when they return for the three or four day celebration here and then go seining or trap-tending for the three canneries located in Klawock and others located at other Indian villages, such as Shakan.

When the fish are biting freely the power trollers sometimes make as much as two and three hundred dollars in a day. The hand trollers in their skiffs of course cannot go so far, nor to the deep water, so their results are more uncertain and are not so great, but when the price is good and the luck, they get fine returns. A troller told me the other day that the largest fish he had caught this season was a 96-pound king salmon which at 16 cents a pound, brought him $15.36.

When the fish are biting the fishermen work hard and live high and they spend their money freely. They seem to crave fresh fruit and the bottled pop shipped up from below, especially— probably due to the thirst caused by their heavy labor and the salt air—and they get away with great quantities of both.

When the season opens the Klawock Commercial Company loads a liberal share of its stock into a big scow fixed up for store purposes, which is towed to Noyes Island and tied up on the beach; and one of the reasons for my being so busy is that George, the native manager, has gone over to the *Hole in the wall* with the scow, and I have had to assume responsibility for the store here and for keeping the scow supplied, goods ordered and bills paid. I planned to write last night, but just as I settled down for work a young fellow came in from the island with his pockets full of money from the scow, and a call for more stock. I spent the evening counting over $400 in change and currency—the receipts of two or three days, and in getting it ready to send out to the bank in Seattle with which we do business.

I have to get fruit, pop, fresh meat and staples in with every mail boat, and grab the first chance to send it over to the island to the scow; and it is a common occurrence to get routed out at any time in the night to make out P. O. money orders for natives who have run in to pay bills due outside, or to stock up with supplies, and must get back in time for the early morning fishing. It is a strenuous life for them while the fish are running and for everyone in any way connected with them. The few people who stay behind in the village during the trolling devote their time to their gardens.

The spring weather has struck us as being rather conservative in its expression, but there is nothing conservative about the growth of the vegetation. I have never seen anything like it before and think I now have some notion of what a tropical jungle is like. The country is densely wooded with spruce, cedar, hemlock and fir, and while from a distance the forest looks negotiable, let one try to penetrate it for a few rods and he will learn a lot in short time. The bed rock lies close to the surface on all of these islands, which are really nothing but mountain tops, so the soil, if one can call it that, is shallow at best; but as a matter of fact, there is almost no soil. What lies above the rock is mostly a tangled mass of sodden, half-decayed vegetation and fallen logs, so soaked with water that actual decay takes place very slowly, and the gardens of the natives are more often than otherwise, simply patches of rotten wood leveled off enough to start some strawberry plants in ridges with furrows in between to drain off the water. In the forests one sees great windfalls covered deep with moss and plant growth from which good-sized trees are growing, like the original branches, which they are not.

At the back door of the teacherage stands a big stump four or five feet in diameter and about six feet high, which looks like a solid mass of moss and organic growth; and on its top grows a ten inch spruce which sends its roots, like feelers, or the tentacles of the devil fish down to the ground along the sodden sides of the stump.

Alongside of the spruce stands a hemlock about as large, growing out of the side of a fallen giant, and further along the same log, grows another spruce and another hemlock. These furnish a natural screen about twenty feet distant from our bedroom window; while between the screen and the house is our garden—the only patch of ground on the property which can be used as such.

In front of the house grows a solid mass of rank vegetation absolutely impenetrable to the human being, which is made up of brush of the salmon berry, which yields a fruit somewhat like the raspberry only much larger, which enters into the living of the Indians to an important degree; the thimble berry, elderberry bushes of great size and loaded with fruit, although a short time ago they were banks of white bloom; a remarkable rank-growing plant which looks like a big squash vine which has tried to change its habits and become a bush, and which the natives call wild celery, in English, and consider quite a relish. They peel off the skin as we do with rhubarb and eat it in the same way. Alma thinks it would work up into salad very nicely.

Without having seen such growth, one could have no idea of its impenetrableness; not even a dog can get through except where there is a well-established trail. And it is such a beautifully verdant greenish-yellow of new growth, as though illuminated by mellow sunlight! It reminds me of the forests of Versailles when I saw them in the spring of 1919, before the Peace Conference.

It is hard to describe the hemlock. It is much more delicate and feathery and graceful in its method of growth and when the sap began to make itself felt, the first evidence was the bright little yellow tips on the ends of the delicate branches, about the size of peas, which produced a very pretty effect against the darker green of the older foliage, as though the tree had been trimmed with sequins. As the growth continued the yellow tips lengthened steadily, but the tree will not be so completely reclothed as was the spruce.

We have not been bothered to the extent one might suppose with flies and mosquitoes, although there is doubtless plenty of time yet to bring about a change. Some of the big bass-singing snow mosquitos were around early, but they are clumsy, heavy fliers and their droning hum, like that of an airplane, gives ample warning of their presence and makes an offensive against them easy. But in the muskegs and swamps of the islands the mosquitoes are said to be like the plagues of Egypt, and the only possible protection against them for those compelled to spend the night in the open, is to build fires on which damp moss is piled to make a dense cloud of smoke nearly as hard on the humans as on the mosquitoes.

Of course the natives have their explanation for the origin of the mosquito, as they have for almost everything with which they come in contact; and there is always someone around the fire to tell the tale to others, and like children, there is nothing the Thlinget likes better than to listen to stories.

"Long time ago," they tell, "long before the flood, a giant and his son lived in the world. The giant was much hungry and much cruel and liked to eat human beings most of all, because he liked their taste; but the really terrible thing about the giant was that whenever the Thlingets tried to kill him the arrows of even their best and strongest hunters would bounce off his body as though shot against a mountainside. The Indians were brave and were not afraid of being killed in conflict if they had a chance to kill their enemy. They did not like to be eaten but that would surely be their fate if they could not kill him. One day, in the midst of their despair, a young man stood up among them and said, "I, me, I will kill the giant or be eaten by him!"

He was a fine, tall young man, straight as a cedar, and he could shoot an arrow straight and far, but his friends did not think he could kill the giant and tried to talk him out of the idea of trying. When he persisted they sang his death song as he entered the house of the giant. He was a shrewd young chap, as well as brave. He knew everyone had a soft spot somewhere—even a hardshell crab—and that he must learn where to find the giant's soft spot before he could kill him. He had no sooner entered the giant's house than he heard a sound and because he could find no other place to hide, he crawled under a pile of blankets on the floor. The giant was so big that when he walked he shook the ground and the young Indian thought his time had surely come

The tale as told, sounds much like that of Jack, the Giant Killer, for when he entered the room he sniffed and wiggled his big nose around and suddenly cried out, "Ho! I smell a man! I'll get an axe and kill him and drink his blood for breakfast!" and he started for his axe. The frightened young Indian crawled out to escape just as the giant's son came into the room to see why his father was making such a noise. At once the Indian raised his bow and threatened to shoot an arrow at the son unless he told him how he could kill the giant. The son was nothing but a child, in spite of his size, and he didn't want to die, so he whimpered, "Shoot him in the ankle." Just then the foot of the giant, who was returning, appeared through the doorway, and the Indian shot an arrow into his ankle. The giant fell and shook the earth with his fall. He squirmed in his pain and groaned till the people far away thought the sound was thunder in the mountains. As he was dying he hissed to the Thlinget who had shot him,

"Even if you burn me, I'll bite you" and he died. Then all the Indians came from far and near and built a great pile of driftwood around the giant and set fire to it. The fire burned fiercely and the terrible enemy went up in a black, greasy cloud of smoke, as when they cremated their own dead. When the giant had gone up in smoke and the fire had burned down to ashes, the natives started to scatter the ashes by kicking them around with their feet, because they did not want anything of the giant to be left around and every particle that was kicked into the air became a mosquito and flew at the Indians to bite them, because the giant had said he would bite the people, even if they burned him. And the Indians are still wondering which is the worse, to be killed and have their blood drank all at once, or to live and have it drank in sips, a little at a time, as the mosquitoes drink it.

Chapter XXXV

DUK-TAT

I wonder if the minds of all the Thlingets are as filled with the legends of their race as is that of Peter Lawrence. He never comes around to see us that he does not tell us some story before he leaves. He was in today and sat and talked when I needed to be at work, or thought I did; but I am glad he came. We couldn't learn the things we do about them on our own responsibility. Any evidence of curiosity shuts them up with a click like a clam shell, but when they are so disposed they will spill anything that happens to come to their minds. Well, Peter "spilled" today, and this is the story he told us:

"Before the white man came, lot sea lions. Indians no have guns—kill sea lions with hands. Only strong mans kill sea lions with hands. Long time not any man strong enough—sea lions don't get killed by mans—grow big, fat.

"Litten boy he hear uncle talk about sea lions. He puff out his front and say, 'I going kill sea lions when I grow big.'

"Uncle laugh—everybody laugh at litten boy cause he weak like rabbit. Make litten boy mad when uncle laugh at him.

"One day uncle tell nephews, 'Come, we go take bath in cold water so you get strong and kill sea lions.'

"Uncle and litten boy and his bruders go down to beach. Water cold—so cold it hard on top like glass. Uncle kick hole in ice, boys go in cold water, splash round like fishes. When boys come out they slap bodies to make warm, but litten boy he won't go bath in cold water—he sit and teeth shake—he say water too cold when hard on top. That make uncle mad. He tell mother of litten boy, 'He no good—he won't make him strong. Let him die—don't give him food—he no good.' And he tell litten boy, 'You not boy—you girl—go stay with women.'

"Litten boy's fader have nother wife — have two wives. Nother wife she young, she sorry for litten boy—give him food when old wife don't look.

"When night come everybodys go sleep. Litten boy he don't go sleep—he go down to beach and kick hole in water like uncle, an he go in water. He splash round like fish and come out. He roll in snow—he put pieces ice under arms an run round like he like it. He get switches and whip body to make it warm. When he get back where everybodys asleep he put blanket over his head and stand over fire to make warm. Fire make litten boy dry, but smoke he make face black like dirty. When everybodys wake up uncle see litten boy. He say, 'See! litten girl who stay with womans got dirty face, he duk-tat.'

"Everybodys laugh—say 'Duk-tat!' That means dirty face in Thlinget. Duk-tat he don't care—he fool uncle an everybodys. When uncle and brudders go to cold water to bathe, uncle show boys broken limb of tree. He say, 'Pull it out!' Boys try—no can do. He show boys tree, small like leg—he say, 'twist tree off!' Boys try—no can do. Uncle say, 'Every day pull tree limb—try twist tree. When can do, Indian boy like strong man . . . go kill sea lions.'

"One night when Duk-tat bath in cold sea he saw man on beach. Man grab him—try throw Duk-tat on ground. Big fight, then man say, 'You do good work, Duk-tat—you grow strong. I East Wind—one day you throw me on ground. When you make me on ground you strong to kill sea lions.'

"Every night when uncle and brudders sleep, Duk-tat go bath in cold sea and whip self with switches. He run on beach in cold to make legs strong. He pull at limb of tree—he twist at odder tree—he get stronger and more stronger.

"Pretty soon East Wind come gain. East Wind an Duk-tat have wrestle match. Duk-tat he so strong he make East Wind on ground. East Wind say, 'You strong nuff, Duk-tat. You pull limb out of tree. You twist young tree.'

"Next night when he bath in sea he pull at limb. Limb come out of tree. He put limb back in like it was before. Then he go and twist at tree. Tree twist round. He know he strong like big man, so he untwist tree like it was before.

"Next day when uncles and brudders swim in sea, uncle run to tree and pull at limb—it come out easy. He surprised—everybodys think he strong like strong mans. He go twist at odder tree—tree twist easy cause been twisted before. Uncle make mistake with himself. He say, 'I strong man now—I go kill sea lions; so all the people take big canoe an go with uncle to kill sea lions. Duk-tat he go too. When canoe get to rocks where sea lions lived, Duk-tat's uncle jump out, run to sea lions to kill them, but uncle foolish with himself—he not strong like he think —sea lion knock him against rock with his tail an make his head broken.

"Duk-tat he stand up in canoe and make talk. He say, 'Uncle

say I girl. He call me Duk-tat, but I pull out limb of tree last night and put it back to make him foolish. I twist young tree last night an I untwist it. I strong like man now—not girl. I throw East Wind on beach odder night—now I go kill sea lions.' an he jump out of canoe.

"When sea lions see Duk-tat come they scared cause they know he strong man, so they try to get away, but they waddle and they flop an Duk-tat catch one. He take sea lion by tail an pull with his hands an pull sea lion in two parts. One part he throw over one shoulder—odder part he throw over odder shoulder. He catch nother sea lion an tear him apart. He kill lots sea lions—sea lions all scared—get in water—swim way off.

"People see Duk-tat big, strong man, not girl, so make him big chief all peoples."

Peter says that was the result of training Thlinget boys to stand cold and hardship, but he doesn't tell how many were killed off in the toughening process. Probably some other explanation was always found when they failed to survive, for there were lots of witches in those days. Peter says so.

He says it was by telling stories of their great men that the boys were trained up in the way they should go, and the chance of some day becoming a chief influenced their lives just as the possibility of some day becoming president of the United States is supposed to stimulate our own boys.

To further illustrate their method of training, Peter told of Kluk-nu-hu-di. He was a spoiled boy, and when he got hungry he teased his mother for food. She gave him a piece of dried salmon which was mouldy on one edge. Whining over a little thing like that, he threw the piece of salmon in a corner on the floor along with bones and other food scraps, and went off to play with his bow and arrows. Sea gulls were floating on the water and he shot at one and killed it. When he waded out to get it, he suddenly disappeared and all the people thought he had been drowned. They felt very sad because always his spirit would be cold and the Thlingets can think of nothing worse that can happen to one. But they couldn't find his body, which seemed strange.

As a matter of fact, he wasn't drowned, but something pulled him down into the water and he walked along the bottom of the sea till he came to a strange country he had never seen before. At last he came to a village and asked for food at the chief's house, but they gave him none. Suddenly he thought he saw some fish eggs on the ground and bent over to pick them up, intending to

eat them, for he was exceedingly hungry, having had no food since
his mother gave him the mouldy salmon which he threw away.
The people saw him and began to laugh at him, to be laughed
at hurts a Thlinget more than being shot at, because they said
he was eating garbage they had thrown away. That made the boy
very cross and he told them he wasn't hungry at all and didn't
intend to eat the fish eggs—just wanted to look at them. The chief
didn't believe that because he knew that Thlinget boys, like all
others, were always hungry, so he ordered his slaves to take the
boy to a brook and make him hug a stork which was feeding there
and listen to it sing. He was a wise old chief—chief of all the
salmon—and knew that hugging often makes cross people feel
good-natured. When he reached the brook there were two storks
feeding and they made him very happy, so when he returned
to the village the chief gave him food. Probably he knew in his
mind, that with an unhappy heart, there would be pain in the
boy's belly.

When the boy's stomach was full and he was contented once
more, the kind old chief explained that he had taken him away
from his home and his people because when he threw the mouldy
salmon away he insulted the chief's sun-dried salmon and he
needed to be taught to be more considerate of the feelings of
others.

Spring came at last and the salmon started on their journey
to the streams that flowed from the land. First went the big king
salmon, then the sockeye, the humpback, the dog, and last of all,
the coho. Finally they reached a stream where some Indians were
fishing, but the boy was inside a coho, so they couldn't see him
and an old man threw a spear and hit the fish. The boy, however,
dodged into the tail of the coho and escaped injury, but when the
salmon was pulled out and taken to the Indian's home, the man's
wife recognized a necklace found inside the fish's belly, as one
that belonged to her family, so she felt certain her son must be
in the fish. She couldn't find him, so she sent for a medicine man,
the best there was in the village, because she loved her son, even
if he was spoiled—in fact, that was why he was spoiled—and she
wasn't going to spare expense. The medicine man couldn't make
the boy come out; nor the others, called in consultation, so finally
someone thought of a young, inexperienced practitioner who had
recently hung out his shingle. In the slang of the day, "he knew
his onions," for he ordered everyone to fast eight days. At the end

of the fasting he danced and shook his rattles and sang eight songs, when lo! forth came the boy!

The lad had learned his lesson of respectfulness towards all and became a great man among his people.

Does that sound like a fantastic fairy tale? It surely does, but to the Thlingets it is no fairy tale, but history. Anyway, it is a lesson in psychology—fish and Thlinget psychology.

The idea seems strange to us, but Peter says that much as the Thlinget fathers love their children, it is not the father who trains them in all they should know, but the grandfather—there is only one—the mother's father, or the uncles, the mother's brothers.

The male members of the family, on the mother's side, are especially indulgent with boys and encourage them to come to them at every opportunity and even to make their homes with them.

The boys are considered more desirable than the girls because men are considered worth more than women—a peculiar view in light of the fact that all inheritance is through the women and all family authority is wielded through the mother's family. It is from the men in the mother's family that the boys learn to hunt, fish and trap. From them they learn the lore of the woods and the knowledge of the sea and its ways. They teach them the history and the legends of their race and train them in all the ways of polite Thlinget society. They teach the boys obedience by telling them the story of the little boy who wouldn't mind his elders. He came home at dark one day and his grandfather told him the world was sharp as a knife and he should be careful not to slip or he might cut himself. The youngster stamped his feet boastfully and shouted, "Grandfather, world big! Lots room— can't fall off." But as he stamped, something sharp punctured his foot, which swelled up and the boy died.

The lesson of obedience is further emphasized when the boy is told about the lad who went hunting with his uncle. They camped on the beach in a cave and went into the brush for the night to sleep, because the Indians never slept near their camp- fires for fear of their enemies. When a sound was heard in the night the uncle told the boy to go to the beach and see if the canoe was fastened, intending as soon as the child had reached the canoe, to rush down and launch the canoe so the two of them could escape before the enemy suspected what was being done. The boy didn't go. Three times was he told, but he did not obey, so the uncle ran and jumped into the canoe and pushed off, leaving the disobedient boy alone on the beach. The boy was captured and made a slave in consequence, and became a lesson to all Thlinget boys.

The indifference of the parents to what the children might do, seems incomprehensible to the whites. They go and come as they please—play without restraint or supervision in the water and on the boats on the beach—wading in, if so inclined, without removing shoes and stockings. There is a possible explanation for such indulgence of the children in the belief of reincarnation which is held by the Thlingets. They consider that it is always possible for the spirit of one who has died, to return to this world in the body of a child, and not infrequently they plan to name the forthcoming arrival after a cherished uncle or aunt, in the hope that the spirit of that particular party may be flattered into taking up its abode again within the family circle. Their disappointment is keen if the sex of the new comer does not fit the intended name. If we bear this in mind, we can see that if they are severe or exacting in their attitude towards the child, there would be chance of their ill-treating some spirit who would take offense and vent its spleen in any of the many ways known to spirits for tormenting humans.

Of course another explanation suggests itself, and that is that there is so little in the Thlinget home that can be injured by children or that costs money to secure, there is no reason for putting any check upon their activities. Maybe so. It's a plausible explanation.

Chapter XXXVI

JULY

It is summer now and we are having a chance to see what Alaska summer weather is like, but it is not so warm as we expected it to be. All the spring the natives had told us how hot it would be when summer came and at first we gave their statements full credence, but as spring slipped into summer and the mercury climbed up close to 70 degrees on occasional days, and the natives began to complain of the heat, we grew a little skeptical about the *hot weather*, and have concluded they call it hot simply because it is warmer than in the winter time.

For a long time we have been going to bed in broad daylight, if we went at a reasonable time, or by twilight at anytime later. At 9:30 at night the setting sun has been yellowing the green of the hemlocks and firs on the ridge behind the schoolhouse, and mellowing the evening landscape with a rich amber light that deepens the shadows, enriches the green of the forests and flows an effulgence over everything, that somehow seems to reach the inner consciousness and stir it with emotions which only a poet can put into words; while the western sky has been a gorgeous sight to behold—one we have never wearied of watching. Generally there would be clouds hanging above the horizon— soft and fleecy, or black, but broken so the light could break through in long streamers. An artist would have trouble depicting the setting sun because of the steadily changing colors. As the sun lowers to the horizon, the clouds flame into rosy masses of cotton, or the heavy clouds take on a Rembrandt lighting that makes them look as though they were bound with rose and gold. As the sun continues to settle into the sea, the rosiness takes on a deeper hue until it drops out of sight; then the color begins to fade and runs from a flaming crimson into a salmon-pink, then a deep orange; gleams of varying shades of red and orange, green and violet, flash forth, suggesting a brilliant display of northern lights. As the evening advances and twilight settles down, the orange fades into yellow and the horizon clouds are suffused with a wonderful golden light. The yellow changes to paler tints and blends into a pale green that softens until only a luminosity is left that suggest phosphorescence. For a month now, except in stormy weather, there has been no time when darkness has overspread the sky. Several times I have had to work at my typewriter until two or three o'clock in order to get necessary mail off on the boat, and have watched the glow of the next day crowd the afterglow of the day before across the sky, and at no time was the night actually dark. There has been something about the blending of one day into the next that has seemed to set the chords of my consciousness to vibrating in a way that clamored for expression, but alas! I am no poet and I shall never know just what I have felt. I wonder if the change from day to day is more impressive further north where it is more pronounced. I am inclined to doubt it, for the delicate touch is always more suggestive than the bold stroke. More is left to the imagination.

This is July. In the pre-whiteman days the Thlinget calendar was one of their own making. They knew no days of the week, for there was no Sunday; nor months of the year, aside from the periodical changing of the moon, but they measured off the passing time by changes that transpired in nature and designated them accordingly. June and July is "The time when everything is born." The period that follows was the time "When everything born commences to fatten"; then followed the time "When all birds come down from the mountains." What would correspond in a measure to our September, was the "Small moon, or Moon-child time," when the berries began to drop and the salmon to run. Then followed the "Big moon," when the first snow appeared on the mountains and the bears began to get fat. Followed the "Time when the snow has to be dug away from the doors." Our December was a time "When every animal in the mother's womb began to have hair." "Goose time," was when the sun began its course back up the sky and the Indians watched for the geese flying north. Next came the "black bear time," when the black and brown bears began to have their cubs and throw them out in the snow. "Fish-egg-time" was when the herring spawned and spring began to quicken. Followed the "Time when things began to grow"; then the "Flower time"; and what would correspond to our May, was the "Time when they knew everything was going to grow"; and "Salmon time" followed that.

Of course such divisions of time were very indefinite—not always the same from year to year, in comparison with our calendar; but time meant nothing to them except in connection with maintaining their existence. Why should they care to measure it accurately? Naturally their seasons varied with the latitude, but each was anticipated because it meant something to be accomplished in connection with their lives. Each was enjoyed in its turn, because they found their pleasures in life in doing what they needed to do. Each was looked back upon with satisfaction because one more step in their daily existence had been taken. Otherwise the passing of time concerned them not. They were children . . . then in time, they were old, but life had been lived and enjoyed in the meantime. They had no great anticipations for the future, save a possible potlatch. They enjoyed talking during the long evenings about the past, but otherwise they lived in the present.

Changes have come into their lives and now living is not so simple as it used to be. Thanksgiving and Christmas are great days with them because they can feast and celebrate, as they did ;n the good old days. Herring and fish-egg-time are still with them. The opening of the halibut season on February 15th has been set by the white men, but it is welcomed as offering a chance to earn the white man's money. Today the passing of time means the passing of *months*, the white man's way of measuring time, and after fish-egg-time, the next big event is the Fourth of July, so after the herring spawn, and the opening of the trolling season had passed, the natives began to talk about that.

The Thlingets, at least here at Klawock, actively engage in trolling up to the Fourth of July. A few continue over at the Hole in the Wall, but the many canneries in Southeastern Alaska by that time are making active preparations for the packing season and they absorb a great deal of labor. There are three canneries here which are able to employ, either directly or indirectly, a large part of the adult population of the village. Many of the women work at the *sliming* of the fish, the cleaning of the fish after the machine, called the "iron chink," has cut off the heads and tails and stripped out the entrails, while the men handle the more strenuous work of the cannery, tend the traps, or engage in seining for salmon on their own responsibility.

The trolling season is a period of arduous work for the fishermen—much exposure and risk when the fish are biting in the deep water of the open sea—but it is a time of happiness for the children who play upon the beach and much enjoyment for all, because it is a return to the freedom and activity of their early life—a reversion to the primitive, such as even the dwellers of the white man's cities find stimulating and renovating after their long months of confinement and hard work.

The season has been a good one so far this year for those

who have been able to follow the fish out to deep water, so everyone has been anticipating the Fourth. A few came back early in the week to make preparations for the great event—Billy Benson and his wife, who run a restaurant—Tom Adams and his wife, she with the reddish hair effectively bobbed, who also run a restaurant on occasion—Peter Anniskett and other small-scale merchants; but on Saturday every half hour brought gas boats put-putting into the inlet and the streets once more became active with children, dogs and adults—and what a dark-complexioned crowd they were, tanned by the wind and the summer sun; and how happy everyone was to be back in town again! They gathered in clumps on the street and laughed and talked merrily. They thronged Bob's and the Klawock Commercial Company's stores in an orgy of spending—of pop drinking and fruit and candy eating. That day the store took in nearly $150 and Bob's must have done better still. It was a gorgeous day, but the mercury didn't quite reach 70 degrees.

George, the native store manager, had insisted there would be a lot of buying when the people returned from the trolling ground, so in his absence with the scow at the island, I had ordered a generous stock of fresh fruit of all kinds from Seattle; candy, casks of pop, and good things to eat out of hand, though not on the extensive scale he desired. On his own responsibility, as a personal speculation, he is strong on personal side-lines, he had arranged with the traveling salesman of a Seattle dry goods house, to express out on consignment a sample line of elaborate dresses. They came, and the first thing he did on his return from the island, was to open them up and display them in the store. Had I had any intimation of any such venture on his part, I certainly would have vetoed it because his time and efforts were being liberally paid for by the company that was employing him and belonged to them. And had I seen the line of gowns, I would still more emphatically have objected. They were not house dresses, but things of crepe de chene, georgette and chiffon, the kind of affairs that women call "gowns," though mere men call them dresses. What could have been more absurd than to bring such things to an Indian village for the Fourth of July festivities? But again I didn't know my Thlingets, for they certainly sold! And it wasn't the snappy young maids and matrons of the new generation who did the buying. Oh, no indeed!

Well the receipts for Sunday, the third, were about $250,

exclusive of the gowns. What George raked down on that speculation of his I have no idea, but it was surely a nice sum.

The Fourth came on Monday and brought a dark and sullen sky with it which proved more or less leaky, but nothing of that kind could stand in the way of the natives' enjoyment of the day.

I don't know what form the celebration took in the forenoon, aside from the traditional ball game between teams from Klawock and Craig, because I was too busy taking care of the store funds and getting them ready to send to the bank in Seattle by the mail boat; in paying bills by check, and in getting off the necessary correspondence, to heed what might be transpiring in the village, but the entire native population assembled on the ball ground in the afternoon with the band, to witness the games. Prizes had been offered, so there was much rivalry among the youth. There were the customary potato sack and barrel races—the barrels used being our empty gasoline barrels; a race of some of the kiddies clad in Montgomery Ward Indian suits down the plank street on tricycles; three-legged races and various other contests, and the grand finale was the tug-o-war. And such a tug as it was with big, blind Jumbo McFee anchored at one end and his counterpart in weight at the other.

The spitting sky seemingly had no terrors for the spectators and the crowd lined up along the sidelines, a picturesque sight outlined against the black, sullen water, and with the black sullen sky above; but even more intriguing were the crepe and chiffon gowns that bedecked some of the older women, and the accompanying display of silk shawls, fancy hats, silk stockings, stylish shoes, and the native bracelets, rings and other finery. The Fourth of July celebration was the Kentucky Derby—the Assembly Ball, among the elite of Thlingetdom—an occasion when wrinkled, weather-beaten faces and shapeless, workworn forms were forgotten, and the fripperies every woman, regardless of color, loves, were enjoyed to their utmost. The first impulse to smile at the incongruous surroundings, attire and wearers, was checked by a welling sympathy for those whose lives were so circumscribed by their environment that they had to grab at any opportunity, no matter how unsuitable for display, to enjoy themselves as white women find enjoyment. In their own day, when their life conformed to their environment, their pleasures and their love for display took forms that were harmonious with the wild life they lived; but today the white man's customs and fashions and something of his tastes have intruded into their lives, although their environment remains the same. It is rather pitiful to see the way in which our much vaunted race has demoralized the lives of those who are not our kind and should not be expected to be. When they become like ourselves, they will not be themselves. Is it any wonder the red men have always resented our presence? Had they attempted to make us like themselves, how would we have received them?

Anyway, the "400" of Klawock were there in their finery. It clearly was the social event of the season and the "squaw" of yesterday was the "fine lady" of today.

The last of the contests was the boat race. In earlier days they would have used the native canoes and it would have been a sight worth seeing, but it was the white man's row boats which were used this time and the broad backs and powerful arms strained to oars instead of the paddles of yore.

As a fitting windup to the great day, a hoarse whistle sounded and the big freighter, the Cordova, sidled around the red light, slipped up to Bob's dock and tied up; and much to our surprise, the editor of our Klawock Daily Bulletin, the Nurse, who had been out on vacation, came down the gang plank accompanied by her daughter and little fairy granddaughter.

We didn't attend the dance that evening in the town hall, and I suspect we missed something by not going, but I felt it was their joy time of the year, so why should an interested, but curious paleface butt in on their play? They had a good time. I know they did because I heard it, but there were no dead Indians lying around the next day, so the good time was probably had by all. We now know what a Thlinget Fourth of July is like.

George has been very grumpy and surly because I cut down heavily the orders he wanted to send in for the occasion, to the wholesale houses, but I am fighting bankruptcy for the store and was determined there should be no more piling up of idle stock. Possibly the sales would have been heavier had there been more stock, but I feel satisfied with the outcome. We cleaned up all the stock ordered for the occasion, and a lot of old stock besides. Our sales for the three days were nearly $600. Bob's must have been as great and may have been much more; while all the little shops did a thriving business, so the aggregate expenditure for the little Indian village of 400, must have been four or five dollars per capita, which was not so bad. And I will guarantee there were nowhere near the headaches the next day there would have been in a similar white man's town.

Chapter XXXVII

LEGENDS

I can conceive no more fascinating study, if one had the time and opportunity, than to make a comparative study of the beliefs and legends of the primitive people in various parts of the world. It would doubtless lead to some interesting revelations, and possibly, if carried far enough, to important additions to our ethnological information.

It astounds us to find a story of the flood current among the Thlingets, with so much similarity to the Biblical account, that the natives accept the latter as the same, except for certain inaccuracies on the part of the white man's version. I have had no explanation offered for the coincidence and think of but one. We do know that the Alaskan islands, and probably much of Alaska itself, have at some time been heaved out of the sea. There is an island today, Bogoloff, which was pushed out of the ocean some years ago and which undergoes alterations from year to year. Can it be that at some time within the history of the human race in Alaska, subterranean commotions have drawn the land beneath the surface, only later, as at Bogoloff, to push it up again? Such a cataclysm would be responsible for such a flood as they describe—the results of sinking land would be similar to those of rising waters. Possibly the geologists may some day be able to tell us what the ethnologists cannot.

It has been interesting to find the belief in the evil-eye and witchcraft among the natives as I found it in Albania; and the similarity between the beliefs and customs of these people and those of the Japanese, has been noted in much detail.

I made quite a study of the raven after my experience with the birds in the mountains of Montana, and found that in Greek mythology the raven was a bird of another color. He had been white up to the time when he carried the gossip to Apollo that one of his sweethearts, Coronia, a Thessalian nymph, was flirting with another sheik. Apollo, mortified and in a jealous rage, killed her, then turned on the raven in his white robe of innocence and purity and in the words of the translator of Ovid,

"He blacked the raven o'er
"And bade him prate in his white plumes no more."

Now I find among the Thlinget Indians the legendary belief
that at one time the raven was white!

At the time the raven secured the light for the world the
Thlingets say he was snow-white, and that after he had freed
the sun, the moon and the stars and made it possible for their
light to shine down upon the world, he became frightened at
what he had done and at the anger of his grandfather, and fled
from his home.

To suddenly have light where they had had only darkness,
filled the mortals on earth with consternation and some, in their
fright leaped into the sea and became fishes; others fled to the
forests and mountains and became wild animals; while still
others changed into inanimate bodies such as trees, stones and
mountains in which their spirits continued to dwell. At this time
there was no fresh water in the world except on Dall Island, not
many miles from Klawock, where there was a spring. That is
vouched for by Mayor Bob. He has never seen the exact spring, but
he knows where the island is—in fact, he pointed it out to us the
day we went to the Hole-in-the-wall with him on his boat, the
Dubrovnik.

It seems that having secured light for the world, Raven
decided to go further and find water for it. That is apt to be the
way with philanthropy: it grows on one and one good act prompts
another. There was one serious obstacle in his way however, in
the form of an old man called Ganook, who was so very conscientious in his guardianship that he would not even allow Raven
to drink at the spring; so to circumvent the old man was Raven's
problem. The old boy appears on some of the totem poles, I have
been told, as a combination of goat and bird. The raven in life,
and in history and legend, is credited with being the slyest and
shrewdest of all beings, and was not overly nice in all his ways,
so one should not be shocked to learn that he deliberately soiled
Ganook, which forced the old man to go and plunge into the sea
for a bath. That was Raven's opportunity and he seized it. He
flew down to the spring and drank and drank of the water until
he could hold no more, then he returned to the house and had
hardly entered the door before Ganook appeared behind him.
Angered at the indignity he had suffered, and at the trick Raven
had played to get the water, he made a rush for Raven, who in a
panic attempted to fly out through the smoke-hole. Ganook, however, called for the aid of his assistant spirits, who blocked his
way so that he was unable to escape before the soot from the fire

had made him black as night. Raven, terribly chagrined, did his best to scrape the blackness off, but could accomplish nothing and ever since he has been forced to wear black. But he had accomplished his purpose, for he had secured the water he was after, so he winged his way over the earth, here dropping a big mouthful of water to make a river, and there, a small one to make a fish creek. That is the way Klawock Creek was made, Bob says. If you don't believe it you can go and see the creek for yourself. He's right! The creek is there!

One good act leads to another, so having furnished light and water for the earth creatures, Raven conceived the idea of putting a creature we call "man" in it. He was inexperienced and tried to make man out of stones, but such a man, though very durable, was so heavy and slow that he gave up that idea in disgust; then he tried sticks, but there were serious objections to the material, he found, although I suspect some people made of that material escaped and have survived; so he tried leaves as a material for man's make-up, which suited him much better, but when he was through Raven found that because leaves fade in the fall of the year, and blow around in the wind when they drop off, so man grows old and dies as well, which has necessitated special effort on the part of the people to properly care for their dead. I have told how they used to put food in the fire at their feasts and cremations, and call the spirits by name to come and partake.

With man created, Raven taught him war and many tricks and ways until he became wise and skilful.

At the time of the flood, Raven rescued his mother from a watery fate by taking her in his arms, and because there was no dry land, he flew up in the sky and stuck his bill in the blue dome, where he hung until a sea gull brought the news that the sea had receded.

After the flood Raven's interference in the affairs of man ceased, and since then he seems to have appeared only in his present-day form, except that his nose is different than it used to be. The Thlingets say that it originally was a fine, straight, beautiful nose, but once upon a time Raven took it into his head to disguise himself as a fish and swim in the sea, where he was caught by a native who broke off his nose. Later, through his shrewdness and wisdom, he found where his nose had been put and recovered it, and by his magic he managed to put it back again. He had no looking glass in which to view himself, so he failed to get it on straight. That sounds plausible; but some claim that Raven bent his nose when he hung by his bill in the sky, the time he saved his mother from drowning. That is possible too, but Charlie Chuck says he bent his bill when he got fire for man. It seems that for a long time the world was without fire, as well as without water, but Raven learned there was fire on an island far away, so he dipped his bill in pitch from a pine tree and flew to the island. There he stuck his bill in the fire and when the pitch got to burning well, he flew back again, but before he got back to the earth, the fire had warmed up his bill so that it warped and bent downward, just the way gutta percha will soften and bend when it is warm. That seems plausible too. Anyway, the raven's bill is no longer beautiful.

The Thlingets feel that they owe a great deal to Mr. Raven, so they treat his present-day counterpart with great respect and indulgence, although they do not revere him. No one will willingly injure a raven, or his cousin, the crow, and they seem careful about talking about him behind his back, but the young generation of Thlingets, as with our own, shows a growing tendency to skepticism. I was quite surprised one day, however, when going through the yard of the native Presbyterian minister, to get to the thicket on the hillside beyond, to find a dead raven hanging from a sapling, along with tin cans, to frighten the marauders from his ripening strawberries. I felt much curiosity, but did not venture to question as to whether he had shot the bird, and what his reactions were towards the legendary history of his people. I would really like to know whether any of the old beliefs still cling to him. Maybe I should say, *which* of the old beliefs, for it would be surprising to have them all eliminated in one generation, in any Thlinget.

Chapter XXXVIII

DEATH OF AN OLDSTER

(This chapter written by Alma)

Bitter the night —

Towering trees writhe and shriek —

Breakers crash with thunderous roar upon jagged rocks —

In a trembling cabin on the storm-beaten shore, a human being stretched upon the floor, breaks the awesome stillness with labored breathing.

Shrunken the form under the heavy blanket—sunken the eyes, like deep wells with a glint of starlight at the bottom —

Brands, burning in a hollow of the earthen floor, crumble and collapse with a shower of sparks.

One from the circle of squatting forms rises, lays a knot upon the glowing coals. Flame runs its length, leaps, illumines the room.

Beside the dying Indian hangs the ceremonial robe of an Eagle.

On the wall at his feet, where his eyes rest upon it, hangs a large American flag.

The form stirs—the eyes turn to the council robe beside him. Guttural speech interrupts the stentorious breathing—haltingly, faintly. The voice gains strength—silently the watching Indians listen to the words of the dying patriarch.

"My sons, there is a power above—You must not lie, you must not steal, you must not kill or the good Ke-an-kow won't give you good luck. He make your arm strong—he make your feet swift—he talk wise words to your ears—listen."

The voice fades—the eyes close—he rests.

Again he stirs—the head turns—his eyes fix upon the flag of stripes and stars, and glow.

Once more the faltering voice breaks the stillness.

"Young men, I am Eagle—long time have my wings beat the air, but I have flown my last flight.

"Maybe you Raven — maybe Wolf — maybe Mink — many, many totems."

"That flag," and he raises a trembling arm to point, "Totem of Great Tribe—Great Tribe over all. Forget not!"

The pointing hand falls to his side. Again the eyes close—the breath comes in gasps.

Once more he rouses—dimming eyes turn to an object revealed by the flickering light—long it is, and narrow—a casket, satin-lined, silver-mounted—glorious in the soft gray of brocaded velvet.

Lingeringly the look takes in the magnificent appointments —only the great are thus honored!

A feeble hand flutters—four of the watching stalwarts raise the wasted form and lay it reverently in the coffin.

A flicker of pleasure about the mouth—a deep sigh of contentment, and the eyes close.

Peace broods within—strife rages without.

The silent group moves only to replenish the fire.

Crash! A tree falls—the eyes flutter open—again they turn to that "robe of honor"—again they rest upon the revered totem of the "One Great Tribe," the stars and stripes—

A sigh!—The brave spirit is winging its way to the "Beautiful Green Island."

THE END